THE FAILED PROMISE OF ORIGINALISM

FRANK B. CROSS

The Failed Promise of Originalism

STANFORD LAW BOOKS

AN IMPRINT OF STANFORD UNIVERSITY PRESS

STANFORD, CALIFORNIA

Stanford University Press
Stanford, California

Printed in the United States of America on acid-free, archival-quality paper

Library of Congress Cataloging-in-Publication Data

Cross, Frank B., author.
  The failed promise of originalism / Frank B. Cross.
    pages cm
  Includes bibliographical references and index.
  ISBN 978-0-8047-8382-8 (cloth : alk. paper)
    1. Constitutional law—United States.   2. Law—United States—
Interpretation and construction.   3. United States. Supreme Court.
I. Title.
  KF4550.C76 2012
  342.73001'1—dc23
                                                              2012015153

Typeset by Thompson Type in 10/14 Janson

Contents

THE FAILED PROMISE OF ORIGINALISM

ONE

The Undeniable Appeal of Originalism

Originalism, the theory that the Constitution should be interpreted according to the meaning or intent of the drafters, has great appeal to Americans. At one time closely associated with the conservative movement, originalism is now commonly held as an important, if not the exclusive, device for interpreting the Constitution. This has not been our historic practice. Over thirty years ago, Munzer and Nickel (1977, 1029) wrote that "one does not have to dig very deeply into the literature of American constitutional law to suspect that many constitutional provisions do not mean today what their framers thought they meant." Yet originalism still has great appeal.

A large number of Americans say they believe that Supreme Court justices should interpret the Constitution solely based on the original intentions of its authors (Greene 2009c, 695–696). In the legal academy, the amount of ink devoted to originalist theory is enormous. The revival of originalism is evident at the Court level. One quick survey found that in 1987 analysis of history figured in only 7 percent of the constitutional cases,

1

but by the 2007 term historical analysis was involved in nearly 35 percent of the opinions (Sutton 2009). While still representing a minority of cases, the trend line appears strong.

There was a time when originalism was considered "dead" and "trounced by many academic critics" (Barnett 1999, 611). One of today's leading originalists declared that if "ever a theory had a stake driven through its heart, it seems to be originalism" (Barnett 2004, 90). The theory was "rebooted," though, and surged in popularity. Conservative academics developed new and more persuasive theories for reliance on originalism. The approach has seen much greater attention in law schools in recent years (Ryan 2006). At the court, some claim that "the originalists have prevailed" (Smith 2004, 234).

Originalism has now gone beyond its conservative "base," and conservative bête noire Ronald Dworkin proclaimed some time ago that everyone should be an originalist (though his application of the theory differed dramatically from that of other originalists). One often hears the claim that we are all originalists now. Indeed, in her 2010 hearings on her Supreme Court nomination, Elena Kagan reported that "we are all originalists." Research reveals a dramatic increase in recent years in law review articles focused on originalism and in the use of certain originalist sources by the Supreme Court (Ginsburg 2010).

While originalism long had severe critics in the academy, especially among liberals, this seems to be changing. In addition to Dworkin, Yale's Jack Balkin has come out for originalist interpretation (Balkin 2009), and other leading liberal scholars go along, at least to a degree. The position is not universal, as a number of law professors reject originalism, with a recent article calling it "bunk" (Berman 2009). However, most concede that originalist interpretation is at least sometimes useful, and many argue that it should serve as the primary basis for constitutional interpretation. The theory is certainly in the contemporary debate over proper interpretation.

The discussion over the use of originalism has largely focused on theoretical debates, sometimes delving into great linguistic detail. This book does not focus on the theory of originalism, on which countless articles and books have been written. Rather, I focus on the practice of originalism and how that informs us of the value of the approach. Some understanding of underlying theory of originalism is important, though, to evaluate the practice. The theoretical argument for originalism obviously has a profound appeal.

The appeal of originalism may be viewed as a sign of respect to the constitutional framers. Madison, Jefferson, Hamilton, and others are held in very high regard today. Ron Chernow (2010) has observed: "In the American imagination, the founding era shimmers as the golden age of political discourse, a time when philosopher-kings strode the public stage, dispensing wisdom with gentle civility."

Americans may treat the founders as giants or saints who created for us the Constitution that formed the backbone of our nation. There has been an "almost religious adoration" of the framers (Miller 1969, 181). Accordingly, some among the public suggest that the Constitution should be interpreted according to the founders' intent for it. The Constitution becomes our secular idol and the founders the prophets.

This simple theory is tantamount to ancestor worship and is hard to justify. Today's originalists commonly reject the approach. Originalism is "not driven by fawning celebration of historical figures" (Whittington 1999, 157). The Constitution and its framers certainly were flawed. The acceptance of slavery is the most prominent example of the framers' shortcomings, but there are others as well. The lack of rights for women is another major example of where the framers' views appear somewhat embarrassing in retrospect. And originalism is not limited to the original framers but would also extend to the later amendments to the Constitution.

Comments at the time suggest that individual framers were not themselves so enamored with the wisdom of other framers. Jefferson said that Hamilton's practice was "a tissue of machinations against the liberty of the country," while Hamilton said Jefferson was not "mindful of truth" but a "contemptible hypocrite." Hamilton said of John Adams that he was "more mad than I ever thought him and I shall soon be led to say as wicked as he is mad." Of course, Adams said that Hamilton was "devoid of every moral principle." It does not sound as if they had great trust in the judgment of their fellow framers.

Nor was it clear that the framers themselves favored an originalist interpretation for their Constitution. Some research into the period suggested that the framers did not expect that future interpreters of the Constitution would rely on the framers' purposes and expectations (Powell 1985), though these findings are contested. The framers carefully debated the language of the Constitution and clearly thought that the text, rather than their particular intentions, should govern. Madison wrote in *The Federalist* No. 14:

> Is it not the glory of the people of America that, whilst they have paid a decent regard to the opinions of former times and other nations, they have not suffered a blind veneration for antiquity, for custom, or for names, to overrule the suggestions of their own good sense, the knowledge of their own situation, and the lessons of their own experience?

Such textualism, though, can be considered a form of originalism. Our leading framers do not seem to embrace originalism. The most compelling evidence of this seems to come from James Madison himself. He was originally convinced that the Constitution did not authorize a national bank but later changed his mind, in light of legislative precedent and his appreciation of the value provided by the bank to the nation (Dewey 1971). In this, Madison plainly embraced a "living Constitution." Of course, this critique applies strongest to reliance on original intent, and today's originalists have a different approach, as will be explained in the following pages.

Had the framers wanted originalism to be the standard, they could have said so explicitly. At the very least, they could have provided a record that made the original intent as clear as possible. They did none of this. Madison took notes during the Constitutional Convention but did not make them public, as would be expected if he thought they should have authority. Records of the ratification debates on the Constitution are also quite incomplete.

At the time of the Constitution's creation, it appears that the standards for legal interpretation did not rest centrally on the intent of a law's creators. Hans Baade's historical analysis suggests that it was the "universal practice" of courts at the time to look only at the text of an act and "never" resort to the "debates which preceded it" (1991, 1010).

The worship of the framers cannot supply the basis for originalist interpretation, though one suspects that it influences many of today's originalist impulses. The framers were great men in many ways but certainly not beyond reproach, and they realized this. A greater justification is required for originalist interpretation.

There is a very cynical position on the appeal of originalism. Jamal Greene attributes its appeal to its simplicity, its catering to populist suspicion of legal elites, and cultural nationalism (2009c). This surely explains some of its appeal to the general public, as originalism is easy to understand and the public is intermittently nationalist and populist. Post and Siegel (2006, 527) suggest that originalism is "so powerfully appealing because conservatives have succeeded in fusing contemporary political concerns with authoritative constitutional narrative" that is "driven by a politics of restoration, which encourages citizens to protect traditional forms of life they fear are threatened."

These motives doubtless underlie some of the public support for originalism. Alternatively, originalism may simply appeal to a "populist taste for simple answers to complex questions" (Berman 2009, 8). One cannot fairly expect the broad general public to appreciate nuances of legal theory. To prevail in the academy and in court, however, originalism needs a stronger basis. Various academic originalists have provided this basis, relying on more robust justifications for originalism.

A stronger case for originalism is simply that reliance on originalism is required for legal decisionmaking. The Constitution, like other legal materials, is a text. When interpreting another legal text, such as a statute, it is typical to use the meanings of its words at the time of its enactment. Many judges look beyond the words of the statute to the legislative history, to attempt to discern the intentions of those who drafted and passed it.

This is considered simple legal fidelity (Solum 2008). The interpretation of any legal material relies on its text. Balkin (2007) argues that fidelity to the Constitution as law must mean fidelity to the words of the text. The words govern. But the meaning of words is impossible to discern outside their "linguistic and social contexts" (Brest 1980, 207). Originalism provides this context. A text is generally interpreted according to the meaning of its words at the time they were expressed. A legal text remains binding until it is repealed or amended. The constitutional text is that of the framing era, as amended. The framers adopted a written constitution, in contrast to England's more amorphous judicially constructed constitution. This was at least in part in furtherance of a desire for stability of interpretation. The drafters believed that the judiciary could not be trusted without a clear governing text (Whittington 1999). The drafters chose their words carefully, trying to anticipate future circumstances, so that they could last (Gillman 1997).

The change in a word's meaning over time should not alter the interpretation of its earlier meaning. When a law continues in force over time, so does the original meaning of its words. If a nineteenth-century novelist referred to a person as "gay," meaning cheery and pleasant, that character should not now be considered to be attracted to the same sex simply because the meaning of the word has evolved. Similarly, a statute retains its original meaning until it is repealed or amended. The word *counterfeit* once meant authentic, and the word *awful* once meant great, but we would not change the meaning of an old statute because those words have transformed their meaning. James Madison noted that the "meaning of the words" contained in the Constitution might change, but the meaning of the Constitution itself should not (Whittington 1999, 58).

Justice Holmes dissented from this vision when he wrote: "A word is not a crystal, transparent and unchanged; it is the skin of a living thought and may vary greatly in color and content according to the circumstances and the time in which it is used" (*Town v. Eisner* 1918, 425). Even originalists recognize that the circumstances are relevant to the correct application of a word, but they would maintain that the word keeps its fundamental meaning.

The Constitution refers to guaranteeing every state a "republican" form of government. This is appropriately interpreted, according to the original meaning, to mean representative government, not government by today's Republican Party (Balkin 2007). The constitutional reference to "domestic violence" is not speaking of spousal abuse but of internal insurrection (Solum 2008). There are plenty of other examples of this phenomenon.

Originalism simply calls for the legal text to be interpreted according to its then contemporary meaning, which is a standard approach to legal or other forms of textual analysis. The process of interpretation arguably calls for nothing else. The framers apparently believed that the Constitution "should be construed to have the meaning attributed to it by some group of persons at the time it was drafted and adopted" (Clinton 1987, 1206). James Madison said that the "true meaning" of the Constitution was that "given by the nation at the time of its ratification" (Dewey 1971, 39).

For a leading current originalist, Randy Barnett, the "intuitive appeal of originalism rests on the proposition that the original public meaning is an objective fact that can be established by reference to historical materials" (2009, 660). If so, constitutional interpretation becomes a question of fact, not one of indeterminate values. Some originalists would maintain that theirs is "the only way to ensure that the Constitution is really law" (Sunstein 2005, 54). Richard Posner (2000, 591) suggests that the "only good reason for originalism is pragmatic and has to do with wanting to curtail judicial discretion."

This is a "rule of law" justification. Without originalism, we have the rule of men and women, specifically the rule of Supreme Court justices. Strictly speaking, judge-created law does not violate the rule of law. The common law is characterized by such judicial discretion, and it is not generally considered contrary to the rule of law. But Justice Scalia suggests that the discretion of the common law is less lawlike than ruling by more rigid tests and that such discretion is inappropriate in the constitutional context. There is no constitutional or other legal authority for justices to create whatever law they desire.

Ultimately, the case for originalism thus appears to be that of the rule of law (Griffin 2008). The constitutional text is the law. If judges do not follow its meaning, they are promoting a rule of judges rather than a rule of law. Only the original meaning, in this view, produces truly lawful decision-making. Bevier (1996) suggests that nonoriginalism is a corruption of the rule of law itself. The rule of law basis for originalism does not make claims about the normative legitimacy of the law, though. Although rule of law is presumably better than no rule of law, its value depends on the legitimacy of the substantive law that it is enforcing. To strengthen its hand, originalism has turned to democracy as a justification for its constitutional law.

Originalism has been considered necessary for true democracy of popular sovereignty (Whittington 1999). The American people exercised democracy to create a Constitution, and its commands should be given effect. This is the basis for the Constitution's legitimacy (Farber 1989). The Constitution was ratified through a democratic process (though democracy of the time was surely imperfect), and it had no force until this time of ratification. Democracy implies that democratic actions that become the law remain effective until legally repealed. Originalism is said to be the only means of interpretation that is faithful to what the people democratically agreed on (Whittington 1999). Allowing unelected justices to alter that popularly agreed-on meaning is to make the justices sovereign, not the people.

The Constitution can be altered through a democratic process of constitutional amendment. Amendment is challenged as a democratic process for constitutional change because as few as thirteen states can block such an amendment, no matter how small their relative population might be. While amendment is difficult and requires more than a simple majority, such supermajority requirements may be democratically beneficial (McGinnis & Rappaport 2007). Any other method of alteration of the original meaning arguably undermines democracy because it denies people the democratic right to make rules (such as the requirements for constitutional amendment) that will be applied in the future.

Originalism could be viewed in tension with democracy. It appears to exalt, in some cases, the ideas of those who died hundreds of years ago over current individuals (the "dead hand" problem). There is little theoretical reason to assume that contemporary Americans necessarily consent to all the terms drawn up in the eighteenth century. Richard Posner (1990, 138) argued that to be "ruled by the dead hand of the past is not self-government in any sense." The nature of American constitutional governance sometimes prevents current majorities from effecting their preferences on policies, demanding the difficult process of constitutional amendment for change. Earl Maltz, a defender of originalism, described democracy as "the most popular defense" for the practice but also the "easiest to dismiss" (1987b, 776–777). The Constitution itself has various antimajoritarian aspects, not least the procedures for its own amendment.

Given the acceptance of a Constitution, though, this criticism of originalism is incomplete. In practice, rejecting originalism permits the originally enacted meaning of the Constitution to be altered by some other entity. In today's system, the judiciary, particularly the Supreme Court, decides matters of constitutionality. The Court, though, is not accountable to the electorate but was made independent of the people. Any judicial changes to the original meaning, therefore, lack a democratic imprimatur. Moreover, permitting judicial modification of the Constitution arguably disrupts the separation of powers conceived at the time of ratification. A set historical meaning with possible amendments could be considered more democratic than one set by judges. This conforms to the belief that "officials charted with *interpreting or enforcing* the law should not usurp the authority of those charged with *making* it" (Bassham 1992, 93).

Perhaps the fundamental appeal of originalism is the fear that "if judges don't follow the original understandings, they will be free to do whatever they want" (Strauss 2008, 973). A central concern of originalism "is that judges be constrained by the law rather than be left free to act according to their own lights, a course that originalists regard as essentially lawless" (Smith 1989, 106). The "best response" to judicial discretion is to "lash judges to the solid mast of history" (Whittington 2004, 599).

Authorizing Supreme Court justices to "do whatever they want" is generally regarded as an undesirable thing. It gives them a governmental power contrary to their role that is difficult to justify. Such authorization appears to create rule by "philosopher-kings" unconstrained by electoral accountability. Moreover, it surely undermines stability and other values of an effective legal system if the justices may alter the content of controlling law at their whims. The prevention of this practice is considered crucial to the rule of law and a central justification for originalism.

From this position, the actual intent of the framers themselves about originalist interpretation is not relevant. The framers might have actively opposed originalism, but that would not refute the contention that the rule of law requires an originalist interpretive practice. It is commonly recognized that the framers' desire that their personal intent be followed does not necessarily dictate our method of interpretation (Bassham 1992). Correspondingly, their desire that their personal intent *not* be followed should not dictate our decisions. If we believe that the rule of law or democracy requires originalism, it scarcely matters that the framers modestly rejected the approach. If the original understanding were unwise or even deemed morally wrong, originalism says that is nonetheless the law, to be applied until it is changed.

A related defense of originalism is that of fairness and neutrality (Maltz 1987). Since the early twentieth century at least, Americans have been somewhat skeptical of the Supreme Court and its motivations. The justices sometimes appeared more as politicians, making rulings driven by their ideological preferences rather than by the law. Because the justices have life tenure and cannot be held accountable in elections, and because constitutional decisions cannot be overridden by elected officials, Supreme Court decisionmaking has intermittently frustrated many Americans. Judges seemed to have overstepped their proper bounds and assumed inappropriate political power. A modern survey of historical analysis at the Court has suggested that it has checked the excesses of both ideologies (Richards 1997).

Reliance on originalism would professedly control such judicial activism. Justices would defend limits to government power but defend only the rights that the framers identified in the Constitution. New rights would not be established out of penumbras. This view applies only to the Bill of Rights, however. It is plausible that originalism in the interpretation of the Articles could produce more activist decisionmaking, such as holding that the Commerce Clause does not authorize certain federal actions, making them unconstitutional. This potentially could radically alter federal government action.

Even with respect to the Bill of Rights, the Ninth Amendment provides an open-ended text that could encourage an originalist to expand the individual rights protected by the Constitution in a fashion that could be labeled as activist. The argument for restraint commonly presumes that the fundamental content of originalism is in fact restraintist, without providing much support. The better case is that originalism preserves the rule of law, whether activist or restraintist. To the degree that this produces undesirable results, it is for the people to change them through democracy.

Some surely defend originalism for nonneutral grounds, though, believing that it will produce their desired conservative results. In this theory, originalism was not successful because of its objectivity or certainty but because of its purported conservatism. Some viewed liberal jurisprudence as "a form of corruption that has degraded the wisdom and virtue found in the Constitution's original conception" (Levin 2004, 109). Rather than truly defending originalism, though, this position simply uses the theory as a convenient instrument for ideological objectives.

The Reagan administration pushed for originalism specifically to counter the Warren Court's liberal decisions. These decisions were viewed as pursuing a liberal agenda independent of what the Constitution truly dictated. The theory was "politically attractive" because it "implied conservative policy results as opposed to the prior wave of liberal Supreme Court decisions" (O'Neill 2005, 9). At this time, originalism became a vehicle for the mobilization of conservatives (Post & Siegel 2006). This conservative originalism, though, collapsed back into the case against "judicial activism." The conservative critics objected that the Warren Court had gone too far in protecting rights.

Originalism's early conservative following resulted from a desire for judicial restraint. Raoul Berger, perhaps the ur-originalist, complained that the Court was usurping power by failing to follow the original understanding (1983). Conservatives opposed Warren Court decisions invalidating statutes as judicial activism and contended that originalism would not have justified such decisions. For Ed Meese, "a jurisprudence of original intent was essential to judicial restraint" (Greene 2009b, 680). He "understood originalism as a way to limit the reach of constitutional adjudication" (O'Neill 2005, 157). Originalism, for example, arguably provided no basis for reproductive rights of the sort found in *Roe v. Wade*. According to Rush Limbaugh, the "only antidote" to "judicial activism is the conservative judicial philosophy known as originalism." This is also the originalism of Robert Bork.

Some of the most prominent contemporary originalists, however, reject judicial restraint as an argument for originalism. Earl Maltz (1994) suggested that originalism was not necessarily consistent with more judicial restraint. They may criticize judicial "passivism" for failing to strike down legislation that violates the Constitution (Whittington 1999). Randy Barnett believes that originalism should be used assertively to limit the federal government's legislative actions. For these leading originalists, originalism may be a tool for aggressive judicial activism in order to return the interpretation of the Constitution to its roots. Many of today's originalists commonly believe that the power of the federal government has far outstripped its constitutional bounds.

Reagan-era originalism was motivated in part by the Supreme Court's expanded recognition of individual rights and invalidation of democratic action (O'Neill 2005). Many of today's leading originalists, though, urge more expanded recognition of individual rights and invalidation of democratic action. Randy Barnett, for example, urges greater judicial activism in support of individual liberty, in direct opposition to the originalist philosophies of Bork and Scalia (Barnett 2005). His originalism is said to be "the antithesis of the originalism of Scalia, Bork, and the many others who seek to preserve democratic rule by limiting the scope of judicial power to interfere with the output of democratically elected legislators" (Colby & Smith 2009, 256).

Whether restraint characterizes originalism is questionable. Consider the voting pattern of the two justices most associated with the originalist philosophy—Scalia and Thomas. Justice Scalia has referred to himself and Thomas as the only originalists on the Court (Scalia 2007, 44). Yet they are among the most activist justices on the current Court (Lindquist & Cross 2009). This is especially true for review of federal statutes, where Scalia and Thomas have a remarkably high rate of invalidation (Lindquist & Cross 2009, 61). Originalism is not clearly associated with judicial restraint.

The argument for restraint is often framed as commitment of its own to democratic processes. By not acting, the judiciary leaves matters to the resolution of the elected branches of government. However, this forms a weak basis for originalism. Restraint in enforcing the Bill of Rights might be seen as democratic, but originalism may not call for restraint. Originalists believe the Constitution should be enforced to restrain democracy. A common call for originalism suggests that the Articles have not been enforced against democratic usurpation of congressional power, which is hardly restraintist in nature. One suspects that the argument for restraint is truly an argument over whether the commenter politically desires the consequences of that judicial restraint.

Whether activist or restraintist, originalism cannot truly be defended based on its political consequences. For any given individual, preferring a particular policy outcome, originalism might seem an appealing way to produce it. However, there is no reason to privilege the preferences of that, or any other, individual. Moreover, as I will show, the policy implications of originalism are not so clear as to ground reliance on originalism on expected results.

Yet another case for originalism might be found in stability, which formed part of Bork's original case for the theory. A stable law has many advantages, including the ability of private actors to adapt their actions in advance to the law. Fixed constitutional language lends stability to the governing law, a value recognized by the framers (Clinton 1987). Of course, stability is not necessarily a virtue; from Chief Justice Marshall on, people have recognized that the Constitution needs to be somewhat adaptable to changed circumstances.

While the true original meaning might be considered fixed and stable, our interpretations of that meaning may not be. With original meaning "a settled constitutional understanding is in perpetual jeopardy of being overturned by new light on the adopters' intent—shed by the discovery of historical documents, re-examinations of known documents, and reinterpretations of political and social history" (Brest 1980, 231). The "most plausible interpretation of a historical text changes over time" as new documents are discovered and old ones reanalyzed (Kleinhaus 2000, 123). Historians frequently change their positions on historical controversies, and reliance on their views could produce "weather-vane jurisprudence" (Bassham 1992, 95). "Revisionist" history is not uncommon.

Reliance on original meaning thus could possibly be relatively less stable than alternative interpretive regimes. Reliance on precedent would arguably be even more stable, at least in today's legal world. Originalism would require an "extraordinarily radical purge" of prevailing law (Bassham 1992, 95). The stability debate is also affected by the relative constraining effect of different legal interpretive methods. To the extent that an interpretive principle is less constraining on judges, it is also likely to yield less stable law. Originalism's effect on legal stability is highly uncertain.

Legally speaking, originalism may require no functional justification. Originalism may be regarded as the linguistically appropriate manner to apply a text, regardless of its association with democracy, or restraint, or stability, or any other external value. Such a simplistic approach may be unpersuasive, though, as constitutional interpretations have significant societal effects. If an approach produced very undesirable effects, there is no reason for society to embrace it simply because it is linguistically more defensible. It is not enough to simply put forward the "how" of interpretation; defending originalism needs a "why" as well.

The best functional case for originalism lies in its claimed objectivity and neutrality. Here it is necessary to distinguish between political appeal and logical appeal. Much of the political appeal of originalism no doubt lies elsewhere, grounded in much weaker rationales often biased by individual ideological assumptions. But this does not itself demean the theory. If a position is amply supported by good arguments, the simultaneous presence of bad supporting arguments does not undermine it. However, the inferior political arguments for originalism may undermine its use in practice.

Some argue that other nations' courts largely eschew originalism (Greene 2009b). If originalism is truly necessary to democracy, or judicial constraint, or the rule of law, this seems odd. Nations such as Canada and Australia, which reject originalism, appear to be democratic and to have a constrained rule of law judiciary. Greene (2009b) suggests that originalism is culturally contingent and has an appeal in this country that is missing elsewhere. However, this claim is not conclusive, and it seems unlikely that other nations utterly ignore original meaning of texts, which is a standard interpretive method.

Because of its political appeal in the United States, originalism may be vulnerable to manipulative use. Justices or others may invoke originalism as rhetorical support for conclusions grounded in other reasons. The earliest examination of the use of originalist evidence found that "while the high tribunal frequently utilizes convention debates and proceedings to rationalize and buttress a stand taken, the intention of the framers thus disclosed will not control the decision rendered" (tenBroeck 1938, 448). Rather than using originalism to find a result, the justices presented it as window dressing to make that result more palatable to readers. Thus, the use of originalism has been called "any-port-in-a-storm expedience" used to justify attractive policy results (Chenoweth 2009, 244). The very public appeal of originalism makes it an attractive device to manipulate.

The strength and weakness of originalism may be seen in the opinions of *District of Columbia v. Heller* (2008), addressing the meaning of the Second Amendment to the Constitution. The Court's majority focused its reasoning heavily on originalism, relying on dictionaries, the ratification debates, and other originalist materials to find an individual right to bear arms. However, the dissent did likewise, using evidence from the ratifying conventions and declarations by Madison and Washington. Both sides relied heavily on originalism. The votes of the justices divided along conventional ideological lines, though, with the conservatives finding that originalism supported a broader individual right to gun ownership and the liberals finding that originalism supported only a narrower right.

Heller reveals the power of reliance on originalist interpretation, given its widespread use, but also the weakness of such reliance, given the Court's division. Both sides in the case found ample originalist support for their opposite conclusions. Some originalists argue that Stevens took the wrong approach to originalism, but this finding, if true, does not cure the problem of originalism's application. The fact that he took the wrong approach would simply demonstrate that justices will take a wrong approach when necessary to justify their preferred outcome. Perhaps Stevens was using originalism in a manipulative fashion. The only thing that kept this hypothesized manipulation from succeeding was apparently the ideological composition of the Court.

The emphasis of the opinions has caused *Heller* to evidence the "triumph of originalism" (Greenhouse 2008, WK4). Yet with the opinion divided five to four along conventional ideological lines, some questioned whether originalism really was the source of the opinions. Nor were the details of the opinion so originalist. When Justice Scalia cited instances when arms could be regulated by the government notwithstanding the Second Amendment, he offered no originalist support whatsoever for his position. Once the right is recognized, the nature of these limitations becomes the crucial legal issue, and Scalia ignored originalism on that crucial issue. A conservative has argued that these details of Scalia's opinion departed so blatantly from originalism that the opinion should not be considered a good one (Lund 2009). *Heller* looks suspiciously as if each of the nine justices began with a preferred outcome to the case and then scoured the originalist record for evidence to support that outcome. Even assuming that an optimal originalism supported Scalia's basic finding, he quickly departed from that when inconvenient to his opinion.

The possibility of insincere (or incompetent) invocation of originalism is the focus of this book. The fundamental strengths of the case for originalism involve decisionmaking according to the rule of law and partisan neutrality. But if originalism is readily manipulated to different ends, it will not achieve those goals. In this event, the appeal of originalism is its downfall. The appeal of originalist interpretation means that insincere justices will claim to rely on originalist materials to legitimize their results, even though originalism had little to do with producing those results. Justice Scalia has cynically suggested that it would be "hard to count . . . on the hairs of one's youthful head the opinions that have in fact been rendered not on the basis of what the Constitution originally meant, but on the basis of what the judges currently thought it desirable to mean" (Scalia 1989, 852).

This manipulative effect is visible in the academic debate over originalism. One suspects that conservatives favored originalism because they believed it would produce conservative results. Liberals originally opposed originalism, perhaps for this very reason. When some liberals have subsequently embraced originalism, it is accompanied by arguments that originalism would produce liberal results. To a degree, Balkin (2007, 518) concedes this point. He notes that interpretive theory may not drive interpretation and argues that one purpose of interpretive theory is "to explain and justify our existing forms of development in hindsight." He sees originalism, in part, as a tool to justify interpretations driven by societal social movements while attempting to preserve some fidelity to the original text. Keith Whittington (2004, 609) argues that the "primary virtue claimed by the new originalism is one of constitutional fidelity." Yet this makes unproved presumptions about its honest application.

The ideological effect of originalism undermines this fidelity, and this problem may be even stronger at the Supreme Court level. Because originalism is appealing, especially to the public, persuasiveness will call for opinions to appear originalist and respond to the political appeal of the theory. Some of the liberals now embracing originalism may be perfectly sincere, but one suspects that others are being only strategic. Laura Kalman (1998, 238) concluded that legal liberals were "stuck with originalism," so that they should use the approach to advance their liberal goals. This recommendation illustrates how originalism may be used as a tool for other ends, rather than a governing principle of constitutional interpretation. The theoretical attractiveness of originalism to the public makes it a particularly desirable tool to pursue other ends and may even embolden the justices to go further than they otherwise might.

This impulse makes it more difficult to evaluate originalism. How does one distinguish true sincere originalism from insincere invocation of the theory to gain greater public acceptance of a holding? If "self-described originalist judges manipulate or ignore historical facts, then the approach is not constraining and of little value" (O'Neill 2005, 211). Of course, occasional insincerity is not condemning if originalism is generally authentic. Even if originalists occasionally manipulate the process to achieve ideological ends, over "the longer term" the reliance on the philosophy may be important (O'Neill 2005, 213). And the claims that originalism is an objective and neutral legal standard, if true, should prevent undue insincere use of the theory. Yet these claims must be tested.

Social scientists have examined the use of *The Federalist* in the Supreme Court, between 1953 and 1993 (Corley, Howard & Nixon 2005). They found that conservatives were somewhat more likely to cite to this source in pursuit of a limited government agenda. They also found that the justices were more likely to cite *The Federalist* in a very divided case, such as a five to four vote, and more likely to cite *The Federalist* when a justice on the other side of the divide cited this source. The justices were much more likely to cite *The Federalist* when their decision struck down a federal law as unconstitutional or formally altered a precedent. From these patterns, the authors concluded that *The Federalist* was cited "in a strategic fashion to bolster the legitimacy of the court when opinions assert judicial power" (Corley, Howard & Nixon 2005, 336). They concluded that use of the originalist source was tactical. Rather than truly relying on originalism for their decisions, the justices were invoking it to lend credence to their decisions. Thus, by "emphasizing reference to the historical document and the meaning or intentions of famous Framers, [justices] can evoke emotional responses that alternatives to originalism cannot directly match" (Wright 2008, 689).

The study gives some reason to question the citations to *The Federalist*. The citations may not be evidence of reliance on the source but instead an attempt to enhance the legitimacy of the opinion. Durschlag (2005, 315) suggests that the source is cited for an "ethos of objectivity" and a "perception of infallibility," as *The Federalist* is the "secular equivalent to citing the Bible." His review of decisions concluded that it was difficult to identify more than a small handful of cases where *The Federalist* even arguably played a decisive role in explaining the decision. Yet Justice Souter has officially declared that at least in one case (*Printz v. United States*, 1997) *The Federalist* determined his position, so it may happen.

Originalism may simply offer an "illusion of objectivity" that is convenient to a judiciary wishing to protect that illusion (Shaman 2010, 92). Another study (Hume 2006) considered a number of "rhetorical sources" including *The Federalist* and found that they tended to be invoked strategically, when the justices render a very controversial decision. The fact that the justices not uncommonly use *The Federalist* in both majority and dissenting opinions (Festa 2007) furthers the suspicion that its use may simply be tactical, to publicly bolster support for their position.

Sometimes, the justices will rely on private letters from one or another prominent framer. I looked for references to the correspondence of John Adams, James Madison, George Washington, John Jay, and Thomas Jefferson. References to the letters of Jefferson were far more frequent than references to any of the others examined. This is somewhat suspicious because Jefferson was not involved in the actual drafting of the Constitution. Nor would one expect that he had greater insight into the text's original meaning than did others. Jefferson is a rather iconic framer, though, and use of his letters might be seen as rhetorically more powerful than reliance on the letters of others.

Justices may "be moved to use slanted or fabricated history to justify results they favor on other grounds (Munzer & Nickel 1977, 1033). The effect of ideology is not a new issue. Justice Marshall's "great decisions consist largely of reading his own Federalist party predilections into the Constitution" (Wolfe 1996, 18). Yet claims of ideological judicial decisionmaking have become much more prominent in recent years. Social scientific studies, discussed later in this book, demonstrate the considerable influence of justices' ideology on the Court's decisions. This is not necessarily malicious; Gadamer contends that it is impossible for even a well-meaning person to understand the past free from his or her own prejudices. Originalism may tempt the justices to decide cases by their own biases and cloak those conclusions in the purported beliefs of the ratifiers, to avoid the need to otherwise justify their biases (Strauss 2008).

Beatty (2004, 9) contends that "no matter how good it sounds in theory, in practice it can't meet the standards it sets for itself." He contends: "Telling judges they must give effect to the original understanding of the constitution doesn't provide them with any guidance or direction and imposes no constraints because there are countless understandings from which they can choose" (Beatty 2004, 9).

Steven Calabresi contends that the justices tend to more often resort to originalism when dealing with issues of great importance (Calabresi 2008). The implication is that originalism is most valuable for the Court in the most salient cases. However, a contrary implication is obvious. Originalism

CROSS, FRANK B.

FAILED PROMISE OF ORIGINALISM.

                              Cloth   228 P.
STANFORD: STANFORD UNIVERSITY PRESS, 2013

AUTH: UNIVERSITY OF TEXAS. STUDY OF VALUE OF
ORIGINALISM APPROACH. A STANFORD LAW BOOK.
LCCN 2012-15153
  ISBN 0804783829   **Library PO#** FIRM ORDERS

		List	45.00	USD
8395 NATIONAL UNIVERSITY LIBRAR	**Disc**	14.0%		
App. Date 2/12/14 SOC-SCI 8214-08	**Net**	38.70	USD	

SUBJ: 1. CONSTITUTIONAL LAW--U.S. 2. UNITED
STATES. SUPREME COURT.
AWD/REV: 2014 CHOS
CLASS KF4550   DEWEY# 342.730011   LEVEL ADV-AC

YBP Library Services

CROSS, FRANK B.

FAILED PROMISE OF ORIGINALISM.

                              Cloth   228 P.
STANFORD: STANFORD UNIVERSITY PRESS, 2013

AUTH: UNIVERSITY OF TEXAS. STUDY OF VALUE OF
ORIGINALISM APPROACH. A STANFORD LAW BOOK.
  LCCN 2012-15153
  ISBN 0804783829   **Library PO#** FIRM ORDERS

		List	45.00	USD
8395 NATIONAL UNIVERSITY LIBRAR	**Disc**	14.0%		
App. Date 2/12/14 SOC-SCI 8214-08	**Net**	38.70	USD	

SUBJ: 1. CONSTITUTIONAL LAW--U.S. 2. UNITED
STATES. SUPREME COURT.
AWD/REV: 2014 CHOS
CLASS KF4550   DEWEY# 342.730011   LEVEL ADV-AC

is important to the Court, not to decide the important cases but to legitimize their decisions in these cases. Rather than a constraint, it is a strategy.

Frank Easterbrook has suggested that originalism *is* the constraint on judges. But one struggles to find a contemporary originalist who believes that the original meaning of the Constitution significantly contradicts his or her own political preferences. Demosthenes reportedly said that "nothing is easier than self-deceit" and that what a "man wishes, that he also believes." The justices "frequently divide on questions of original meaning, and the divisions have a way of mapping what we might suspect are the Justices' leanings about the merits of the cases irrespective of originalist considerations" (Primus 2010, 79). If this tendency influences originalist interpretation, it undermines its value. Scalia and others suggest that precedents are not truly constraining because they can be readily distinguished and evaded, but the same principle may apply to originalist interpretation.

This issue is the central question behind this book. I will elide the theoretical debate over the correctness of interpretive originalism, because this debate would be irrelevant to the actual law, if originalism could not be formally realized. If originalism is so manipulable in practice, the debate over its validity could have a theoretical philosophical value but lends little to actual judicial decisionmaking practice. The test of application, though, is not whether originalism is perfectly constraining on judges but whether it is relatively constraining, perhaps only "better than the next best alternative" (Macey 1995, 306). Thus, for Justice Scalia, originalism is a "lesser evil" (Scalia 1989), flawed but better than any alternatives. It may be that a theoretical dedication to originalism as an interpretive method may become instilled in the justice's mentality and overcome his or her ideological objectives (Gillman 1997). Such a finding alone would not justify reliance on originalism, but it would be a significant supporting prop.

Originalists may suggest that the only alternative to originalist interpretation is unbridled judicial discretion. Sometimes they suggest that the absence of any competing theory of interpretation makes originalism inevitable as "it takes a theory to beat a theory." These analyses are too simplistic; other factors such as precedent may bind justices today, and they are amply grounded in theory. Originalists are correct, though, in making the matter a comparative one. Originalism need not be a perfect theory to be justified; it need only be better than the alternatives.

Originalism is often juxtaposed with the notion of a "living" Constitution. The latter notion, though, has little content. It recognizes a need to adapt the original Constitution but contains no intrinsic directions on how this should be done. The living Constitution is not itself an interpretive theory.

In practice, the essential alternative to originalism in Supreme Court interpretation is now typically pluralism (Griffin 2008). Cardozo embraced this approach, referring to it as a "wise eclecticism" of methods. Pluralism means that the justices would choose the interpretive method (such as originalism, or precedent, or pragmatism), depending on the facts of the case before them. Ideally, they would choose the theory best suited for the individual case, but their ability and willingness to do so is unestablished.

Logically, it seems that giving such added flexibility as to interpretive method in pluralism would increase the discretion of the justices and, by so doing, increase their ability to manipulate results for ideological ends. Thus, exclusive reliance on a single interpretive method such as originalism could well be more constraining that the alternative of choosing among multiple methods. Many defenders would argue that originalism would be the most constraining of *any* single method available to the Court. Originalism is thought to offer a "comparative advantage in being able to constrain justices by providing fairly objective and specific criteria to evaluate judicial performance" (Whittington 1999, 39). Originalists recognize indeterminacy but believe that their methods will resolve important contested questions that are determinate. Justice Scalia (1997) has argued that originalism is at least somewhat limiting, as no originalist would have concluded that capital punishment or restraint on abortion was unconstitutional.

If, however, originalism is not in fact constraining on the justices, that fact totally undercuts the case for the method. While it most obviously undercuts the constraint justification, it also undermines the democratic justification and the rule of law justification (because the theory is manipulated and inauthentically applied). The debate over the theory of originalism has generally overlooked the practice, but the theory is of little real value if it cannot be operationalized in practice.

Justice Scalia (1989) has recognized that exclusive originalist decision-making at the Supreme Court is rare. The "vast majority of Supreme Court decisions interpreting the Constitution have been nonoriginalist in their methodology" (Shaman 2010, 87). While originalism is said to have "substantially reoriented constitutional theory, its influence on the Court was not as deep" (O'Neill 2005, 205). Originalism seems one alternative for use by the pluralist Court. Yet there has been a dearth of actual scholarship on the use of originalist sources in judicial opinions (Festa 2007), so any conclusion can only be a tentative one.

The vast majority of constitutional decisions at the Court are decided on the basis of precedent or other materials, without any reference to original meaning (Fallon 1997, 106). Yet every justice in the Court's history has relied to some degree on originalism (Merrill 2008). The Court's use of originalism has increased over the years, and at least some recent decisions rely centrally on the method. Some argue it should be used much more in constitutional interpretation. This book reviews the history of its use, with an eye on the promise of possible greater reliance on originalism. My analysis of usage is confined to that of the Supreme Court. This is arguably too narrow, as the Constitution is interpreted by lower courts, legislators, executive officers, and the citizenry, but the Court is the primary determinant of constitutionality and where most of the dispute over originalism lies.

Using originalism to interpret the Constitution has great appeal. As the Supreme Court is increasingly the subject of public attention, that appeal has been recognized by many justices. Even critics of originalism have "understood intuitively the persuasive power of an appeal to historical authority in legitimizing legal arguments" (Festa 2008, 492). As they invoke originalism, though, the process may represent a sincere attempt to uncover the original meaning of the constitutional text, or it may be just a means of cloaking a decision founded on other grounds with the mythic status of the framers. Although a great deal has been written about originalism, this issue is the crucial one and has been largely unexplored.

A claim that originalism is the ideal method of constitutional interpretation has little real value if that ideal cannot be realized in practice. The debate over originalism has generally been quite abstract, however. Those who have debated the theory of originalism "rarely test their views on the merits of originalism by reference to the realities of constitutional adjudication" (Rosenthal 2012, 1187). To be practically meaningful, a theory must be tested in practice (Friedman 1998, 668).

This book examines the practice of originalism at the Supreme Court. I review the history of its usage throughout the centuries with an emphasis on the recent era. Originalism has in fact gained great prominence recently, perhaps because of the perception that the Court wields great government power. In many cases, though, the apparent use of originalism appears to be a fig leaf covering other motivations for a decision of the Court. By reviewing the use of prominent originalist sources by the justices, I search for evidence of the method's constraining effect.

The Meaning of Originalism

This chapter examines the theoretical meaning of originalism. I caution the reader that the focus of this book is not theoretical, and my discussion will elide some of the finer theoretical points of the theory. A basic understanding of the theory's meaning, though, is vital to appreciating its application, and this chapter will provide at least a summary of the debate. Many people do not appreciate that originalism is not a single theory but various different approaches to interpreting the Constitution.

Basic principles of originalism have long been with us, but the theory first coalesced politically in the 1970s (Solum 2008). At this time, originalist constitutional interpretation was presented as reflecting the original intent of the framers; that is, "What would Jefferson think about this question?" It is reflected and lampooned in Justice Alito's statement at oral argument: "What Justice Scalia wants to know is what James Madison thought about video games," to which Scalia responded that he truly wanted to know "what James Madison thought about violence" (Liptak 2010). This position had an appeal to those who held the framers in the highest regard. Today's justices could find answers by attempting to channel the thoughts of the leading individuals who wrote the Constitution. This original intent originalism, though, was fraught with problems, as discussed in the following pages.

This traditional view has sometimes been called "original expected applications" originalism. It asks what the framers might have thought about the question immediately before the Court and how they would have believed the case should be resolved. This approach is considered "original intention" originalism. Edwin Meese was a leader in the early promotion of originalism, and he insisted on a "jurisprudence of original intention" based on "the original intent of the Framers" (Meese 1985). This was a search for the subjective beliefs of those who wrote the Constitution, such as James Madison.

A contemporary controversy illustrates the issues over original expected applications originalism. The Constitution prohibits cruel and unusual punishment. Some originalists maintain that if a punishment was in existence at the time of the Constitution (and unchallenged constitutionally), it must not be unconstitutionally cruel and unusual. It apparently was not seen as unconstitutional by those living at the time. This view appears to be held at least to some degree by Justices Thomas and Scalia of the current Court. Of course, practices such as ear cropping and flogging were also accepted punishments at the time (Greenberg & Litman 1998), and one doubts that they would be upheld today (a point Scalia concedes).

For about a century, it seemed to be "generally agreed that the amendment was originally understood to prohibit only barbarous and torturous punishments of the sort that had been common in Tudor and Stuart England" (Bassham 1992, 95). As society evolved, this made the provision relatively unimportant, as such punishments were abandoned. The Court shifted to recognize the Amendment's control of contemporary disproportionately severe punishments, based in part on original meaning evidence.

The prevailing majority of today's Court has employed an "evolving standards of decency" doctrine to interpret cruel and unusual punishment (*Roper v. Simmons* 2005). Even Justice Scalia has admitted that unconstitutionality could be evaluated by "the demonstrable current standards of our citizens" in addition to originalist text (*Stanford v. Kentucky* 1989, 369–370).

While original expected applications can resolve some questions about the meaning of cruel and unusual punishment, it cannot answer them all. Consider a form of physical punishment that was not in existence at the time of the framing. Original expected applications could not evaluate its constitutionality, and originalists would simply try to apply the principles of the original expected applications to the new circumstances of the case. A slightly more difficult case would arise when a form of punishment, used at the time of the framing, is found to have consequences unknown at that time. Perhaps that form of punishment causes excruciating pain, of which the framers were unaware. In this case, the answer of the original expected applications originalist is uncertain. Was their intention based on the punishment itself or its perceived consequences? A further question is the effect of changing social standards of morality. Our assessment of what punishment is "cruel" will change over time. In this case, the original expected applications originalist would be expected to rule out this development as a basis for constitutional interpretation. Such originalists would leave such cultural changes to be reflected in constitutional amendments.

Because this provision also refers to "unusual" punishment, though, it seems to ask for a more contemporaneous assessment and evolving standards. The Court has conducted a similar "evolving standards" analysis under the First Amendment (when evaluating Sunday closing laws, a tax exemption for churches, prayers in legislative assemblies, setting school district boundaries) and other constitutional provisions (Lain 2009). This particular originalist approach has not pervaded the Supreme Court's analysis, as will be discussed in following chapters. Several problems have been identified with this reliance on original expected intent originalism.

One difficulty of original intent was that associated to ascribing intentions to a collective group (such as the framers or those who ratified the Constitution), in contrast to an individual. While collective intentions are theoretically possible (all members of a group may agree precisely), the nature of the drafting makes this unlikely or at least inaccessible (Solum 2008). The numerous people who drafted the Constitution or voted for ratification may not have and almost surely did not share intentions as to the meaning of all the specific terms. Jack Rakove (1987, 229) questions "how one can assign any coherent intentions to groups of individuals acting with a range of purposes and expectations and reaching decisions through a process of bargaining and compromise." History "makes clear that there was frequently no strong consensus on the specific principle or proposition expressed by a given provision" (Bassham 1992, 85). To "admit the relevance of such a large number of states of mind is to set forth a task virtually impossible to fulfill" (Wofford 1964, 509), and the framers prominently disagreed on some issues. The presence of some conflicts, though, does not mean that there was not a collective intention as to *some* constitutional meanings.

If a group were viewed as a single entity with a single intent in the absence of universal assent, presumably the views of the majority of that group would be taken as the collective intent. However, this approach runs into the problem that it is possible that, of the majority who saw a given intent, a majority of them voted *against* ratification but accepted the Constitution on other grounds. Ratification may have succeeded only because of the votes of those who took the minority interpretation of a provision's meaning. This would undermine the democratic basis for originalism.

Solum (2008) notes that using the intent of the majority supporters implausibly implies that there was no meaning to the language before it had the support of the majority. However, there may in fact have been no accepted or understood meaning of some terms. It is very possible that a single set of words could have different meanings to different people. With multiple meanings, it is possible that no single one had majoritarian support. Dworkin suggested that there was "no such thing as the intention of the Framers waiting to be discovered" but "only some such thing waiting to be invented" (Dworkin 1981, 477).

Moreover, individual framers had very different views of the meaning of the Constitution. The original intent theory could not tell us *which* framer to consult about the proper interpretation. Perhaps only one framer spoke on the relevant question of the day. While he would be an obvious candidate for interpretive use, there is a distinct possibility that other framers believed differently but never even expressed their opinions or that their expressions have been lost in the historical record. If multiple framers spoke, and they took contradictory positions, original intentions originalism becomes an uncertain choice.

This original intent theory could also be lampooned as a "time travel" approach to interpretation. There was no way to discern what a framer, in his eighteenth-century position, would have thought about a modern legal question. Moreover, circumstances have changed so greatly that one would have to imagine a Jefferson, at 300 years old, having lived the entire course of American history with unchanged views. Harvard law students skewered this approach in a mock article decrying the destruction of Justice Scalia's time machine, asking, "How will we ever know about what Jefferson would have thought about fake Twitter accounts as grounds for libel claims?" (Wells 2009).

Yet another problem with original intent is legal. However wise the framers may have been, they do not have legal authority. Indeed, they did not create the Constitution as law. The Constitution governs only because it was ratified by the people of the states. As the source of the Constitution's legal authority via democratic vote, it is these people, rather than the framers, who seem legally relevant. Perhaps the ratifiers endorsed the views of the framers on the Constitution, but this endorsement could extend only to those views of which they were aware. The ratifiers may have had a very different intent from that of the prominent framers typically used for discerning original intent.

Not least among the problems with original expected applications originalism is its implications. Whittington (1999, 173) asks: "In an originalist America, would not the government engage in flogging and branding of criminals, forced sterilization, white supremacy, electronic eavesdropping, silencing of evolutionary teachings, and so on?" While the framers are greatly admired, few would desire to constitutionalize all their expectations for America.

For these and other reasons, the original intent of the framers was largely though not entirely abandoned as the appropriate guide to constitutional interpretation. Originalism "has itself changed—from original *intention* to original *meaning*" (Barnett 1999, 620). A leading originalist has declared that the "fact that the Framers in Philadelphia . . . expected a certain application of the text is of no moment at all" (Calabresi & Fine 2009, 666). This abandonment of framers' intent provided the impetus for the rebirth of a more persuasive and powerful form of originalism.

The "new originalism" distinguished itself from the earlier originalism in several ways. The originalism of the Reagan era was described as only a "reactive and critical posture" (Whittington 2004, 604) that was committed to judicial restraint, while the new originalism had no such necessary presumptions about the judicial role. Larry Solum (2008) terms this new approach "semantic originalism," which implies that the true meaning of the constitutional provision was fixed at the time of ratification by the meaning of the words of the text. Today's originalism claims to be more objective both in interpretation (as opposed to seeking the subjective intent of the framers) and in implications (not necessarily yielding results desired by conservative original intent group).

The "new originalism" eschewed reliance on the subjective thoughts of the leading framers. The current "academic defenders of originalism have been disavowing expectation originalism" (Berman 2009). Instead, it focuses on the original meaning of the words of the Constitution, at the time of its ratification. While one might think this generally correlated with original expected applications, that is not necessarily the case (Greenberg & Litman 1998). Because the written Constitution was an expression of popular consent to a form of government, it was the original ratifiers who made a democratically validated decision to approve particular constitutional language (Solum 2008) and not the drafters themselves. The original "public understanding" of the Constitution's terms should govern its interpretation (Lash 2004, 339). Should the views of the people change, they may amend the language of the Constitution, per the terms of the original text.

In today's originalism, the standard is "not what went through the minds of the framers as they wrote and ratified the particular constitutional provisions they did, but rather the contemporaneous public understanding of the language comprising the doctrine" (Goldford 2005, 117). Calabresi (2007, 15) argues that "there is no reason to think that the unenacted, idiosyncratic intentions of particular Framers are law." Justice Scalia has thus said that he may be consulting the writings of the framers not because "their intent is authoritative" but instead because "their writings, like those of other intelligent and informed people of the time, display how the text of the Constitution was originally understood" (Scalia 1997, 38). This position was that taken by James Madison himself, who once referred to the "intention of whose who framed" the Constitution but then quickly corrected himself to say "or rather, who adopted" it, indicating that the ratifiers were the relevant authority (Maggs 2009b), though this still refers to intention and not meaning. Thomas Jefferson also said that constitutional interpretation should conform to the probable meaning of the text at the time (Meese 1985).

The ratifying individuals may still be considered the best source for originalist interpretation. Some suggest that originalism refers to "what the persons who participated in the state ratifying conventions thought that the Constitution meant" (Maggs 2009b, 461). The originalist objective is finding the meaning of "the text of the Constitution, as originally understood by the people who ratified it" (Calabresi & Prakash 1994, 551). The ratifiers' understanding "can be taken, at least provisionally, as an adequate approximation of the original public understanding" (Perry 1991, 677).

Still, the ratifiers themselves may not be conclusive. The governing standard of "original meaning" inevitably raises the question of "original meaning to whom?" Randy Barnett expresses the common view of original meaning as referring "to the meaning a reasonable speaker of English would have attached to the words, phrases, sentences, etc. at the time the particular provision was adopted" (Barnett 2001, 105). While one would expect this to correspond with the views of the ratifiers, this may not be the case. Originalists could maintain that "it matters not what any (much less all) of the Ratifiers actually *intended* or *understood*, but what the hypothetical reasonably well-informed Ratifier would have objectively understood the text to mean with all of the relevant information in hand" (Kesavan & Paulsen 2003, 1162). Thus, the "proper object of constitutional inquiry is a *hypothetical* mental state, not an actual mental state" (Lawson & Seidman 2002, 90). This has been called objective public meaning originalism that does not particularly concern itself with "how the words of the Constitution were actually understood by the Framers, the ratifiers, the public, or anyone else" (Colby & Smith 2009, 254). In this view, the standard is the "reasonable American person of 1788" (Lawson & Seidman 2006, 47). While theoretically more appealing in several ways, this approach obviously complicates the application of the theory, as we have no imaginary hypothetical person on whom to rely in interpretation.

This view conflicts with the theoretical grounding of other leading originalists, however. Some still emphasize the subjective intent of the ratifiers of the Constitution (Berman 2009). These are the individuals who gave legal authority to the Constitution. In this vision, it is the majority view that is privileged. Consequently, original public meaning would not necessarily "distinguish the writings of Hamilton and Madison from those of any literate hack of the day" (McGowan 2001, 756–757), but they might still rely on intentions. Whittington (1999, 36) argues that the Constitution cannot be taken to mean what the "best" minds of the period thought and that interpretation should focus on identifying the thoughts of the ratifiers, who provided the democratic basis for the Constitution's authority.

I suspect that the strongest theoretical grounding for originalism would hold that the objective original meaning is the guiding principle and that the beliefs of whose who ratified are strong evidence of this objective original meaning, but not conclusive evidence. However, a modern interpreter should surely be modest about his or her ability to discern an original meaning different from that of the the ratifiers, who lived at the time. Thus, ratifier understanding of the semantic meaning of constitutional language is a very good proxy for original meaning.

Whether the ratifiers' subjective views should govern the original meaning can be disputed. It can be argued that the ratification "was an intentional act and we cannot understand what it accomplished independent of what the people involved in it thought they were doing" (Kay 2009, 706). What is to count is "the document as understood by the American People who ratified and amended it" (Amar 2000, 29). This is the interpretation of Thomas Jefferson himself, who declared that he would administer the Constitution "according to the safe and honest meaning contemplated by the plain understanding of the people at the time of its adoption" (Berger 1977, 366–367). Originalists may thus refer to "ratifier intent" as governing (Lofgren 1988, 79). McConnell (1998, 1136) argues that originalism "is the idea that the words of the Constitution must be understood as they were understood by the ratifying public at the time of enactment." The importance of the subjective views of the ratifiers is also relevant to the democratic justification for originalism, though they are not necessarily theoretically controlling, as they were in earlier formulations of originalism.

Keith Whittington, who may be regarded as one of the framers of the new originalism, justified originalist interpretation on the grounds of democracy. The Constitution was adopted through democratic processes and thereby given legal authority. The original meaning therefore has the democratic imprimatur. Alternative theories of constitutional interpretation arguably lack this democratic basis. If democracy is the grounds for originalist interpretation, one might think that the subjective intent of the voters should control. The hypothetical, well-informed ratifier was not necessarily the voter who approved the Constitution. When electing a president or other official, we do not attempt to evaluate the intent of the hypothetical, well-informed voter.

This democratic argument for subjective ratifier intent is not necessarily the case, however. Thus, when interpreting a statute, Justice Scalia and others eschew reliance on the subjective beliefs of members of Congress, as evidenced by the legislative history and other materials. For them, democracy is a process in which a text is adopted, and that text should be given its objective meaning. This is more of a rule of law justification.

In practice, the distinction between the subjective actual ratifier and the hypothetical well-informed ratifier is probably a trivial one. The objective original meaning for the hypothetical ratifier will presumably mirror that of the actual ratifiers. The subjective mental states of the subjective actual ratifier likely parallels the linguistic semantic meaning of the objective ratifier. The ratifiers obviously acted based on contemporary understandings of the words' meaning.

Robert Bork has therefore argued that "what the ratifiers understood themselves to be enacting must be taken to be what the public at that time would have understood the words to mean" (Bork 1990, 144). Surely contemporaneous actual intended application is a close guide to contemporaneous reasonable understanding (presumably better than most retrospective estimation) (McGinnis & Rappaport 2007). It seems likely that the "longer the temporal gap between an event and its investigation, the less reliable an investigator's perceptions are likely to be" (Samanaha 2008, 1340). The early expectations of the text applications, including those of the framers, are thus highly relevant to original meaning originalism. Ratifiers' subjective intention may not demonstrate original meaning, but it is possibly the best available evidence of such meaning.

While much has been made of the evolution of originalism, the changes may be exaggerated. There may not be great difference between original expected applications originalism and new semantic originalism. Original expected application of the Constitution presumably would typically be in accordance with its original meaning. McGinnis and Rappaport (2007,

378) note that "it is hard to understand what constitutional provisions mean without reference to expected applications." Calabresi and Fine (2009, 669) respond that this is not necessarily the case and that "Congress often passes statutes with a mistaken impression of what they mean or how they will apply." In the short term, at least, most expected applications would be consistent with original public meanings. As times and circumstances change, though, this association may become more remote.

Justice Scalia's vision of original meaning has been considered by many akin to original expected application originalism (Balkin 2007). While semantic originalists would not embrace original expected applications as necessarily equivalent to meaning, they would consider it as relevant evidence as to meaning. Although the new originalists have gone to great lengths to distinguish themselves from early originalists, the difference may not truly be so great.

There may be some cases in which there is a plain difference between the intent of the framers and the ratifiers. During the Constitutional Convention, a number of framers suggested an intent that treaties be self-executing, but records from the state conventions suggested that ratifiers did not believe this to be the case (Maggs 2009a). So there are surely some differences in the proper sources for originalist interpretation.

Some maintain that there is no true current meaning to the term *originalism* (Colby & Smith 2009). Some still adhere to the earlier original expected meanings interpretation. Others reject this in favor of original public meaning but differ as to whether this conclusion measures the subjective meaning assigned the text by those who ratified it or some objective contemporaneous meaning to be assigned the text. The theory has been embraced by liberals, as well as conservatives, with widely diverging views of its proper application. Some originalists are more fainthearted than others. The "self-professed originalists on the bench who have claimed to endorse one particular brand of originalism, to the exclusion of all others, have in fact bounced around among originalist theories from case to case" (Colby & Smith 2009, 292–293). Consequently the nature of originalism has been called "mushy and confused" (Fallon 1996, 492). All originalists presumably concur that the meaning of the Constitution was fixed at the time of ratification, but they take different approaches to discerning this meaning. Some preserve a role for original expected applications.

Robert Bork suggests that originalism does not mean that judges must "decide cases the way the Framers would if they were here today," but also that "many cases will be decided that way" (Bork 1986, 826). Original meaning and original expected application thus "will tend to converge in practice even if the two concepts remain distinct in theory" (Nelson 2003, 558). The original applications "will often be some of the best evidence of what meaning is" (McGinniss & Rappaport 2007, 378). Many original-ists view original expected applications as very strong evidence of original meaning, but they recognize some differences. In many cases, one suspects there was no thought given in original expected applications for modern-day controversies. Great changes have occurred since the framing, which take our disputes well beyond their anticipations. Of course, the framers were aware of this problem. They "strove for a Constitution that would survive changes in American society" (Hamburger 1989, 325).

Bork highlighted the effect of technological change on interpretation. This is one obvious area in which original expected applications should not prevail. There could be no original expected application when the framers were entirely unaware of the possible application that developed later. This is an inevitable concession to the effect of changing circumstances on even an immutable text. The Second Amendment right to bear arms is thus not limited to those arms, such as muskets, that were available to Americans at the time. In *Heller*, this theory was not pursued by those who favored gun control.

This practice is a larger concession to nonoriginalism than often rec-ognized. The fact that the framers favored a right to bear arms available at the time does not intrinsically mean that they would favor a right to bear weaponry available today, which is certainly more destructive. Applying the Constitution to new technologies necessarily involves some abstrac-tion. What was the purpose of creating a constitutional right to bear arms? Perhaps it was self-defense. If so, the Second Amendment should be applied so as at least to allow ownership of those arms that are necessary and ap-propriate to self-defense in a modern society. But, as recognized by *Heller*, this self-defense right is not boundless. The interpretation of the bounds on this right is inevitably influenced by contemporary conditions. If original-ism can shed light on the bounds to Second Amendment rights, the *Heller* opinion offered none of it (Lund 2009).

The problem of technological change on the Constitution is ubiquitous. The founding era could not possibly have contemplated anything like the Internet. This makes it difficult to apply principles such as the Bill of Rights to the Internet. The drafters of the Commerce Clause could have no appreciation of today's technologies driving commerce (Strang 2009). Justice Scalia has observed that jurisdictional understandings must be altered in light of "changes in the technology of transportation and communication, and the tremendous growth in interstate business activity" (*Burnham v. Superior Court* 1990, 616).

Technological development may not be the only relevant changed circumstances. Surely, the international position of the United States and military authority has changed markedly. The Constitution was not written for a nation that was by far the richest of the world and a preeminent military power. Other nontechnological changes involve mores about sex and religion, and the law arguably should adapt to such cultural changes (Strang 2009).

The United States has shifted from being a rural agricultural nation to being urban and focused on manufacturing and services. This has involved cultural changes as well as technological. Originalists recognize that such changes should influence constitutional interpretation. Rakove (2003, 1346) tells of a colloquy with Ed Meese, in which he suggested that originalism would limit the executive prerogative over national security, to which Meese responded something like: "You have to realize . . . that the Constitution had been written in a very different period and world, and that much had changed since then." Bork (1990) acknowledges that the First Amendment originally did not apply to defamation cases but suggests that changed circumstances made it clear this protection was necessary. But he recognizes that this is a slippery slope (Bork 1990, 169) that could be used to destroy true originalism. He offers no clear principle to stop the slippery slope, however.

While originalists acknowledge the need to respond to effects of societal change, they claim that their method is amply adaptable to it. First, the broad principles underlying the Constitution, if not the original expected intent, can still inform decisions today. Thus, when the Court considers whether the new technology of the thermal image scan of a house (revealing to some degree interior contents) violates the Constitution, the Court will apply the broad principles of the Fourth Amendment (*Kyllo v. United States* 2001) and the types of privacy it was meant to protect. By abstracting fundamental principles from the text, a broader meaning can be found to adapt to changed circumstances. This is reasonably consistent with the intent of the framers, who used broad language for defendants' rights in anticipation of changed technology (Wray 2005), and it can be consistent with original meaning, which goes beyond original expected applications of the Constitution.

Justice Scalia has noted that the effect of changing circumstances on constitutional interpretation goes beyond technology (*Georgia v. Randolph* 2006). He observes that "our unchanging Constitution refers to other bodies of law that might themselves change" (*Georgia v. Randolph* 2006, 144). Today's treaties are very different from those of the past, and the major international organizations did not exist at the time. For another example, the Constitution provides protection for property but does not control what matters are protected *as* property. As different forms of property are recognized, the law must define the rights those forms possess. Thus, while the language of the constitutional provision does not change, its practical effect could change considerably due to changed circumstances.

Moreover, the inevitable concession to technological change alone may have much broader applications. As already discussed in connection with cruel and unusual punishment, not only are new technologies developed by society, but we gain learning about the scientific implications of even earlier technologies. The relevance of such information to originalist interpretation is unclear. Some originalists would hold that if the framers were incorrect about a simple matter of fact, their resultant views need not govern (McGinnis & Rappoport 2007). The framers presumably did not mean to enshrine in law their factual conclusions, if they were later found to be incorrect. If the framers believed a given disease to be contagious, but it is not, we shouldn't adhere to their mistaken belief (Greenberg & Litman 1998). Christopher Eisgruber (2001) cites a grandchild's promise to "eat only healthy food" and the difficulty of using the promise's original meaning as we change our understanding of what foods are healthy. Thus, "changed circumstances may undermine the relevance of framing-era understandings or practice to contemporary circumstances" (Rosenthal 2012, 16).

But if developments in factual knowledge are reason to modify original intent, why would other developments not provide a similar justification? For example, should cultural or moral changes, such as changing evaluations of what is cruel, be reason for interpreting the constitution differently? Most originalists and even critics of originalism (Berman 2009) would reject this view. If the constitutional text must be adapted to technological change, without the requirement for formal amendment, why should it not be adapted to other forms of change? With semantic originalism, it is possible to argue that a fixed original meaning can yield different results with changed facts but not changed cultural views, unless the meaning has an underlying cultural referent.

Even excluding culture, changes besides new technologies may alter the Constitution's application. With our economic growth, many activities that once were not "commerce among the several states" have become so (Greenberg & Litman 1998), which alters the implications of the commerce clause. The law may also change. Today we recognize contracts that would not have been recognized at the time of the Constitution's adoption (Greenberg & Litman 1998), but the Constitution should presumably protect the rights of such contracts. Original expected applications originalism has difficulty accommodating such change, but original meaning may be better able to do so.

A change in surrounding law called the original understanding into question in *Tennessee v. Garner* (1985). In the framing era, the Fourth Amendment permitted warrantless arrests on probable cause for a felony. But in *Tennessee v. Garner* (1985, 13), the Court held that "because of sweeping change in the legal and technological context, reliance on the common-law rule in this case would be a mistaken literalism that ignores the purposes of historical inquiry." Justice White noted that, in the intervening time, there had been a considerable change in the types of offenses classified as felonies. Justice Scalia has similarly acknowledged that a change in the surrounding legal rules may change the original understanding of when a warrant is required (*California v. Acevedo* 1991). This is not necessarily contrary to original meaning originalism but complicates it, as factual changes lead to legal changes, which lead to possibly dramatic changes in constitutional meaning. It can be difficult to say how the original meaning of language should apply to very different circumstances, not contemplated by the drafters or ratifiers.

Regulatory takings provide an example of the impact of nontechnological change on constitutional interpretation. The constitutional prohibition on taking of property addressed its physical expropriation by government. The clause was so interpreted for over a hundred years, and this appeared to be its original meaning (Treanor 1995). In *Pennsylvania Coal Company v. Mahon* (1922), Justice Holmes extended the takings clause to cover regulation that unduly diminished the value of property. Though Justice Scalia recognized some question about regulatory takings and original meaning (*Lucas v. South Carolina Coastal Council* 1992), he affirmed the doctrine. Some conservatives have sought to reconcile original meaning and restrictions on regulatory takings by arguing that circumstances have changed and that the doctrine is required by the broad principles of the takings clause.

Perhaps the key controversy that differentiates original expected applications originalism from newer semantic originalism is the question of abstraction. If the words of the Constitution do not install specific expected applications, they instead can sometimes be viewed as statements of broad principle. The "provisions of the Constitution stand for principles, not for lists of impermissible practices" (Greenberg & Litman 1998, 580). Ed Meese (1985), though often associated with more specific original intent, has said that his originalist approach "seeks to discern the particular and general principles" expressed by the Constitution.

The guarantee of free speech, while it obviously had some intended applications at the time of the framers, might stand for a broad principle that went beyond those applications. This approach allows for adaptation to new technologies, for example. We need simply evaluate the technological facts at issue and apply the Constitution's broader principles to find the correct conclusion. Robert Bork (1986) explains that the Constitution creates a "core value" such as free speech as a major premise. This is then applied to new electronic media, the changing impact of libel litigation, and other developments since the time of ratification. He notes that this approach may not yield the exact result that the framers would reach but at least channels judicial discretion.

It is this original principles-based originalism that has been aggressively embraced by some liberals. By interpreting the original constitutional principles broadly, liberal opinions, including reproductive rights, may be brought under the umbrella of originalism. Most conservative originalists accept the notion of principles-based originalism, to some degree, but disagree about application. Bork (1986), for example, believes originalism is governed by the principles of original meaning but takes a much narrower view of those principles than does Balkin. For example, he recognizes the Fourteenth Amendment's principle of equality but notes that it was limited at the time to racial equality and argues that a justice cannot apply any higher level of abstract generality (for example, sexual equality) in applying the principle to override democratic choice (Bork 1986). Allowing such generalization makes originalism "quite an open-ended process" (Farber 2001, 178). One need only define the "core value" to be protected. Berman (2009) questions whether broad generality can truly be reconciled with originalism, but many originalists recognize its possibility.

The debate becomes one of the proper level of generality to ascribe to originalist principles. Some conservative originalists, such as Robert Bork, commonly wish to restrict that generality, bringing originalism closer to an original intended applications approach. They argued that interpreters should adopt the "most specific level of generality" (Friedman 2009b, 311). Such an approach would surely reduce judicial discretion, an important goal of originalists.

For many contemporary originalists, though, the most narrow level of generalization is not the appropriate one. They argue that the level of generality is a "contextualized historical one" (Whittington 1999, 187). While fine as a theoretical point, this is not terribly helpful. How would one identify historically the correct level of generality? Doing so seems to ask for evidence on original expected applications, which is now largely disregarded as a rule for originalism and one that fails to reflect changing facts to which the Constitution must be applied. It is difficult to find a rule to tell us the appropriate level of generality for constitutional language. It is widely accepted that the general principles for interpretation cannot contradict the text (Balkin 2007), but this allows considerable room for maneuver.

Some conservatives argue for a narrower abstraction of constitutional language by returning to the restraintist justification for originalism. They suggest that allowing greater abstraction allows contemporary justices much freer rein in interpretation. They claim that a "Constitution that was established to place limits on future government actors would not delegate power so generously" (McGinniss & Rappaport 2007, 378). Yet it is not clear that a narrower abstraction would necessarily place greater limits on future government actors. Take, for example, abortion. Finding that the Constitution protects reproductive rights places greater limits on legislative and executive actors. It may empower the judiciary, but a greater focus of the Constitution was on limiting legislative powers more than judicial powers.

The appropriate level of generality presumably should be dictated by the language chosen. This was Justice Frankfurter's two-clause theory. He believed that there was a single correct reading of specific clauses of the Constitution but that more open-ended clauses reflected values that admitted more flexibility in interpretation. When the Constitution used a very open-ended phrase (such as "due process"), we presumably should interpret it with greater generality. A bill of attainder, by contrast, has greater specificity. In these instances, it appears that the framers delegated considerable interpretive authority to later Courts. They could have chosen narrower words, but they did not. Originalism would counsel for more abstraction. But this still does not tell us the correct level of abstraction to apply to particular provisions.

Conversely, when the constitutional text is more specific and concrete, the level of abstract generalization should be less. When the Constitution sets a minimum age for the president, little generalization seems appropriate. This is an easy case, though, and one that is not typical of the Constitution's language. Most of the constitutional language contains an intermediate level of generality, which varies by provision. Assigning the correct degree of abstraction is a daunting and quite indeterminate task. The process of abstraction provides considerable discretion for the interpreter, especially in light of change.

The proper level of generality will inevitably be somewhat vague. If our hypothetical ratifier were asked whether the right to bear arms should extent to grenade launchers or machine guns, one suspects that he would be stumped. To the extent that his conducting further investigation would answer, one suspects that the content of this answer would likely reflect his own ideology and views of weaponry, rather than an objective original meaning. Surely it is hard to claim that the ratifiers had any consensus view on the Second Amendment's coverage of grenade launchers.

Perhaps all the terms of the Constitution should be viewed in the abstract. When Eisgruber's grandchild promised to eat healthy food, the grandfather may have very specifically understood this to mean drinking much whole milk and avoiding red wine. However clear this original meaning may have been, science has taught us to shun whole milk and drink red wine in moderation for health. With some abstraction of this meaning, the opposite of the original understanding might prevail because of greater knowledge. This is potentially consistent with original meaning originalism, though obviously quite contrary to original expected applications originalism.

It may be instead that none of the terms were meant to be abstracted. It is unclear that the framers or ratifiers intended the constitutional language to express any broad concepts, as opposed to specific commands (Bassham 1992). The ratification debates focused more on applications than principles, though the latter were discussed. The constrained approach, though, is unappealingly constricting in practice and would, for example, vastly reduce the scope of free speech. Moreover, it is semantically dubious—if the text includes a word of great generality, how can we ascribe it a narrow meaning? The only way to do so would be to revert to original expected applications, an approach largely rejected and hard to apply to modern circumstances.

The framers and ratifiers of the Constitution meant to accomplish something with their choices of text, and the task of originalism is to ascertain that meaning. But the general view of the search for that meaning may be unduly circumscribed. Original expected applications originalism presumes that the framers meant to eternally enact particular expected applications, but this is not proved. As soon as one accepts some level of generalization or abstraction in interpretation, one is called on to define the appropriate level. There may be little originalist evidence about the precise abstract principle that the enactors sought to enshrine (Balkin 2007). Lund (2009) suggests that use of broad generality enables a moderately clever judge to reach whatever result he or she wishes. Barnett (2006) likewise suggests that reference to unwritten principles underlying constitutional language allows interpreters to adopt whatever principles they personally prefer. This fact plainly undermines the value of originalism as an interpretive method.

The result of the abstraction to generality question is to leave considerable uncertainty about the proper scope and application of originalism. Original expected applications originalists strive to avoid this difficulty, but they truly cannot. Unless the framers considered the precise issue in today's case, some analogy is required, and this analogy requires a determination of the correct level of generality for originalist interpretation.

Ideally, an originalist would simply say that the proper level of generality was the level that was originally understood by the ratifiers and that the language could reasonably bear. Words may be broad or specific in their meaning (Wofford 1964). But ascertaining the precise level for abstract generalization is difficult. Esteemed jurists Learned Hand and Felix Frankfurter could not agree whether the privilege against self-incrimination should be considered a broad general protection or a narrower specific one (Wofford 1964, 515). Laurence Tribe suggests that assigning the correct level of generality to a constitutional provision is functionally impossible (Scalia 1997). The correct level is surely not simply binary (broad or narrow) but requires a more particular titration. Without a clear way to measure the choice of generality, originalism can collapse into great discretion. Kay (2009) worries that, if use of original expected applications are abandoned, the ability to generalize purposes from constitutional text will make originalism relatively useless for interpretation.

One final issue about the meaning of originalism is contested—should anything else matter in constitutional interpretation? If it is true that the original meaning of the contextual text governs, it could trump other legal materials, such as precedent, in interpretation. A true exclusive originalist would plausibly say that precedent is irrelevant. If prior decisions got the original meaning wrong, they should be reversed, no matter how solidly entrenched they are. For some, more extreme, originalists, the only relevant consideration in constitutional interpretation is the original meaning of the document. Merrill (2008) suggests that originalism and precedent inhabit two orthogonal universes, but they must be reconciled, and precedent should not be abandoned.

Barnett argues that originalism's essential content is that the meaning of the Constitution should remain fixed until properly changed and that none of the branches of government, including the judiciary, have authority to change that meaning (Barnett 2005). Consequently, the doctrine of reliance on precedent is potentially inconsistent with originalism. Michael Stokes Paulsen suggests that any theory of precedent inevitably "corrupts" originalism (Paulsen 2005). If the polestar is original meaning, there is no reason to rely on latter precedent rather than going back to the original meaning. If precedent were consistent with the original meaning, it would be correct but superfluous.

Robert Bork rejected the extreme version of originalism, declaring that even an incorrect Supreme Court decision may have become so embedded in the law as a precedent that it should not be changed. Scalia likewise would allow a role for precedent. Calabresi (2007, 37) suggests that even when contrary to original meaning a given issue may be "closed at this point as a matter of *stare decisis*." This is an interesting rejection of originalism in favor of stability in the law. But, if the value of such stability can trump originalism, why should not other values also do so?

Some have argued that originalism can be reconciled with reliance on precedent because the framers and ratifiers intended for courts to rely on precedent (McGinnis & Rappoport 2009). The common law practice was well established at the time of ratification and logically part of the judicial function authorized by the Constitution. Whittington (1999) suggests that justices may rely on precedent out of humility, recognizing the wisdom of the prior justices, and only gradually redirect constitutional law toward more originalist bases. Such humility is surely appropriate but not clearly due except insofar as the prior justices considered original meaning.

There is a question over whether the true originalist theory should be "exclusive" originalism, contending that the only legitimate test of constitutional meaning is its original meaning. Berman (2009) calls this hard or strong originalism and claims that it represents the essence of contemporary originalism. The Reagan administration's commitment to originalism insisted that "no other method of interpretation was legitimate" (Friedman 2009b, 307).

The exact number of such exclusive originalists is uncertain, but it appears that many self-professed originalists would give at least some credence to other sources of constitutional meaning, such as precedent. In the presence of a plain conflict, though, one suspects that most originalists would give priority to original meaning over contrary precedent, except perhaps in cases where precedent is long settled. Thus, some "limited respect" may be given to "nonoriginalist constitutional precedent because of the larger societal and constitutional goal of effectively pursuing the common good" (Strang 2006b, 421). Yet the scope of this caveat on originalism is not well defined. In general, originalists would privilege original meaning over a line of contrary precedent. An originalist is at least "suspicious of precedent" (Posner 2008, 345) and would be more likely to compromise its direction.

Berman (2009) suggests that only exclusive devotion to originalism can be true originalism, noting that there is scarcely an individual to be found who utterly rejects consideration of original meaning as one factor in constitutional adjudication. This thesis seems too binary, however. Much of the debate revolves around the *relative* primacy of originalism. Some would be relatively more willing to compromise original intent in a constitutional dispute, while others believe it is worthy of greater reliance, even if not wholly exclusive. An originalist, at minimum, grants relatively greater importance to originalist materials and lesser importance to precedent, though the latter may be considered. Originalism may be considered on a continuum rather than as an all or nothing proposition.

The exact degree of the primacy of originalism is somewhat undertheorized. But one who believes that originalism should rule except in the case of long-settled precedent is still a fairly strong originalist, much more than many others and as Berman (2009) recognizes. Yet even if precedent represents one exception to originalism, judges might still place original meaning as primary. Originalism is sometimes characterized as weak, moderate, or strong. This simply reflects a continuum of dedication to the theory, and there is no need to create categories. It seems most logical to consider the fundamental *theory* of "originalism" to be exclusive originalism and then recognize that even those who call themselves originalist may recognize some exceptions and need not always follow the practice; yet they would remain originalists.

It is sometimes said that "we are all originalists now," which basically invalidates the theory. The most prominent originalists do not believe everyone else has joined them. Dedication to originalist interpretive theory falls along a spectrum. At one end are those who believe originalism is utterly worthless, and the other end represents exclusive originalists. Even if no one truly exists at these ends, one's relative originalism is shown by one's position on the spectrum. Some plainly prioritize originalism more than others as a method of constitutional interpretation. Presumably, even if there are no pure originalists or nonoriginalists, people occupy different places on the spectrum of importance placed on original meaning.

Originalism itself remains of unclear meaning, however. While original public meaning is now the majority position among academics, there are some who continue to adhere to original intention or other variants. Among those committed to original meaning, there are more subtle differences in the standard. Moreover, this book is about the practice of originalism in the courts, not the academy, and judges appear to have many different views about originalism. Hence, for my purposes any reliance on evidence from the framing area qualifies as originalism, whether in pursuance of original meaning, original intention, or some other theory. An original meaning theorist might argue that one who relies on original intent wasn't a true originalist and got an interpretation wrong. But this is the point of my book—that those who use originalism may "get it wrong." This chapter's review of originalism is not evaluative but is simply meant to enhance the reader's understanding. For my purposes, originalism is broad enough to encompass all the theories discussed in the preceding pages.

THREE

The Materials of Originalism

A justice's decision to use originalism for constitutional interpretation is just the first step. The justice must then figure out how to carry out that intent. Original meaning begins with the words of the Constitution itself. But the meaning of those words must be discerned, according to not their contemporary meaning but instead the original meaning. This requires some reference to materials of the era.

Use of originalist materials, though, to find original meaning, can be quite a difficult task. Justice Scalia has explained the complexity of the process (Scalia 1989, 856):

> But what *is* true is that it is often exceedingly difficult to plumb the original understanding of an ancient text. Properly done, the task requires the consideration of an enormous mass of material—in the case of the Constitution and its Amendments, for example, to mention only one element, the records of the ratifying debates in all the states. Even beyond that,

it requires an evaluation of the reliability of that material—many of the reports of the ratifying debates, for example, are thought to be quite unreliable. And further still, it requires immersing oneself in the political and intellectual atmosphere of the time—somehow placing out of mind knowledge that we have which an earlier age did not, and putting on beliefs, attitudes, philosophies, prejudices, and loyalties that are not those of our day.

The task of the originalist is plainly a daunting one. In this chapter, I focus on the first requisite—evidence of original intent or meaning. An interpreter relying on original intent or original meaning requires evidence of that meaning. A variety of sources have been used to discern the original meaning, with some much more prominent than others. Some may be considered direct evidence of the intent of the ratifiers, while others are more indirect evidence and might go to the original expected intentions of the framers of the Constitution.

My assessment of the materials of originalism is limited to those of the original Constitution, the era of the framers. Of course, this addresses only part of originalist interpretation, much of which involves later constitutional amendments, especially the Civil War amendments. Originalism has focused heavily on the original Constitution, though, for which we may have the best available materials. Indeed, applying originalism is easier for the original Constitution than for the subsequent amendments, due to the availability of resource materials (Friedman 2009).

There is considerable debate over which historical materials are most useful for an originalist interpretation. Under modern semantic originalism, the key question is the original meaning of the text at the time of its ratification. To assess this meaning, one might first turn to direct sources of the meaning of the terms of the Constitution at the time. While the subjective intent of the framers is less relevant to this form of originalism, their thoughts may also reveal the meaning of the text.

It is possible that the proper interpretation of the meaning of the original Constitution may have legally changed via intervening amendments. The term *due process* was found in the Fifth Amendment of the original Constitution but also in the Fourteenth Amendment of the post–Civil War constitutional amendments. The meaning of "due process" changed, however, during the intervening years (Balkin 2007). This perhaps should change the proper interpretation of the Fifth Amendment, due to the intent and meaning of the amenders, though they did not formally alter the meaning.

This may be true for other provisions as well. Balkin (2007) suggests that it was unclear that the Second Amendment enshrined a right to self-defense but that this concept was widely accepted at the time of the Fourteenth Amendment. He suggests that finding such a right is appropriate for constitutional interpretation, even if it were not explicitly intended by the framers, because it is consistent with the original text and underlying principles.

The later changes need not present a serious problem to relying on evidence from the time of the framers, however. The amendments have done little to change the structural components of the original Constitution, and the bulk of the Constitution remains unamended. The Civil War amendments did not explicitly change the content of the original Bill of Rights, and the courts have not focused on the theoretical potential impact of the amendments on this content. When the Supreme Court evaluated the right to bear arms in *Heller*, they focused on the original intent of the amendment, not that behind the later amendment. I likewise focus on the original era. In any event, the original era provides a test case for analysis, even if it is incomplete.

In the remainder of this chapter, I will consider the primary source materials for proper originalist interpretation. I begin with *The Federalist*, surely the most famous originalist source and renowned for its status as political philosophy. I also consider the ratification records of *Elliot's Debates* and the notes that James Madison took at the Constitutional Convention. These appear to be the three most frequently used originalist sources for the justices. I further consider some other sources, such as the use of dictionaries of the era and the Declaration of Independence. Though their use is less common, they raise interesting questions. Various other sources could also be considered for original meaning, with greater or lesser validity, and I review them as well.

Defenders of originalism generally do not set forth which resources should be used in application. There is no prioritized list of "best" originalist sources, and countless different materials have been used. Different sources are surely applicable to different controversies. Because this book is about the application of originalism I will focus primarily on the sources that have been most commonly invoked by the Supreme Court.

The Federalist

Perhaps the most prominent source of original meaning is *The Federalist*, written by leading framers to promote the ratification of the Constitution. This source has been called "the most important of originalist sources" (Corley, Howard & Nixon 2005, 329). The famous historian Clinton Rossiter said, "It would not be stretching the truth more than a few inches to say that *The Federalist* stands third only to the Declaration of Independence and the Constitution itself among the sacred writings of American political history" (Rossiter 1964). Between 1953 and 1984, the Court cited to this resource more than twice as many times as any other originalist source (Corley, Howard & Nixon 2005, 330).

The importance of *The Federalist* to discerning the original meaning of the Constitution was set out by Thomas Jefferson, who regarded it as "evidence of the general opinion of those who framed, and of those who accepted" the Constitution (Rossiter 1964, 227), which is precisely the evidence sought by semantic originalists. Madison, though perhaps biased as an author, declared that *The Federalist* was "the most authentic exposition of the text of the federal Constitution, as understood by the Body which prepared & the authority which accepted it" (Dewey 1971, 47).

The Supreme Court has declared that *The Federalist* "papers were received by the people of the States as the true exponents of the instrument submitted for their ratification" (*Prigg v. Pennsylvania* 1842, 594). The Court later wrote that *The Federalist* papers were among the sources "usually regarded as indicative of the original understanding of the Constitution" (*Printz v. United States* 1997, 910). A leading contemporary originalist has called the source the "best single extra-textual source in explicating the Constitution" (Amar 1987, 1498). *The Federalist* was written to explicate the Constitution to the ratifying public, explaining and justifying its terms, so it should be a good source of original meaning.

The Federalist was the product of James Madison, Alexander Hamilton, and John Jay. Under pen names, they wrote eighty-five essays that explained the proposed Constitution to the people and urged its ratification. The focus of the letters was the ratifying convention of New York, where approval of the draft Constitution was highly contested. Several New York City papers published the essays. Some journals outside New York reprinted their content, and Hamilton and Madison personally distributed them to supporters elsewhere (Maggs 2009a).

One might think that the relevance of *The Federalist* is colored by the fact that the authors were admitted advocates of ratification. The authors to some degree sought to describe what was intended in the Constitutional Convention but also sought to present the text in a light that would encourage ratification. Under an original meaning approach, though, this does not undermine the reliability of *The Federalist*. If the ratifiers based their votes on its content, that fact alone is dispositive. When the textual interpretation of *The Federalist* diverges from that of the Constitutional Convention, that fact may be quite salient. The authors, particularly Madison, knew what was believed at the Convention. If they presented the Constitution in a different manner in *The Federalist*, that very fact suggests that its representation of given meanings was necessary to achieve ratification and thus a more reliable source of original meaning.

Despite its iconic status, the significance of *The Federalist* as evidence of the ratifiers' understanding of original meaning is uncertain. In the ideal model, the ratifiers would have read *The Federalist* to learn of the meaning of the proposed Constitution and then voted on the basis of this understanding. In such circumstances *The Federalist*, like a congressional committee report, should provide a sound basis for drawing conclusions about the text's meaning.

Unfortunately, most of the ratifiers of the Constitution appear to have been largely unaware of the content of *The Federalist*. While the essays were published in New York, they had a relatively small circulation even there and were not widely distributed throughout the country. None of the essays was published in Connecticut, New Jersey, Delaware, Maryland, North Carolina, South Carolina, or Georgia (Maggs 2009a). Papers in other states may have published one or two of the essays (Maier 2010). One study found that *The Federalist* "did not reach an audience of any significant size" (Crane 1964, 591). Even when the essays were available to ratifying individuals, one cannot assume that they read them or were persuaded by their content. Those voting for ratification may well have made up their minds before the conventions, representing either Federalists or Anti-Federalists. There is "no good evidence that anyone, even in New York, relied on *The Federalist* as the basis for voting to ratify" (McGowan 2001, 756).

The irrelevance of at least some of the essays is obvious from the timing of their publication. At the time of Delaware's ratification, only seventeen of the eighty-five essays were in print. Pennsylvania ratified with only twenty of the essays published and New Jersey with only twenty-two (Maggs 2009a, 826). Some of the most important essays, such as *The Federalist* No. 78, justifying constitutional judicial review, were not published until after a majority of states had ratified the Constitution.

The accuracy of *The Federalist* has also been questioned. The Virginia Supreme Court observed that they were "a mere newspaper publication, written in the heat and hurry of the battle" (*Hunter v. Martin's Lessee* 1813, 27). Because it was a piece of advocacy, it may lack "usefulness as a window into the reasonable ratifier's likely understanding" (Manning 1998, 1354). Various objective errors have been identified, including an incorrect count of the members of Congress, inaccurate description of the vice president's authority, and misunderstanding about the process of electing the president (Tillman 2003). In some places, the essays appear to be contradictory (Maggs 2009a, Mason 1952), and we know that Madison and Hamilton differed on fundamental matters.

For these or other reasons, *The Federalist* was not heavily relied on in the days of the early American republic as a source of constitutional meaning. In the debates of the day, neither the Federalists nor the Republican-Democrats gave much credence to the arguments of the essays (Lynch 2000). The Supreme Court declared that the source was due "respect" but that the "correctness" of its claims could not be presumed (*McCulloch v. Maryland* 1819, 433). Although *The Federalist* has mythic status in our history, its reliability as a source of original meaning is questionable.

The use of this source in court has been criticized for failure to recognize its limitations. It is invoked as "a handbook to constitutional interpretation that is never discussed as the hastily written and often inconsistent polemic that it is" (Richards 1997, 889–890). The justices are said to systematically cite its passages "as authority without even a cursory examination of the validity of the surrounding text or the document as a whole" (Tillman 2003, 618). This practice suggests that its citation may be more for its iconic status than as an attempt at authentic historical exposition.

It is difficult to claim that the ratifiers adopted the Constitution in reliance on the statements made in *The Federalist*. This does not entirely demean the sources as evidence of originalist understanding. It is evidence of what some leading framers believed the Constitution to mean but hardly conclusive of what the general population thought. Yet its paramount significance may be questioned.

Although some have questioned *The Federalist* for its strategic objectives, its use as an advocacy document may strengthen its value. *The Federalist* was written to persuade voters to ratify the Constitution and consequently was presumably drafted in a way that made the proposed Constitution appear desirable to the voters. Consequently, *The Federalist* may be a good representation of what the ratifiers of the time would approve. This argument is undermined, though, by the fact that *The Federalist* was aimed at ratifiers of New York. As a result, its arguments would be "naturally skewed toward" positions "that would sway New Yorkers" and away from those appealing to ratifiers of other states (Bhargava 2006, 1766). Thus, *The Federalist* may simply reflect original public meaning in New York State.

Ratification Records

If it is the ratifiers who provide the best source of original meaning, the ratification records are an obviously useful originalist resource. The classic source of ratification evidence is *Elliot's Debates*, published originally in 1836. Since that time, others have sought to put together improved materials from the ratification process, but these have been unavailable to the Court for nearly all of our constitutional history. A study found that, from 1953 through 1964, *Elliot's Debates* was the third most cited originalist source at the Supreme Court (Corley, Howard & Nixon 2005, 330).

Under original meaning originalism, the ratification record might seem to be the dispositive source for constitutional interpretation. The ratifiers are the persons who gave the Constitution its legal standing. They presumably voted according to its public meaning, as they perceived it. Of course, some caution must be employed in using these records, as the views of one particular individual arguing for or against ratification may not have reflected the common understanding of the text.

The available records of the ratification debates have other problems as a resource for originalist interpretation of the Constitution. The records are quite incomplete, and truly extensive records of the ratification debates exist only for the conventions held in Pennsylvania, Massachusetts, Virginia, and New York. More fragmentary records exist for the conventions of Connecticut, Maryland, South Carolina, and New Hampshire. For five states, there are no records at all. We have data for only a minority of the content of the ratification debates, and the representativeness of this information is uncertain.

Moreover, the ratification records we have are of uncertain reliability. Inadequate "stenographic skills" reportedly compromise the available evidence (Hutson 1986, 21). Comments of the speakers were summarized rather than inscribed verbatim. Elliot himself warned that his records "may, in some instances, have been inaccurately taken down, and, in others, probably, too faintly sketched" (Levy 2000, 289). Elbridge Gerry of the Philadelphia Convention complained that the debates "as published by the short-hand writers were generally partial and mutilated," while the editor of the debates for the Massachusetts Convention reportedly "doctored some speeches, altering the meaning of the speakers, and provided some spurious speeches as well" (Levy 2000, 289). James Madison himself told Eliot that parts of the record for the Virginia Convention were "defective" and "more or less erroneous" (Levy 2000, 290). James Hutson (1986, 1–2) studied the period and questioned the "integrity" of *Elliot's Debates* and whether it represented a "faithful record" of the events of the time. The Pennsylvania and Maryland debates were recorded by an ardent Federalist who simply deleted record of speeches he disliked (Farber 1989). Thus, we cannot rely on the records for an accurate depiction of the views of the ratifiers.

Even if the record of the ratification debates was perfectly accurate, it would still present problems for interpretation. Different ratifiers apparently had very different views of word meaning. Indeed, "each of the ratifying conventions may have had a different understanding of the Constitution" (Maggs 2009b, 491). Justice Story, of the era, observed that in "different states and in different conventions, different and very opposite objections are known to have prevailed, and might well be presumed to prevail . . . to remove local objections, or to win local favor" (Story 1833). The states of "Georgia and Virginia and Delaware and New York did not all think alike when in convention assembled" (Dewey 1971, 41). Thus, "supporters and opponents of ratification offered conflicting accounts of the Constitution's meaning" (Smith 2006, 630). There may not have been a common view of the public meaning of the ratified text. This conflict is surely more profound the more one seeks to abstract general principles from the meaning of the text.

The ratification debates even saw significant conflict in interpreting meaning within individual states. When different states are compared, the conflict grows. If "the Constitution means whatever its ratifiers understood it to mean, then different conventions arguably ratified different things" (Nelson 2003, 586). Friedman (2009b, 309) argues that the ratifiers were a "motley bunch" that did not reveal their assessment of constitutional text on many important questions. Use of the ratification debates to fix a given contemporary meaning to the words of the Constitution is questionable, at least in some cases.

Original meaning originalists have recognized that conflicting intentions of the framers and ratifiers undermine the original intent approach to originalism (Solum 2008). It has been suggested that, to be binding, a text must contain an intention held by a sufficient majority of the founders (Whittington 1999). Yet they sometimes seem to ignore the degree to which this same problem may infect original meaning. Those who adopted the Constitution may have done so with very different ideas of what the words meant. Originalists seem to assume that there is one true original meaning. But this is hard to sustain in light of the vigorous debates of the time over what the Constitution meant. When different meanings were expressed, it may be difficult or impossible to ascertain the most common interpretation.

The ratification debates were substantially a fight between groups called Federalists and Anti-Federalists. The Federalists supported the proposed

Constitution, while the Anti-Federalists argued against ratification. The Anti-Federalists were skeptical of national government power and feared potential restrictions on individual liberty. The primary objective of the Anti-Federalists was defeating the ratification. The Federalists carried the day, and the text was ratified. Yet the statements of the Anti-Federalists about constitutional meaning remain part of the historical record. They commonly contradict statements from Federalists about textual meaning.

Some of these conflicts of the time might be resolved simply by discounting the views of the opponents. Levy (2000, 4) contends that "much of the Anti-Federalist literature was trash based on hysterical assumptions or on political calculations intended to deceive and incite fear of the Constitution." John Yoo's discussion (1999) of the treaty power suggests that Anti-Federalist claims about meaning were simply exaggerations to provoke the defeat of the Constitution. It is often presumed that the opponents of a proposal are driven by an incentive to provide misleading information to make it appear more extreme than it truly is (Austen-Smith & Riker 1987).

This is consistent with modern views of statutory interpretation, which relatively discounts the expressed views of a statute's legislative intent spoken by opponents of the legislation. From this perspective, the claims of Anti-Federalists about constitutional meaning might be disregarded. The ratification may be viewed as a rejection of the Anti-Federalist position. But this is not necessarily true; the Constitution may have been ratified because of a common agreement with that perspective. Perhaps ratifiers accepted the Anti-Federalist interpretation and nevertheless approved the Constitution. Moreover, the fact that the Anti-Federalists lost the war over ratification does not mean that they lost every battle about the meaning of specific terms (Smith 2004).

In practice, the Anti-Federalist positions of the time have not been disregarded. The "modern originalist . . . believes that Anti-Federalist views deserve equal time in the quest to determine the original understanding" (Smith 2006, 663). The Supreme Court has occasionally referred to the fears expressed by Anti-Federalists as evidence of constitutional meaning (Smith 2004). It is commonly thought that the Federalists created the Articles and the Anti-Federalists were responsible for the Bill of Rights. Yet the Anti-Federalists have been relied on in interpreting the Articles, especially on questions of federalism. Justice Thomas relied heavily on Anti-Federalists to interpret the commerce clause (Smith 2004).

The content of the ratification debates in many states were largely a reflection of a contest between Federalists who favored approval and Anti-Federalists. Both had a self-interest to describe the Constitution, not accurately, but in a manner that would further their objectives. The ratification record has been described as a "cacophonous debate in which squibs, parodies, wildly fantastic predictions, and demagogic rhetoric alternated with the more serious analysis" (Rakove 1997, 1600). The accuracy of particular claims of the record therefore is highly uncertain.

The presence of such inconsistency and conflict is a serious problem for originalism. It was the ratifiers who gave legal effect to the Constitution, and their perceived meaning is often taken to govern original meaning. Yet if different ratifying states gave different meanings to the words of the Constitution, how can it be interpreted? Would the Constitution have been ratified if only one meaning prevailed? If so, which of the different meanings would yield that result? Such conflict need not doom all reliance on originalism. In many cases, there may have been no conflict. When it occurred, many originalists acknowledge that originalism cannot resolve every interpretive controversy. The disagreements over original meaning expressed at ratification may be a broader problem, though, because there may have been other conflicts over constitutional meaning not even disclosed in the ratification debates.

Some have contended that the ratifiers are not reliable originalist sources because they were limited to an "up or down" vote on the entire text and could not amend. It is possible that the ratifiers strongly disapproved of specific provisions, but not enough to reject the overall Constitution. As a legal matter, though, this criticism seems irrelevant. The law does not defer to the political views of the ratifiers, just their acts. If the ratifiers understood the meaning of constitutional language and ratified that language, it matters not that they hated that language; they still transformed it into law.

DICTIONARIES

A dictionary from the framing era would seem to be strong evidence of the meaning of the words used at the time. The reliance on this resource is complicated by the fact that no American dictionary existed at the time of the Constitution (Wofford 1964). However, one suspects that American English of the era closely paralleled that spoken in England, where dictionaries were available. Moreover, American dictionaries appeared not too long after the framing period.

Dictionaries have various problems, though, for ascertaining the original meaning of the constitutional text. Justice Holmes declared that the meaning of the constitution was "to be gathered not simply by taking the words and a dictionary" (*Gompers v. United States* 1914). Dictionaries define words in isolation, without context. Typical dictionaries contain multiple meanings for individual words, which occasionally may even be contradictory. A classical example is the word *sanction*, which may be defined as either the punishment for an action or the approval of an action. The proper meaning of the word requires consideration of its context, including the other words of the phrase and even the overall document in which it is found. Amar (1999, 791) notes that legal words "can sometimes be used as terms of art, with nuances of meaning not well captured by standard dictionaries." Understanding a sentence requires more than understanding the definition of each of its component words (Rubin 2010). Originalists themselves have provided examples of how definitions of isolated words could miss the true originalist meaning (Kesavan & Paulsen 2003, 1203).

The earlier dictionaries existing at the relevant time were typically prescriptivist in nature, setting forth how words *should* be used, according to the author, and not necessarily describing how they were commonly used (Sonpal 2003). These dictionaries were "written by elites who wished to convey the correct usage" of words but not how they were currently used (Weinstein 2005, 658). Consequently, they may not describe the word understandings of those who ratified the Constitution or the true original public meaning. Nor has it been established that the framers or ratifiers were aware of the content of any particular dictionary. If due only to lack of resources and this theoretical approach, older dictionaries are generally less reliable (Rubin 2010).

Dictionaries may differ in their definitions, and there is also a question of which dictionary to use in originalist interpretation. This may be relevant, as commentators have reached different interpretations of the proper constitutional meaning of the word *commerce*, depending on the dictionary chosen (April 1998). Justice Scalia may simply choose a dictionary depending merely on its availability in his chambers (Sonpal 2003), which would not seem to be a reliable cue to original meaning in disputed cases.

While the availability of a dictionary is at worst a random standard, reliance on this resource may contravene sincere originalism, through "dictionary shopping" for a definition that suits a desired interpretive conclusion of a justice. The justices may simply seek out the dictionary that best suits the result that they wish to reach. Anyone familiar with dictionaries knows that they may offer multiple definitions of the same word and that different dictionaries may offer somewhat different definitions for a given word. Justice Scalia purportedly relies on a dictionary for meaning "only when it supports the ideologically conservative outcome" (Rubin 2010, 176). Both the majority and the minority in *Heller* relied on dictionaries, but neither examined the relative validity of their choices and that of the sources of the other side.

Two dictionaries of the founding era appear to have the most frequent usage by the justices. I will rely on them for my study. Samuel Johnson produced *A Dictionary of the English Language* in 1773, which is often used by the Court. In 1796, Thomas Sheridan produced *A Complete Dictionary of the English Language*. These resources are roughly contemporary with the framing and appear to be good resources for word meaning of the era. Focusing on these two helps limit the effect of dictionary shopping. However, they were from England and may have ignored the American meaning of words at the time, to the extent they differed (Sonpal 2003).

RECORDS OF THE CONSTITUTIONAL CONVENTION

One prominent source of originalist constitutional meaning is the records of those who drafted the Constitution at the Convention. While some records were published as early as 1819, the full compilation came later. The classic resource for these records is Farrand's *The Records of the Federal Convention of 1787*. It was not published until 1911, but it quickly became the standard reference work (Kesavan & Paulsen 2003) for this source. This resource focused on the contemporaneous notes of James Madison but also included notes and letters by many other participants of the Convention. While others also took notes during the proceedings, Madison's were more comprehensive and have carried the field as an interpretive resource (Kesavan & Paulsen 2003).

The records of *Farrand* were the second most used originalist source by the Supreme Court between 1953 and 1984 (Corley, Howard & Nixon 2005, 330). Of course, this resource evidences only the beliefs of the drafters and not the ratifiers who gave legal effect to the text. It might therefore be considered a source only of intent and not of meaning. Yet it is surely at least indirect evidence of the original meaning of those words.

James Madison suggested that the Convention debates had no authoritative character but could provide "presumptive evidence of the general understanding at the time" (Berger 1990, 736). However, he also declared that "the sense of that body should never be regarded as the oracular guide in expounding the Constitution" (Dewey 1971, 40). Yet, on other occasions, he treated conclusions of the Constitutional Convention "as if they were authoritative in determining the meaning of the Constitution" (Dewey 1971, 43). Such conflicts make one wonder if even James Madison did not seize on the interpretive method that suited his ends at the time.

One shortcoming of the convention records is their incompleteness. Madison probably "reported no more than ten percent of an average hour's proceedings" at the Convention (Bittker 1989). These records have also been challenged as to the accuracy of what Madison did record. He may have biased the record and recorded his own speeches "at greater length than the speeches of others" (Levy 2000, 287). He may have "tampered with the notes . . . in order to suit his own political advantage and that of his party," though this claim has been disputed (Hutson 1986, 25). Hamilton challenged the veracity of the record (Hutson 1986, 25). Madison probably embellished his own speeches and "abbreviated, short-shrifted, or even omitted speeches that contradicted his views" (Collier 1988, 142). He himself suggested that his notes "ought not always be taken at face value" (Collier 1988, 142). Madison was human, and his notes were surely biased.

As with the ratification records, there are conflicts among those at the Constitutional Convention regarding the meaning of the text they would propose. There were differences about phrasing and its implications. Levy (2000, 294) elaborates:

Sometimes Framers who voted the same way held contradictory opinions on the meaning of a particular clause. Each believed that his understanding constituted the truth of the matter. James Wilson, for example, believed that the ex post facto clause extended to civil matters, while John Dickinson held the view that it applied only to criminal cases, and both voted for the clause. George Mason opposed the same clause because he wanted the states to be free to enact ex post facto laws in civil cases, and he believed the clause was not clearly confined to criminal cases; but Elbridge Gerry, who wanted to impose on the states a prohibition against retroactive civil legislation, opposed the clause because he thought it seemed limited to criminal cases.

How is today's originalist to make sense of the proper expected application of the Constitution's ex post facto clause? The ratification debates reflect similar direct opposition on the meaning of the clause (Nelson 2003). On other issues as well, it was "clear that those involved in formulating our Constitution held conflicting views based on different assumptions" (Alexander 1986, 321).

This presents a serious problem for originalism. If those who actually wrote the Constitution openly ascribed different meanings to the language, how can there be said to be an original meaning? There were surely other cases in which the framers gave different meanings to language but did not openly address the issue, perhaps they were unaware of the existence of the differences in interpretation. And if the smaller number of those at the Convention thought the text had different meanings, one can imagine far more disagreements among the ratifiers.

Another issue with the reliance on *Farrand* is its contemporary secrecy. Garry Wills has suggested that if the records of the Constitutional Convention, then secret, had been available at the time of the ratification debates, the Constitution never would have been approved (Wills 1984). Indeed, Rufus King suggested that Madison's reports should be destroyed or hidden, lest they be used to preclude ratification (Clinton 1987, 1195). Some have objected to relying on the Convention records because they were secret at the time of ratification. The secrecy does not demean the resource as a contemporary assessment of textual original meaning, however, under an original public meaning view. The source has been called the equivalent of a "contemporaneous dictionary" (Prakash 1998, 537), though it would be a dictionary unavailable to the ratifiers.

While the ratification records provide more direct evidence of original meaning for the relevant parties of the time, those records have numerous limitations, as already discussed. It's suggested that "the difficulties of ascertaining the intent of the ratifiers leaves little choice but to accept the intent of the Framers as a fair reflection of it" (Monaghan 1981, 375). Moreover, the ratification debates provide only the interpretations of individual ratifiers, who may be unrepresentative. The views of individual framers might be considered at least equal to those of individual ratifiers. Indeed, some suggest that the statements at the Convention may be "more reliable evidence of original meaning than partisan statements made by the same Framers (and others) under the public eye" at the ratification debates (Kesavan & Paulsen 2003, 1189). Although the journals were not made public at the time, they were preserved to, in the future, rebut false suggestions about the meaning of the constitutional text (Clinton 1987, 1196). They were used by framers in the First Congress to argue what the Constitution meant (Clinton 1987, 1197–1198). This counsels for crediting the record as an originalist resource, though its relative significance might be challenged. The Court has sometimes privileged the subjective intent expressed at the Convention over the original meaning of the text (tenBroek 1938), though this is inconsistent with prevailing contemporary visions of originalism.

DECLARATION OF INDEPENDENCE

One other primary source deserves particular attention. The Declaration of Independence has no obvious relevance to originalist interpretation. It predated the Constitutional ratification by years and could not possibly have addressed the text of the Constitution. It was written by different people and for a very different purpose. Raoul Berger (1990, 732) rejected its use as the product of "rebels and revolutionaries" in contrast to the "men of substance who drafted the Constitution itself." Justice Scalia (1997, 134) declared that the Declaration was simply aspirational, while the Constitution was "a practical and pragmatic charter of government" that contains no "philosophizing."

Yet for some, the Declaration is fundamental to constitutional interpretation because it provided the base on which the Constitution was structured. The Declaration is said to lie at the "heart of the Constitution" (Gerber 1995, 3). It may be considered "fundamental to a proper understanding of the Constitution" (Himmelfarb 1990, 170). If the Constitution's purpose was to further the fundamental rights claimed in the Declaration, then the latter document would be relevant to interpretation of the constitutional language.

Today, the "vast majority of scholars, including the vast majority of originalist scholars, do not include any unique role for the Declaration in constitutional interpretation" (Strang 2006, 432). Both liberals and conservatives are said to be "united in their near universal disregard for the role of the Declaration in constitutional adjudication" (Robinson 1996, 128). In fact, neither the framers nor the ratifiers made much reference to the Declaration in their proceedings (Detweiler 1962). Not only is there no evidence of reliance on the Declaration in constitutional formation, but the record appears contrary (Cooper 1994).

Defenders of reliance on the Declaration argue that it was not commonly discussed because it was assumed to be the settled foundation for the Constitution and its significance therefore assumed. The Constitution was simply the means by which the principles of the Declaration were to be effected in the nation (Arkes 1990). The original Constitution, though, was a response to the failed Articles of Confederation, which were more directly grounded in the Declaration. Rather than foundational, some historians have suggested that the Declaration was "forgotten" by the framers and ratifiers (McDonald 1999, 179). There was "scant evidence from the time of the Framing and Ratification that anyone was thinking of the Constitution as an extension of a political theory announced in the Declaration" (Cosgrove 1998, 134). However, there is evidence from the time that fundamental natural rights theories such as those of the Declaration were relied on and ultimately produced the Ninth Amendment (Clinton 1987). *Dred Scott* found the Declaration so plainly important to original understanding that the majority felt the need to distinguish it (*Dred Scott v. Sanford* 1857).

Reliance on the Declaration has a major limitation—it is not contemporaneous with the adoption of the Constitution. For originalists, meaning is fixed at the time of enactment, not over a decade earlier. However, it was reasonably proximate in time, and available dictionaries are not perfectly contemporaneous either. The Declaration was not clearly incorporated by documents of the framing era, but neither were dictionary definitions.

The Declaration of Independence has one considerable advantage over the other sources commonly used for originalist interpretation—its entire content is known. Records of the Constitutional Convention and ratification debates are incomplete, and the records that do exist are of uncertain reliability. The substance of the Declaration is well established, and it was a corporate statement, not the opinions of one or a few individuals, known to those of the time. Of course, the meaning of the words of the Declaration might need the same exegesis as those of the Constitution for it to be valuable in interpretation.

While the Declaration might seem not to shed much light on the original meaning of the Constitution's words, which were written later, it can carry greater weight when it comes to generalizing the implications of those words. Text must be read in context, and the Declaration arguably provides the context of the Constitution and gives important cues to deciding how abstractly or generally that terms should be read. The Constitution, in this view, should be seen as "a reflection of larger moral truths" (Whittington 1999, 30) that are provide by the Declaration.

Use of the Declaration may be considered a way of generalizing the broader principles of the constitutional text. The Declaration arguably tells us the purpose of the constitutional text. Jaffa (1994, 31) argues that the focus on the text in isolation, without consideration of the Declaration's moral philosophy, produces originalist decisions such as *Dred Scott*. If abstraction of constitutional meaning is to be grounded itself in originalism, the Declaration is a logical place to look for the basis of such abstraction.

Use of the Declaration as a tool for interpreting the Constitution is highly contested. It is not the sort of direct evidence about the meaning of the text, as provided by the Constitutional Convention or the ratification debates. A primary expounder of Declaration-based originalism (Jaffa 1994) declares Justice Brennan the best justice, though Justice Brennan has explicitly rejected originalism. To the extent that the Declaration's broad rights principles did not show up in the constitutional text itself, originalists would say that they lack legal authority. However, it allegedly informed the content of the Constitution, and it has its own iconic status as a great

American document. The Declaration of Independence has occasionally been used in constitutional interpretation, though not so frequently and with little explanation of its importance.

OTHER ORIGINALIST SOURCES

While the sources listed in the preceding pages are the most commonly invoked bases for originalism, there is really no limit to the possible sources that could be used to facilitate originalist interpretation. Scalia suggests a judge must immerse him- or herself in the time of the framing to correctly understand the originalist meaning of the Constitution. Perhaps even novels of the time should be read to gain an understanding of word meaning. However, some sources appear relatively more useful.

An originalist source sometimes used by the courts includes the private correspondence of prominent framers. This source roughly parallels the records of the Constitutional Convention, as evidence of framer subjective intent. While private correspondence might seem less relevant, such letters may be relevant for perceived original meaning. Keith Whittington (2004, 610) notes that the "discovery of a hidden letter by James Madison revealing the 'secret, true' meaning of a constitutional clause would hardly be dispositive to an originalism primarily concerned with what the text meant to those who adopted it." But the letter could provide relevant information.

Correspondence from prominent framers could be considered to have the virtue of sincerity, and the Court has occasionally cited to correspondence of Jefferson, or Madison, or some other leader of the era. Public declarations may be posturing for political purposes, while private correspondence may be more sincere. The nonpublic nature, though, means that the ratifiers were unaware of its comments. Such correspondence can represent the views of only a single person, and they may have been expressed precisely because of broader uncertainty about the correct meaning of a particular provision.

Another possible source of originalist interpretation, sometimes used by the Courts, is existing judicial opinions, sometimes those of England. The legal interpretation of then-existing texts could be said to establish the original understanding of words found in the Constitution, and these are sometimes used by the Court. This approach might imply that the ratifiers or people of the time generally were familiar with these existing opinions, which seems questionable. Even in today's world, with much greater distribution of judicial opinions, the populace is unfamiliar with their content. Use of such opinions, though, could be relevant to the view that originalism should be based on the understanding of the hypothetical, fully well-informed individual of the day.

Moreover, it may be that the ratifiers adopted a text in reliance on prevailing judicial interpretations, even if they were unaware of them. When the Constitution refers to "letters of marquee and reprisal," the ratifier may not have known the precise meaning of those terms but understood that the terms had an existing precise meaning. The ratification of the constitutional language may therefore have been a deference to the then-existing judicial opinions that fleshed out this meaning.

This is not necessarily the case, of course. The Constitution was the result of a rebellion against England and its laws. Controversies over executive power in the Constitution may turn on whether it meant to copy English practice of the time, which is quite uncertain (Scalia 1989). Although the new American legal system relied in part on traditional English law, that fact does not mean that it embraced all of it. James Madison "flatly denied that the American courts could refer to English common law unless authorized to do so by the legislature" (Dewey 1971, 49). Some was changed by the Constitution. If the question is whether the Constitution changed the traditional English legal rule, the nature of the traditional legal rule should not govern its interpretation.

Reliance on framing-era judicial opinions (and sometimes earlier and later opinions) is a fairly common source for originalist interpretation at the Court. As noted, though, it is not clear that the Constitution incorporated these or that original public meaning could be equated with legal meaning. Moreover, it is dubious that the ratifiers of the Constitution were closely familiar with the contents of these decisions, which calls their relevance for original meaning originalism into some question. It is also difficult for me to comprehensively search for such opinions citing early cases, which share no common phrasing, so they are not included in my analysis.

Another possible piece of evidence for originalist interpretation involves the actions of the First Congress, essentially contemporaneous with the framing period. The members of this Congress were surely intimately familiar with the original public meaning of the Constitution when enacted; many of them had been involved in the writing and/or ratification of the Constitution. Madison considered the actions of the First Congress a reasonable source of constitutional meaning (Dewey 1971) and suggested that decisions of this Congress could serve as binding precedents for constitutional interpretation (Miller 1969). John Marshall found the source so reliable that he could not conceive that an action of the First Congress might violate the Constitution (Bhargava 2006). Justice Scalia suggested that early congressional enactments provided "contemporaneous and weighty evidence of the Constitution's meaning" (*Printz v. United States* 1997, 905). On occasion, the Supreme Court has relied heavily on this resource to interpret the Constitution (Bhargava 2006).

But there is very good reason to challenge reliance on the decisions of the First Congress as evidence of the Constitution's original meaning. Its members were "political actors, responding to political as well as legal influences, who are eminently capable of making mistakes about the meaning of the Constitution" (Lawson 2002, 398). Legislators may be relatively indifferent to the constitutionality of a measure, if that measure is politically attractive (Bhargava 2006). Some prominent originalists maintain that the fact that the First Congress engaged in a practice is poor evidence that that practice was necessarily constitutional (Calabresi & Lawson 2007).

Early legislators had many of the same incentives as those of today, seeking reelection and certain policy goals. They may have pursued these goals at the expense of faithfulness to the Constitution. Justice Brennan stated that legislators, "influenced by the passions and exigencies of the moment, the pressure of constituents and colleagues, and the press of business, do not always pass sober constitutional judgment on every piece of legislation they enact, and this must be assumed to be true of the Members of the First Congress as any other" (*Marsh v. Chambers 1983*, 814–815). Madison himself "voted in Congress for a bill that he later, in a private capacity, stated to be unconstitutional" (Brown 1993, 186). Reliance on the acts of the original Congress contains an implicit presumption that government action must have been constitutional, a presumption that defeats the very purpose of judicial review and that was surely undermined by the result in *Marbury v. Madison*, which invalidated a law passed by the First Congress.

Actions of the First Congress are like what is called "postenactment leg-islative history," where legislators declare the meaning of a statute some-time after it was passed. Such postenactment legislative history is largely discredited, however, as a basis for statutory interpretation. It is considered "simply a legislator's attempt to accomplish after the fact what he or she could not accomplish during the debate of the measure" (Aleinikoff 1988, 41). Yet these postenactment sources are sometimes used, and, in *Heller*, Justice Stevens criticized Justice Scalia for reliance on them. In addition to the uncertain reliability of the source, the records of the proceedings of the First Congress are poor (Bhargava 2006), so the Court may use a result but with little explanation of the legislators' constitutional analysis or even if they engaged in constitutional analysis.

The Court has sometimes used Joseph Story's *Commentaries* or the views of other roughly contemporary learned legal commentators as bases for constitutional interpretation. Story is by far the most commonly used by the Court (Kesavan & Paulsen 2003) and follows only *The Federalist, Far-rand,* and *Elliot's Debates* as a source used between 1953 and 1984 (Corley, Howard & Nixon 2005, 330). These resources reflect the views of only one person, though. Story's views were published about a half-century after the time of ratification, and he had his own biases. He had a nationalist perspec-tive on governance that arguably did not reflect the views of the framing generation (Kesavan & Paulsen 2003). Justice Thomas has thus declared that Story's views do not represent the original understanding but only "his own understanding" (*U.S. Term Limits, Inc. v. Thornton* 1995, 856).

A somewhat more contemporary source for interpretation used by the court is that of William Blackstone in his *Commentaries on the Laws of En-gland*. His writings have been considered a primary source for the framer's efforts in drafting the Constitution (Schwartz 1993). Of course, the title of his book makes clear that he was describing the laws of England, against which the country rebelled. He was describing English law of the time, which American courts had already altered in some cases (Meyler 2006). Some constitutional provisions were intended to extend existing British practices of the time, but others were aimed at rejecting those practices. Some early state governments actually prohibited their courts from relying on Blackstone, for fear of English influence on American law (Law 2005), surely calling into question whether it is a good source for originalist constitutional interpretation.

Moreover, the reliability of Blackstone can be questioned. His was a subjective recapitulation of English common law of the time, much like our current *Restatements* of law. Like the *Restatements*, his work may have involved some channeling the law toward a desired, coherent end. Meyler (2006, 562) suggests that he did not present a "sophisticated account of English common law" but instead sought to manipulate English legislation. Moreover, it is unknown the degree to which the ratifiers, the relevant party, were familiar with the writings of Blackstone at the time of the Constitution's adoption or shared his view of the law's meaning.

While I have emphasized some originalist materials and downplayed others in this research, there is no clear or absolute rule as to the proper ones. For original meaning originalism, the best sources are those that provide evidence of ordinary usage of the language at the time. Contemporary newspapers could be a good source, but ideally an originalist would want to look at hundreds of pieces of evidence from the era and seek a clear pattern. In reality, though, this is seldom done, and justices typically rely on a few classical sources, such as *The Federalist*.

INDETERMINACY OF ORIGINALIST MATERIALS

The discussion in the preceding pages makes clear that there is no single authoritative originalist source. There are various available sources, but they tend to be incomplete in their coverage, which leads one to wonder about the content of omitted material. They are also of uncertain reliability, with records compromised by incompetence or purposeful bias. The records that do exist are not infrequently contradictory in their direction. To the degree that history tells us anything, it is that the adoption of the Constitution "involved processes of collective decision-making whose outcomes necessarily reflected a bewildering array of intentions and expectations, hopes and fears, genuine compromises and agreements to disagree" (Rakove 1996, 6). Given this indeterminacy, pursuit of originalist interpretation has been called "questing after a chimera" (Brest 1980, 222). By indeterminate, I am truly speaking of underdeterminacy—the materials do have some meaning, but it cannot be ascertained with precision.

One area in which originalism has been commonly invoked is the First Amendment's religion clause. Scholars and the Court have analyzed original meaning, focusing on matters such as whether there was truly intended a separation of church and state. Research on the question has been conducted by "highly reputable scholars," yet they have reached "very different conclusions" (Brownstein 2009, 197). The scholars rely on different sources, and the ability to emphasize particular sources enables different conclusions, not to mention the difficulties of generalizing from the text.

The indeterminacy of original understanding is clearly a problem, and the history of Madison and Hamilton is illuminating. They are surely two of the leading framers and, as authors of *The Federalist*, considered to be perhaps the best originalist sources or at least the most commonly used. Yet, once the Constitution was ratified, they "clashed repeatedly" and came to "radically different conclusions about what the Constitution allowed" (Bhargava 2006, 1767). If Madison and Hamilton could not agree upon the original meaning of the constitutional text, what makes one think that a justice of today could identify the correct original meaning?

Some suggest that problems with the historical record doom any attempts to reconstruct original meaning. Hutson's review (1986, 2) suggested that the sources had been "compromised—perhaps fatally—by the editorial interventions of hirelings and partisans," such that to "recover original intent from these records may be an impossible hermeneutic assignment." The "best professional historians" allegedly "know better than to be originalists," though "constitutional lawyers and scholars who have taken the turn to history do not" (Barber & Fleming 2007, 111).

Additional difficulties with originalist interpretation can be seen in the fight over the Jay Treaty in 1796 (Clinton 1987), when the House demanded a role in approving a treaty. Even such a straightforward matter was contested, with framers taking both sides and disputing the relevancy of the record of the Constitutional Convention. Even "after thorough and careful historical research, scholars disagree on the original meaning of almost every constitutional provision" (Farber & Sherry 2002, 14). This calls into question the ability to perform an accurate and sincere originalist inquiry.

Describing one case, Justice Scalia said that there was "plenty of room for disagreement as to what the original meaning was, and even more as to how that original meaning applies to the situation before the Court" (Scalia

1997, 45). Other justices have been even more dubious about the ability of originalism to resolve controversies before the court. Justice Brennan argued that it was "arrogant to pretend that from our vantage we can gauge accurately the intent of the framers on application of principle to specific, contemporary questions" (Rakove 1990, 25). David Strauss (2009, 3) claims simply that originalism is "not doable" as it is "hard enough to figure out what the Framers were thinking more than two hundred years ago," and even if we could do that, we would have to apply those "thoughts to our completely different world—one which the Framers could not possibly have foreseen." The materials of originalism "rarely contain clear evidence of an understanding of the particular constitutional question before the court" (Smith 2004, 280).

Throughout this chapter, I have identified numerous flaws in the primary sources for originalist interpretation. Records may be unreliable, incomplete, or even contradictory. These flaws need not fully demean the originalist process, though. In some cases, there was a "remarkable unanimity" of opinion at a ratifying convention (Berger 1990, 738). James Madison wrote that the "sense of the Constitution" could be found "in the proceedings of the Convention, the contemporary expositions, and above all in the ratifying Conventions of the states" (Farrand 1911, 474). John Quincy Adams declared Madison's notes to be a "correct and tolerably clear view of the proceedings of the Convention" (Wofford 1964, 504). No legal analysis is ever perfectly informed; perhaps originalism can resolve some important legal disputes.

As with any historical analysis, one should not rely on a single piece of evidence. Each piece of evidence, though, is relevant evidence of the original meaning. Rakove (1997, 1604) notes that the historical record has limits but can still "provide informative and bounded accounts of the range of potential meanings that Federalists and Anti-Federalists attached to particular clauses." Even if originalist methods cannot resolve all questions with certainty, they may focus the resolution and "lead toward increased agreement on questions of constitutional interpretation (Kay 1988, 258).

One suspects that originalist history will rarely answer conclusively modern-day legal disputes, but it may still be informative. The history may provide "sufficiently parallel normative questions from which inferences can be drawn about the issue at hand" (Clinton 1987, 1269). Of course, the ability to apply such parallels depends crucially on the level of generality given to the relevant constitutional text. If the text is given a high degree of abstraction, many parallels may be found. If viewed more narrowly, the parallels might seem much less analogous.

Problems with relying on available records do not necessarily doom historical analysis but may simply instead counsel for better history.

It is possible that if originalism became the controlling method of constitutional interpretation, that could motivate better historical analysis of the period. Historians never have perfect documentary records, but that does not stop them from trying to establish historical propositions with some accuracy. But "professional historians understand that interpreting the past is akin to viewing the world through a distorting prism" that becomes more opaque as intervening time grows (Bhargava 2006, 1770). Whittington (2004) acknowledges this effect but believes it can be overcome by a disciplined effort to appreciate the context of the time in which the Constitution was written.

Originalists recognize that materials from the framing era cannot resolve all of today's constitutional disputes. The framers failed to address may of the issues of legal interest today (Farber 1989). Some constitutional terms are sufficiently vague that their original meaning cannot be precisely ascertained (Solum 2008). Vague terms admit of unresolved borderline cases and hence underdetermine the application of language in such borderline cases.

Today, many (but not all) originalists emphasize "construction" as well as mere interpretation of the Constitution. Construction recognizes the possibility that the original meaning of the text simply does not address and resolve the relevant question before the Court. While interpretation is considered legal, construction is political (Whittington 1999), which would seem to considerably unleash judicial discretion. Solum and others concede that construction may commonly be necessary to settle today's controversies over constitutional meaning.

In construction, the justices have discretion to choose among meanings that are consistent with the original meaning of the constitutional text, though not determined by this meaning. Balkin argues, for example, that reproductive rights can be found in the constitution by this means. Various principles may be used for construction, including the equity of the result and the principle of deference to the elected branches. However, construction remains constrained by originalism inasmuch as it cannot violate the original textual meaning. It is not "unlimited" in scope but constrained by the constitutional text. The extent of this constraint still depends on the determinacy of the original text.

When originalism was gaining credence as a theory, Raoul Berger argued that it was the antidote to living constitutionalists trying to fulfill their "libertarian hopes" (Berger 1977). Yet, to some leading modern-day originalists, the theory is central to the fulfillment of their own "libertarian hopes." These modern-day libertarian originalists rely in part on the natural rights expressed in the Declaration of Independence, with the Ninth Amendment as central evidence of this philosophy. Thus, originalism has been conceived as both strongly antilibertarian and extremely prolibertarian, which might cause some to question its determinacy.

The libertarian originalists certainly present a plausible case for their historical interpretation, but in the process they call originalism itself into question as an interpretive theory. Their approach is directly contrary to that of originalists such as Berger, Bork, and Scalia. Other nonlibertarian originalists critique the libertarian originalist position. All are presumed to be making sincere attempts to uncover the authentic original meaning of the Constitution. Yet they come to starkly different interpretations of that meaning.

A leading contemporary originalist, Steve Calabresi, has challenged the modern libertarian originalists, Randy Barnett in particular (Calabresi 2005). He notes that they interpret the Articles' authorization of government power narrowly but the Bill of Rights protections quite broadly and create a presumption for liberty in the "total absence of textual or historical evidence" (Calabresi 2005, 1088). This pattern might suggest manipulation of the historical record to reach desired policy ends. Another prominent conservative originalist, Michael Stokes Paulsen, believes that the Articles provide very broad authority for federal government action (Paulsen 2008), which is quite contrary to the libertarian originalist position.

Much of this conflict is not so much over the content of actual originalist materials, though, as over the proper level of abstraction for the text. The libertarians think that natural rights animate the Constitution and provide a basis for interpreting limitations on individual rights narrowly but affirmations of such rights more broadly. Calabresi and others disagree. Yet this debate within what is considered the conservative movement illustrates the great difficulty of any authentic descriptivist originalist undertaking. Not only are the original resources themselves indeterminate, but so is the interpretation they should be given.

The indeterminacy of the originalist record seems daunting, but ultimately the question is whether the theory can be well operationalized. In my study, I consider the leading originalist sources employed by the Court (*The Federalist*, *Elliot's Debates*, and *Farrand*), as well as leading roughly contemporary dictionaries and the Declaration of Independence. I will examine how the justices have used these sources, in hopes of illuminating the value of originalism in Supreme Court practice.

FOUR

Originalism before the Warren Court

This chapter begins a brief survey of the history of the use of originalism at the Supreme Court. Ultimately, the test of any constitutional theory must lie in its practice. Most originalists are consumed with the theory and "do not typically focus on the actual interpretive practice of the Supreme Court" (Griffin 2008, 1197). Yet it is practice that is truly important, and originalism can best be evaluated by its usage in practice. Some originalists have suggested that originalism has been a method followed by courts from the beginning years of our nation (Griffin 2008).

It is not clear that true originalism was in play historically. The theory of originalism, especially prevailing original meaning, is relatively recent in its development. The theories of today's originalists were not available to early justices. Yet the general notions of the theories can be found in some early cases. The notion that a law should be interpreted according to the ordinary meaning of its words is not a new theory.

In the Supreme Court's first years, the justices themselves had firsthand knowledge of the meaning of the Constitution, as understood by the framers or ratifiers. Chief Justice John Jay was one of the authors of *The Federalist*. Chief Justice John Marshall had been a delegate to the convention responsible for ratification of the Constitution. They participated in the original understanding of the Constitution. Their personal understanding surely affected their decisions (Miller 1969), but their opinions also required some outside legal justification.

In the first few decades, the primary originalist source used by the justices was *The Federalist*, as many other records were not yet published and available to the court. There were some records, such as newspaper accounts of the ratification debates, though they "were not well indexed or widely and simultaneously available" (Clinton 1987, 1277). Perhaps such references would be unnecessary for the original justices. They lived of the time and personally knew the original meaning of the text, just as any ratifier would. Thus, "when a provision is interpreted roughly contemporaneously with its adoption, an interpreter unconsciously places the provision in its linguistic and social contexts, which she has internalized simply because she is of that society" (Brest 1980, 208). Those of the time know what the words mean to those of the time. While Justice Marshall's opinions tended to make historical assertions without support, subsequent historical investigation suggests that his assertions were generally accurate (Kelly 1965). The justices' memories "bridged the temporal distance between the Founding and the case at hand" (Friedman & Smith 1998, 11).

One might expect the earliest opinions to ignore external sources of original meaning because the justices were themselves such sources. Cases that come to the Court are contested, though, and I have noted how even members of the First Congress disagreed over the original meaning of constitutional terms. Consequently, one might expect the justices not to rely entirely on their own impressions but to seek additional evidence of original meaning.

Justice Marshall, dissenting in *Ogden v. Saunders*, seemed to make clear his reliance on original meaning. He declared that the intention of the Constitution was critical to interpretation and that its words were to be "understood in the sense in which they are generally used by those for who the instrument was intended" (*Ogden v. Saunders* 1827, 332). This sounds like today's understanding of original public meaning originalism. Yet this was in dissent, and the opinion did little to elaborate how he would discern the original understanding of constitutional text.

Several references to originalist materials could be found even in the earliest days. The first material citation to *The Federalist* occurred in 1798, in *Calder v. Bull*. That opinion relied on the resource, not as an explication of original meaning but because the author had "extensive and accurate knowledge of the true principles of government" (*Calder v. Bull* 1798, 391). It was not cited for original meaning but for the knowledge and wisdom of its authors (a reliance of uncertain legal significance). Likewise, in 1803, the Court cited *The Federalist* as the product of "men high in esteem of their country" (*Stuart v. Laird* 1803, 304). This case, at least, also makes reference to original meaning, explaining the relevance of *The Federalist* as a "contemporaneous exposition" of the constitutional text.

Chief Justice Marshall first extensively referred to *The Federalist* in the very important decision of *McCulloch v. Maryland* on taxing authority (*McCulloch v. Maryland* 1819). He declared that the source was "justly supposed to be entitled to great respect in expounding the constitution" and that "no tribute can be paid to [its authors] that exceeds their merit." This reference appears to defer as much to the quality of the source as to its standing as evidence of original meaning. He also declared that the content of the Constitution could not be changed without formal amendment, which conforms to originalist inclinations.

Marshall cautioned, though, that justices should not simply assume the "correctness" of *The Federalist* in individual cases. Moreover, this case is the source for the famous quotation that "it is a constitution we are expounding," one that must be "adapted to the various crises of human affairs." This point created something of a loophole in original meaning interpretation and has been used as a reason not to constrain interpretation to originalism. However, during the nineteenth century, this language "was never cited in support of the proposition that the meaning of the Constitution . . . could change over time" (Gillman 1997, 205).

Marshall made considerable use of *The Federalist* in several opinions (Pierson 1924). He used it heavily in *Cohens v. Virginia*, a case involving the supremacy of the federal judiciary over state courts on matters of federal law. Here, he wrote (*Cohens v. Virginia* 1821, 418–419):

> The opinion of the Federalist has always been considered of great authority. It is a complete commentary on our constitution; and is appealed to by all parties in the questions to which that instrument has given birth. Its intrinsic merit entitles it to this high rank; and the part two of its authors performed in framing the constitution, put it very much in their power to explain the views with which it was framed. These essays having been published while the constitution was before the nation for adoption or rejection, and having been written in answer to objections founded entirely on the extent of its powers, and on its diminution of state sovereignty, are entitled to more consideration where they frankly avow that the power objected to is given, and defend it.

Here we have a case for reliance on *The Federalist* (a) because of the quality of its authors, (b) because of their role as framers in knowing the original intent behind the Constitution, and (c) because of its influence on the ratification process, evidencing the original meaning of the words to the ratifiers. These rationales are all distinct, and the justice did not explain the independent relevance of each.

The influence of the source may have exceeded its citations of the time. Marshall did not cite *The Federalist* in *Marbury v. Madison*, but his opinion appears to draw strongly on the source (Clinton 1987). Just like an original understanding of the words of the Constitution, the content of *The Federalist* may well have lurked in the minds of the justices, influencing their decisions.

The Federalist played some role in the resolution of many of the most important cases of the early Court (Maggs 2009a). While it was cited but once in the years before Marshall became chief justice, it was then cited in fourteen cases between 1800 and 1840 and cited in seventeen cases in the period from 1840 to 1860 (Clinton 1987, 1218). Inferior courts also frequently cited *The Federalist* during this time period (Clinton 1987, 1218). The source was clearly considered of value in constitutional interpretation.

Although *The Federalist* was invoked during the era, the Court did not appear to consistently rely on what some consider to be originalism. Rather, it was a heavily textualist court, interpreting the words of the Constitution as written (O'Neill 2005) but without much exploration of their meaning at the time of ratification. Because the early decisions were so contemporaneous with the drafting of the Constitution, the justices may not have needed external sources on original meaning. They lived through the era and had their own knowledge of original meaning. Thus, the original textualism was arguably true original meaning originalism because the justices were of the time of the original meaning.

The early Court also relied on precedent. The Marshall Court "sometimes made clear they felt confined by precedent" (McGinnis & Rappoport 2009, 821). In the earliest days, there obviously was very little existing U.S. Supreme Court precedent to rely on, but the justices relied to a degree on prior English precedent or that of state courts. As past opinions of the Supreme Court grew, so did its reliance on precedent. Overall, the justices of the Marshall Court "drew upon a range of sources to justify their decisions: the text of the Constitution, the plan or ordinary meaning of words, common law definitions or principles, natural law, local practices and rules, principles of equity, and what they termed 'general principles of republican government'" (White 1988, 114). Pluralism began in the initial days of the Court. Originalism was a common theme of a number of early opinions, but it was by no means the only method used by the justices. Some suggest that this era revealed that originalism "was little more than a myth that obscured the true nature of constitutional adjudication" (Shaman 2010, 87). Of course, this contention may be evidence of judicial construction and not the open rejection of originalism.

When Justice Taney acceded to the Court as chief justice, the political direction of the Court shifted. The justices' personal memory of the founding era had waned, so reliance on *The Federalist* continued and even accelerated. In 1848, the Court quoted *The Federalist* and wrote that it was "an historical truth, never, so far as I know, denied, that these papers were received by the people of the States as the true exponents of the instrument submitted for their ratification" (*The License Cases* 1848, 607). Here we have a clean exposition of the source based purely on finding the original meaning of the constitutional text. The source was significant because it declared that meaning. During this period, the Court even unambiguously emphasized original meaning, writing that it should "give the word the same meaning as prevailed here and in England at the time it found a place in the

Constitution" (*Ex Parte Wells*, 1955, 311). Justice Taney essentially followed the originalist approach in his constitutional interpretation (O'Neill 2005).

By this time, there were more available records from the Constitutional Convention, in the form of Madison's notes. In addition, there were records of the ratification debates from the newspapers of the day, though they were not yet compiled in a convenient source. Outside *The Federalist*, though, originalist resources were not broadly used in constitutional interpretation by the Supreme Court. Early originalism was based largely on textualism, drawing conclusions from the words of the Constitution without relying much on extrinsic evidence of meaning, save the occasional reference to *The Federalist*.

In the first fifty years, the Court focused on textual exegesis of the Constitution without truly addressing the importance of original meaning. The Court sometimes referred to originalist materials and sometimes even relied heavily on them. The theoretical basis for their invocation was not perfectly clear. Sometimes, the Court used *The Federalist* simply as a persuasive source, but at other times it was discussed as a source of original meaning. In the very earliest years, of course, the justices were presumably aware of the original, then largely contemporary, meaning and used it naturally in their textual analysis. They may have had little reason to need outside sources for the meaning of constitutional language.

The justices of the era were clearly influenced by more than the mere text of the Constitution, however. They relied on animating philosophies of the Constitution, such as those principles of natural rights reflected in the Declaration of Independence. Thus, in *Calder v. Bull* (1798), Justice Chance wrote:

> The people of the United States erected their constitutions . . . to establish justice, to promote the general welfare, to secure the blessings of liberty, and to protect their persons and property from violence. The purposes for which men enter into society will determine the nature and terms of the social compact; and as they are the foundation of the legislative power, they will decide what are the proper objects of it. The nature, and ends of legislative power will limit the exercise of it. . . . There are certain vital principles in our free republican governments, which will determine and overrule an apparent and flagrant abuse of legislative power, as to authorize

manifest injustice by positive law; or to take away that security for personal liberty, or private property, for the protection whereof the government was established. An act of the legislature (for I cannot call it a law), contrary to the great first principles of the social compact, cannot also be considered a rightful exercise of legislative authority.

This language seems to be a rejection of original meaning and even the language of the Constitution itself. Rather, it is a very broad and general notion of original intent, as expressed in the Declaration of Independence. Chief Justice Marshall's opinions also were influenced by the philosophy of natural rights (Clinton 1987). Of course, this could be considered an invocation of originalism at a higher level of generality in the application of originalism, though it doesn't pay much heed to the original meaning of the constitutional words.

The early court, roughly current with the framers, themselves, took various approaches to constitutional interpretation. The references to *The Federalist* show that they took originalist materials seriously, though not always clearly from their role as evidence of original public meaning. Other factors, such as precedent and a natural rights philosophy, were also important to decisions of the time. The interpretive approach of this area need not govern us. Contemporary originalists thus call for use of original meaning, regardless of whether this was the framers' intent or the practice of early justices. This era does, though, begin to tell us how the Supreme Court justices would make use of originalist materials. A dedication to originalism by the Marshall Court does not mean the justices got the results right, however. Madison challenged the correctness of such decisions (Clinton 1987, 1210). Indeed, many originalists do not view Marshall as a true originalist justice.

Although not perfectly consistent in its application, some say that "a commitment to original meaning was the announced rule of both the Marshall and Taney Courts" (Gillman 1997, 204). In the nineteenth century, some suggest that the view that "the Constitution should be interpreted according to the original intent of the Framers dominated the legal landscape" (Bhargava 2006, 1757). Perhaps this should be unsurprising; as less time had passed since the ratification of the text, there was less need for adaptation of original meaning from changed circumstances. Yet, even during this era, some argued that the judiciary was not simply applying original meaning but shaping the law, in contrast to prevailing rhetoric, which had the justices as mere "servants" of the law (Gillman 1997, 21). Clearly, changing views on matters such as the constitutionality of the national bank evidenced some limits of original meaning, but the devotion to the method persisted. Yet the "method" was imperfectly defined. As already noted, contemporary theories were not yet developed, and the justices sometimes appeared to use original intentions.

Unfortunately, the apotheosis of originalism, at least for the early years, appears to come in the greatly lamented opinion of *Dred Scott* (*Dred Scott v. Sanford* 1857). This is probably the most loathed Supreme Court opinion in American history. The Court at that time held that a person of African ancestry could not claim citizenship in the United States.

The decision for the Court, written by Chief Justice Taney, relied heavily on originalism. The opinion urged that blacks were not citizens of the United States at the time the Constitution was adopted. It relied on the fact that the Constitution "speaks not only with the same words, but with same meaning and intent with which it spoke when it came from the hands of the framers, and was voted on and adopted by the people of the United States." Per the opinion, the framers "perfectly understood the meaning of the language that they used . . . and they knew it would not in any part of the civilized world be supposed to embrace the negro race." This is plainly devotion to originalism, both in intent and meaning.

The opinion referred to two constitutional clauses suggesting that blacks were not to be treated equally and the fact that laws of the time, even in Northeastern states, demonstrated the "inferior and subject condition of that race at the time the Constitution was adopted." It also noted that legislation in the First Congress confirmed this view. Taney declared, surely correctly, that the slave states never would have ratified the Constitution had it provided equal rights to blacks. At the time of its issuance, *Dred Scott* was arguably more explicitly and extensively devoted to original meaning than any Supreme Court opinion that had been issued to date. Justice Taney stressed that it was "not the province of the court to decide upon the justice or injustice, the policy, or impolicy, of these laws" regarding slavery, a quote that sounds much like the contemporary originalist's criticism of judicial activism. It's said that "no one, on or off the Court, has ever expounded the theory of original intent with greater eloquence or conviction than Chief Justice Taney in the case of *Dred Scott*" (Jaffa 1994, 13).

A dissenting opinion in *Dred Scott* also employed originalism, though. It relied on *The Federalist* to argue for congressional power to change the status of blacks, regardless of how they were perceived at the time of the framing. Moreover, it noted that blacks could vote in multiple states at the time of the ratification, a fact that the majority opinion got wrong.

Given the status of the *Dred Scott* opinion as an embarrassing episode in our history, modern originalists have understandably sought to distance themselves from its opinion. They have analyzed the opinion and found it to be wrong as a matter of correct use of originalism (McConnell 1992). Some have even claimed that the opinion is the fault of the rejection of originalism and a "living Constitution" (Rehnquist 1976). It is suggested that originalism was but a fig leaf for the ideologically racist true motivations underlying *Dred Scott.*

Others have argued that *Dred Scott*'s originalism, while imperfect, was roughly accurate. But the ultimate accuracy of the opinion's originalism is somewhat beside the point as a practical matter. The relevant fact is that the opinion of the Court relied heavily on originalism in reaching its conclusions. It is not enough for originalists to say that learned commentators, writing a century later, can identify originalist conclusions correctly. For the theory to be valuable, it must be reliably exercised by the judiciary of the time. If it was an erroneous intentionalist opinion, that means that the justices used originalism erroneously, which is relevant to the value of originalism at the Court.

Suppose that *Dred Scott* was wrong as a matter of originalism. Some originalists have contended that it relied unduly on intentionalism rather than the original public meaning of the constitutional language. This could possibly be the result of simple judicial incompetence. Justices are not historians, and they may well get the originalist record wrong. Alternatively, the judgment may be the product of insincere originalism. Justice Taney may have reached his conclusion for political or other extralegal reasons and employed originalism only to justify his preconceived conclusion. For such an important case, a justice might be expected to invoke the venerated framers in support of his ruling. This possibility of course suggests the problem of originalism's manipulability. *Dred Scott* is but a single opinion, and the general validity of an interpretive method should not be determined by such a small sample size. However, the opinion does highlight potential problems with depending on originalism at the Court.

Originalism again became controversial when the Court was called on to assess the constitutionality of paper money. The Court initially found such paper money to be unconstitutional in an opinion that relied upon the "spirit of the Constitution" (*Hepburn v. Griswold* 1870). Many leading constitutional scholars at the time concurred with this view (O'Neill 2005). The Court quickly overruled this opinion, though, and held that paper money was constitutional (*The Legal Tender Cases* 1870). The majority opinion urged that the language of the Constitution had to be "construed with reference to [its] purpose so as to subserve it" (*The Legal Tender Cases* 1870, 531). Congressional powers, it held, need not be found directly in the text but could be presumed from the overall document, which seemingly creates quite a loophole in originalism.

This latter majority opinion was a very broad, perhaps Balkinian, vision of originalism. Some have suggested that the opinion's originalism was "superficial at best and even indifferent to the Framers' intent" (Dam 1981, 382). The best evidence indicates that the framers intended to prohibit the use of paper money (Dam 1981, 389), in light of concerns at the time. Nevertheless, a little creative originalism, using intentionalism, saved the practice.

More traditional originalism remained influential in the late nineteenth century. In *McPherson v. Blacker* (1892), the Court held that, when the constitutional text was ambiguous, evidence of early practice was warranted great weight in interpreting the text. When attempting to discern the constitutionality of the income tax, the Court examined "what, at the time the Constitution was framed and adopted, were recognized as direct taxes" and what "those who framed and adopted it [understood the] terms to designate and include" (*Pollock v. Farmers' Loan & Trust Co.* 1895, 558), using the Constitutional convention debates and *The Federalist* as support. The Court wrote that "in the construction of the language of the Constitution here relied on, as indeed in all other instances where construction becomes necessary, we are to place ourselves as nearly as possible in the condition of the men who framed that instrument" (*Ex Parte Bain* 1887, 12). The Court later declared that "the Constitution is a written instrument. As such its meaning does not alter. That which it meant when adopted it means now" (*South Carolina v. United States* 1905, 448). In 1905, "the justices, even when in disagreement, were united in the belief that constitutional meaning meant original meaning" (Gillman 1997, 227). These opinions read as a strong commitment to original public meaning originalism. Even at this time, though, the Court did not closely analyze original meaning with any extrinsic evidence (O'Neill 2005). The Court was textualist, though, in focusing on the specific language of the Constitution, although it did not closely seek out the meaning of that language.

Although originalism was important to some of the Court's decisions of this era, it was not truly dominant. In *Sparf v. United States* (1895), dealing with jury rights, the majority decided entirely on precedential grounds to establish that the law was the judge's province and not that of juries. A two-justice dissent, though, undertook an extensive historical analysis of old English practice and the originalist record, including the ratification debates, to support the claim that the jury could decide points of law. The majority saw no need to respond to this, however, in its opinion.

Although not perfectly consistent, it seemed that from "the time of the founding throughout the nineteenth century, there was a consensus in court opinions and legal treatises that judges were obligated to interpret the Constitution on the basis of the original meaning of constitutional provisions" (Gillman 1997, 192). The fealty to this approach was intermittent and the accuracy of the judicial determinations debatable, but the theory was commonly held. This approach plainly changed in the early twentieth century.

The change may simply be explained by the felt political needs of the day. Originalism apparently "posed problems for the emergent twentieth-century central administrative state" of the New Deal (Gillman 1997, 1996). Justices at the time appeared to believe that such government regulation could not be reconciled with original meaning. Some used this finding to strike down the government regulation, but others chose to adopt a position of great deference to the legislature and avoid originalist decisions invalidating the new laws. This might be considered part of legal realism's revolt against formalism, originalist or otherwise (O'Neill 2005).

In the progressive era of the twentieth century, originalism was plainly in decline, at the Court at least. Justices such as Holmes and Brandeis believed in a pragmatic interpretation of the Constitution, which could change to suit changing circumstances. Justice Holmes wrote that a case "must be considered in light of our whole experience and not merely in that of what was said a hundred years ago" (*Missouri v. Holland* 1920, 433). He also declared that "the provisions of the Constitution are not mathematical formulas having their essence in their form; they are organic living institutions" whose significance required some consideration of the "line of their growth" (*Gompers v. United States* 1914, 610). His was truly a living constitution, not an originalist one.

Justice Brandeis wrote that clauses "guaranteeing to the individual protection against specific abuses of power, must have a similar capacity of adaptation to a changing world" (*Olmstead v. United States* 1937). For Brandeis, the language of the Constitution should not be confined to original expected applications but should be adapted to changing needs. This approach is arguably consistent with original meaning interpretation with a broader abstraction of meaning, though he did not expressly employ such reasoning.

Another member of America's judicial pantheon, Justice Cardozo, likewise sought escape from originalism. In one case, he initially wrote in a concurrence that upholding a particular law "may be inconsistent with things that men said in 1787 when expounding to compatriots the newly written constitution" but emphasized that those men "did not see the changes in the relation between states and nation or in the play of social forces that lay hidden in the womb of time" (Gillman 1997, 223); he later withdrew the opinion in light of a change in the majority opinion. In his view, the beliefs of the framers about the constitution had to be adjusted to new circumstances. For Cardozo, it was "possible to be more faithful to the framers' objectives if we were willing to depart from their expressed beliefs" (Gillman 1997, 223).

This approach is illustrated by the Court's venture into the cruel and unusual punishment clause in a case where an individual was given hard labor for forging a public document (*Weems v. United States* 1910). The punishment could not be seen as torturous under the original meaning of the provision, but it seemed greatly disproportionate to the crime. The Court wrote (*Weems v. United States* 1919, 373, 378):

Time works changes, brings into existence new conditions and purposes. Therefore a principle to be vital must be capable of wider application than the mischief which gave it birth. This is peculiarly true of constitutions . . . [the cruel and unusual punishments prohibition] may be therefore progressive, and is not fastened to the obsolete but may acquire meaning as public opinion becomes enlightened by a humane justice.

This language is commonly invoked as a commitment to a "living Constitution." It fits reasonably well within a Balkinian originalism grounded in general principles rather than expected applications, but this type of originalism did not appear to be the Court's vision. The opinion is clear that constitutional interpretation should evolve with the times. Interestingly, justices who would be more associated with originalism joined the opinion, while Justice Holmes joined a dissent.

The period when the justices were striking down statutory regulation as unconstitutional has come to be associated with the case of *Lochner v. New York* (1905), which struck down a state law regulating the hours of bakers. *Lochner* itself did not rely on originalist interpretation, and the opinion has been roundly criticized by many originalists as improper judicial activism. The opinion itself relied more on a natural rights theory which, though arguably originalist in spirit, did not focus so directly on original meaning (Richards 1997) of the constitutional text. The justices made no attempt to justify their outcome with originalist principles and relied generally on a substantive due process approach that was generally rejected by originalists. However, O'Neill (2005, 26) suggests that originalism remained an important, though "tacit," concept in the period.

In connection with *Lochner*, the court struck down many laws based on a substantive due process theory. This theory, which later became associated with liberal individual rights vindication, has been repudiated as nonoriginalist by many. The justices who have used the theory have generally not relied on originalism. Yet there is some basis for finding an originalist basis for substantive due process (Phillips 2001). While there is no reason to think this motivated the justices, it is noteworthy that even renowned nonoriginalist decisions could possibly have been cast in originalist clothes.

This was an era of legal realism, in which the value of the formalistic bonds of originalism was increasingly doubted. Scholars questioned whether justices ever truly "followed the law" in the classic sense. Realists maintained that judges first identified the outcome they desired and then justified it with selective use of legal materials. Although they did not commonly address originalism, tenBroek (1938) suggested that the Court purported to use originalism but manipulated it to support a previously held political position.

Much of the important constitutional litigation of the era involved government regulation of business, but the Court was also called on to address a major structural problem involving the unilateral power of the president to remove executive officers in *Myers v. United States* (1936). Congress sought to condition the removal of postmasters on the approval of the Senate, while the president maintained that the Constitution gave him the exclusive power to make such decisions.

The majority opinion, of Chief Justice Taft, relied heavily on a related debate in the First Congress. While he recognized that a congressional construction of the Constitution was not conclusive, Taft emphasized that the "Congress numbered among its leaders those who had been members of the [Constitutional] Convention" (*Myers v. United States* 1936, 136). The opinion's reliance on originalism was qualified somewhat by emphasis on continued practice throughout the intervening years, suggesting that the "acquiescence" in this interpretation was a crucial factor. Justice McReynolds dissented, though, and pressed evidence from the more relevant time period, including *Farrand* and reference to contemporaneous understanding of the Constitution's meaning.

In a separate dissent, Justice Brandeis also relied heavily on history to tell a contrary tale. His sources were also arguably better than Taft's, including *The Federalist*, Story, and the underpinnings of *Marbury*. Brandeis also relied on a pattern of intervening practice through the nineteenth century. Some suggest he got the better of the argument, and his historical review was more exhaustive. The Court in the majority opinion arguably got the originalist interpretation wrong and used originalism simply as a "shield for political values" (Miller 1969, 68). Taft's conclusion was "far more than the facts of history warranted," while the Brandeis "historical argument was persuasive and authoritative" (Daly 1954, 206). Originalism was plainly relevant to this decision, if not the exclusive driving force, but both outcomes could be justified by reference to originalism. The originalist evidence on the issues before the Court was quite conflicted (Bhargava 2006), and it is not clear whether the justices were motivated by that evidence or simply used it to justify their preferred results.

In general, the ethos of the era was not an originalist one. Originalism "remained firmly on the margins of constitutional law" (Greene 2009a, 330). This was an era of a living Constitution. Justices such as Holmes and Brandeis were pragmatic and thought that the Constitution should be applied in light of the contemporary circumstances and needs, which could require updating the original meaning.

Originalism was not wholly absent from opinions of the era. Justice Sutherland argued that "the meaning of the Constitution does not change with the ebb and flow of economic events" (*West Coast Hotel v. Parrish* 1937). But this expression of originalism was in dissent. Other cases also saw reliance on originalism by a majority, including extensive references to Madison's notes, on matters such as admiralty jurisdiction (*United States v. Flores* 1933) or the scope of presidential pardon powers (*Ex Parte Grossman* 1925). But these were typically not among the more politically salient cases of the era.

One possible exception, where originalism survived, was found in the opinion in *Carter v. Carter Coal Company*. Justice Sutherland argued that the Constitutional Convention "made no grant of authority to Congress to legislate substantively for the general welfare" (*Carter v. Carter Coal Co.* 1936, 298). While not relying on originalist references, he emphasized the fundamental principles of the original Constitution and the limits of the enumerated powers. This represented something of a nod to original meaning, though it wasn't extensively fleshed out. Still, the opinions of the Court of this time "were, for the most part, devoid of any serious attention to history or mention of the Founders" (Friedman & Smith 1998, 16).

A revealing and very important case of the era was *Home Bldg. & Loan Ass'n v. Blaisdell* (1934). The Minnesota legislature had restricted mortgage foreclosure sales in light of the Great Depression, and the state's action was challenged under the Constitution's contract clause. The Court's majority upheld the provision, stressing the emergency situation of the nation. Justice Sutherland wrote in dissent that "the whole aim of construction, as applied to a provision of the Constitution, is to discover the meaning, to ascertain and give effect to the intent, of its framers and the people who adopted it" (*Home Bldg. & Loan Ass'n v. Blaisdell* 1934, 453). The original meaning allowed no exception for emergencies and in fact was adopted to prevent such responses to emergencies. Yet the majority disregarded this originalism.

The originalist record in the case was on the side of the dissenters (Miller 1969). Rather than trying to obscure this issue, the majority was straightforward in making a pragmatic ruling contrary to the original understanding of the Constitution's meaning. While the majority pointed to originalism, citing *The Federalist*, it did not use the method to reach its result. Indirectly, though, the majority may have simply been relying on originalism at a higher level of abstraction. The purpose of the contract clause, they noted, was furtherance of the smooth functioning of the economy. Hence, the strict language of the provision could be considered inapplicable if it would interfere with its designed purpose. Of course this sort of generality could eviscerate the text itself (Miller 1969), so the opinion is hard to justify on originalist terms. Instead, the majority held that the claim that "the great clauses of the Constitution must be confined to the interpretation which the framers, with the conditions and outlook of their time, would have placed upon them . . . carries its own refutation" (*Home Bldg. & Loan Ass'n v. Blaisdell* 1934, 442–443). This was perhaps the highest point of the Supreme Court's rejection of strict originalism.

The majority was essentially rejecting originalist interpretation, in light of changed circumstances and new knowledge. The opinion declared that "in earlier days, it was thought that only the concerns of individuals or of classes were involved" but that "it has later been found that the fundamental interests of the State are directly affected; and that the question is no longer merely that of one party to a contract as against another, but of the use of reasonable means to safeguard the economic structure upon which the good of all depends" (*Home Bldg. & Loan Ass'n v. Blaisdell* 1934, 442). The opinion also declared that "the whole aim of construction, as applied to a provision of the Constitution, is to discover the meaning, to ascertain and give effect to the intent, of its framers and the people who adopted it" (*Home Bldg. & Loan Ass'n v. Blaisdell* 1934, 453). This was a "living Constitution" holding, with a bit of intentionalism but no acknowledgment of original public meaning.

The opinion in *Home Bldg. & Loan Ass'n v. Blaisdell* (1934) did not immediately presage a shift to allowing greater government regulation of business. The court for a time remained true to the standard of *Lochner*. The *Lochner*-era Court often put its constitutional vision in the way of progressive change. The impulse for such change, though, put pressure on the Court. In the showdown between originalism and Roosevelt, the president won. While this might be attributed to the limited political power of the Court, rather than argument over interpretive theory itself, the Court changed.

Nonetheless, it remains significant that the Court chose to adapt to this pressure, not by attempting to find in originalism a basis for the legislative changes but instead by abandoning originalism. Perhaps they could not support their preferred outcomes via originalist interpretation. A congressman at the time declared that the New Deal was so outside original meaning that the framers, on viewing its actions, "would not recognize their own handiwork" (Gillman 1997, 223). So the era first recognized the notion of a "living Constitution."

The Court did not fully eschew originalism, and in the important decision of *United States v. Curtiss-Wright Export Corporation* (1936) the Court discussed constitutional history and cited *Elliot's Debates*, but the discussion was perfunctory by modern standards. The justices of the era no doubt recognized the respect commanded by the framers but felt little need to display fealty to their words or intentions.

It has been said that originalism "was largely abandoned by constitutional scholars and the Supreme Court itself following the triumph of New Deal liberalism" (Bassham 1992, 1). Yet originalism was truly interred before that time. Justice Sutherland apparently cried out for originalism in dissent to opinions upholding government regulation. Yet, in other *Lochner*-type opinions where he was in the majority, he showed little interest in originalist interpretation. His votes were consistently conservative, whether or not they were grounded in originalism.

The progressive New Deal court was openly committed to deference to the judgment of legislatures. While this is consistent with the theme of restraintist originalism opposed to judicial activism, it came in a rejection of originalist interpretation of the constitutional text. The Court seemingly concluded that legislatures were best positioned to collect the data necessary to adapt to change. The New Deal was not an originalist period, perhaps out of the perceived pragmatic needs of the day. The constitutional principles of the New Deal carried over into following years.

Youngstown Sheet & Tube Co. v. Sawyer (1952) arguably cried out for originalist analysis. It presented a unique and significant dispute over the separation of powers and foreign policy. President Truman sought to seize the steel mills in support of the Korean War effort. The issues of the case were those lying at the heart of the original constitutional Articles and the respective authority of the various branches.

Yet *Youngstown* saw some of the clearest rejections of originalism in Supreme Court history. The plurality ignored the theory. Justice Jackson, in his very influential concurrence, wrote: "Just what our forefathers did envision, or would have envisioned had they foreseen modern conditions, must be divined from materials almost as enigmatic as the dreams Joseph was called upon to interpret for Pharaoh" (*Youngstown Sheet & Tube Co. v. Sawyer* 1952, 634–635). He suggested that the occasional quotations supporting one side of the dispute or the other simply cancelled one another out. Justice Frankfurter considered the originalist record but wrote that it was "an inadmissibly narrow conception of American constitutional law to confine it to the words of the Constitution" (*Youngstown Sheet & Tube Co. v. Sawyer* 1952, 610). The text, in this view, had to be updated to deal with modern circumstances. This opinion may have been the true nadir of originalism at the Court.

The Court has never wholly ignored originalism. References to original meaning or original intent intermittently recur throughout its history. However, originalism appeared more important in the latter half of the nineteenth century. By contrast, the first half of the twentieth century was plainly a time when originalism was declining in importance. At no time prior to the Warren Court was originalism clearly the primary theme of Supreme Court jurisprudence. Originalism was used but was not predominant in the cases, and the theory of originalism was underdeveloped at the time.

FIVE

Originalism since the Warren Court

The modern era of Supreme Court history arguably begins with the Warren Court. As noted, the Warren Court began at a time when originalism was not at the forefront of interpretive methods and arguably rejected by the Court. The Warren Court is sometimes considered that classical anti-originalist Court, expanding the Constitution's dictates, especially those of the Bill of Rights, far beyond that originally conceived. This pattern of decisions produced a backlash, largely from the Reagan administration, that sought to restore originalism to its rightful place in constitutional interpretation. This chapter examines this history of the recent era and finds that the reality of originalism's role at the Court in this time is more complex than the standard story.

Warren Court

The Warren Court was often accused of ignoring the original meaning of the Constitution (Smith 2006). Liberals commonly accept the conservative criticism that the Warren Court dismissed originalist interpretation (Kalman 1998). Robert Bork (1990) essentially argued that the Court never issued an originalist opinion. Originalism was "submerged and marginalized" (O'Neill 2005, 39), as the Court became more openly results oriented. It was the decisions of the Warren Court that reinvigorated originalism.

In fact, however, a closer examination shows that originalism survived and even grew in importance during the Warren Court era. The Court made "inconsistent, but frequent, resort to originalist history to expand constitutional rights" (Friedman & Smith 1998, 24). The continuation of originalist sources in opinions of the period will be shown in Chapter 7. The early Warren Court did not rely on originalism, though, in the crucial early opinion of *Brown v. Board of Education* (1954).

If *Dred Scott* is the most reviled Supreme Court decision in history, *Brown v. Board of Education* may be the most applauded, in forcing an end to segregation. The Court actually heard reargument in *Brown*, largely for originalist purposes, to attempt to discern the original meaning of the Fourteenth Amendment. However, the justices found the historical investigation to be inconclusive. They were unable to find originalist support for their opinion. On this issue, the opinion declared that the Court "cannot turn the clock back to 1868 when the Amendment was adopted" but had to "consider public education in the light of its full development and its present place in American life throughout the nation" (*Brown v. Board of Education* 1954, 492–493).

Brown was functionally an antioriginalist opinion. It has been called "poorly reasoned" and an "ad hoc assertion of power" (O'Neill 2005, 56). Some nonoriginalists have questioned the expressed basis for the holding in the decision. But virtually no one, conservative or liberal, originalist or nonoriginalist, criticizes the outcome, at least in the sense of favoring a reversal of the outcome in *Brown*. Various commentators have agreed that originalism could not support the outcome, and there is a widespread belief that the decision was inconsistent with the original understanding of the Fourteenth Amendment.

Originalists have sought to say that *Brown* could have been decided on the basis of authentic originalism, with the same outcome. Michael McConnell (1995) has engaged in an extensive historical analysis to argue that segregation was in fact not consistent with the original meaning of the Fourteenth Amendment. Klarman (1995) has disputed this, noting that racially segregated schools were the rule at the time of the Fourteenth Amendment and that McConnell relied on evidence from years after its adoption to support his claims. Overall, the originalist case for the opinion in *Brown* finds relatively little support in the research on the historical record (Hall 2010).

Some originalists have sought to justify *Brown* under originalism simply by elevating the level of generality ascribed to the equality demands of the Fourteenth Amendment. A more common originalist argument suggests that the outcome was defensible under the privileges and immunities clause, had the scope of that constitutional provision not been severely limited by incorrect nineteenth-century precedent. Of course, neither the Court nor the advocates for desegregation sought to rely on this theory, apparently out of respect for the precedent. Since that time, the Court has continued to defer to the precedent limiting the privileges and immunities clause.

The outcome of this debate may be important to legitimate originalism as a matter of theory by showing it is consistent with *Brown*. McConnell (1995, 952) notes that any theory unable to accommodate the decision in *Brown* would be "seriously discredited." Pam Karlan likewise contends that "every constitutional theory must claim *Brown* for itself" (Karlan 2009, 1060). However, reconciling the outcome in *Brown* does little to legitimate originalism as a matter of practice at the Supreme Court. The Court in that case proved unable to justify its decision with originalism and hence turned to other rationales. A theoretical possibility could exist, but the Court was unable to find an originalist basis for its opinion.

Finding that the decision in *Brown* was consistent with correct originalism is not truly helpful to support the theory in practice. Such a finding means that "the best lawyers in the country, the best historians in the country, the Supreme Court justices and their clerks, with all the resources available to them and every incentive to discover the original understanding did not succeed in recovering that original understanding" (Strauss 2007). Originalist interpretation must be supported by justices using the method to find the correct result, not justices blundering into the correct originalist result by other means.

Brown was not an originalist opinion, but neither was it antioriginalist. In its decision, the Court essentially concluded that originalism could not resolve the question before it. The Court was plainly interested in originalism, though, insofar as it could help decide *Brown*. The decision may show the limits of originalism but does not stand as an attack on the interpretive theory. Indeed, the Warren Court sometimes openly embraced the theory of originalism. Justice Brennan wrote in a concurrence that "the line we must draw between the permissible and the impermissible is one which accords with history and faithfully reflects the understanding of the Founding Fathers" (*School District of Abington v. Schempp* 1963, 294).

One of the more controversial Warren Court opinions prohibited state officials from requiring the recitation of an official state prayer in public schools (*Engel v. Vitale* 1962). This opinion was quite originalist in orientation. The court relied centrally on the views of Jefferson and Madison and actions taken by the states in the period leading up to the American Revolution. It proclaimed that this history demonstrated concern for the "dangers of a union of Church and State" (*Engel v. Vitale*, 429). The use of originalism in the opinion, though, was highly contested, and a strong case was made that the result did not conform to the original meaning of the Constitution (Rice 1964). Originalism was used, but perhaps inaccurately. The opinion was extraordinarily controversial at the time, but it is now generally accepted, regardless of its originalist accuracy.

In the reapportionment cases, though, which logically might want originalist evidence, the Court did not rely centrally on the approach, though it was discussed. The limited role for originalism here was perhaps because originalism could not support the outcomes (Maltz 1987, Berger 1977). These cases may simply illustrate the ability of the justices to avoid the method when it seems inconvenient. When Justice Black sought to justify the apportionment cases on originalist grounds (*Wesberry v. Sanders* 1964), his efforts were effectively rebutted by Justice Harlan (O'Neill 2005). Justice Black's majority opinion, though, used originalism, even if inaccurately. At the time, these decisions were heavily criticized for interfering in political processes and for the weakness of the occasional attempts to rely on originalist evidence (Kelly 1965).

There is a general belief that the reapportionment decisions cannot be justified by any originalist analysis (O'Neill 2005). Yet these decisions, controversial at the time, are now generally accepted and even lauded for their role in promoting democratic governance. Forcing the justices to decide based on a contrary originalist record, if possible, would have prevented outcomes that are now almost universally approved. Originalists, of course, may bite the bullet and concede that their theory does not result in the pragmatically preferable outcome in every case. The Constitution may be amended to correct bad originalist outcomes. Of course, the weakness of the originalist justification for the reapportionment decisions did not prevent the Court from presenting it as supportive evidence, illustrating the appeal of the theory as a rhetorical device at least.

Another controversial Warren Court opinion, issued in *Griswold v. Connecticut* (1965), invalidated a state law against use of contraceptives. The majority found a right to privacy in the Constitution through the vague evocation of penumbras without concern for originalism. Justice Goldberg's concurrence sought to find a more explicit basis for the right in the Ninth Amendment, but Justice Black's dissent (relying heavily on *Farrand*) argued that this claim turned somersaults with history. Kelly (1965), though generally a critic of Black's historicism, agreed. Although there is a near consensus that *Griswold* was not originalist (Balkin may disagree), few disagree with the holding itself, though many argue with its progeny. Again, originalists may concede that the theory will produce inferior outcomes in particular cases, even if the overall use of the theory was beneficial or necessary to the rule of law.

In other Warren Court cases, originalism was debated more openly. A couple of decisions in 1967 on Fourth Amendment rights saw impassioned originalist dissents from Justice Black, arguing inter alia that it did not cover electronic eavesdropping (Kerr 2010). The majority, though, adopted a more pragmatic and progressive approach that contended that the Amendment had to be adapted to modern technologies.

Other Warren Court opinions from the 1960s had some openly originalist orientation in majority opinions. The court examined history to ascertain the meaning of the constitutional protection against double jeopardy (*Benton v. Maryland* 1969), the scope of jury trial rights (*Duncan v. Louisiana*

1968), and the nature of the constitutional right against self-incrimination (*Miranda v. Arizona* 1966).

This era saw a number of references to the Declaration of Independence in support of the Court's opinions. Typically, these references were simply in support of a very broad principle, such as free speech, or equality, or even the right to try to promote a revolution. Perhaps the Court sincerely found the Declaration inspiring in support of its conclusion, though the very high level of generality suggests the possibility that the Court was merely "decorating" its opinion with powerful originalist sources.

Bork (1990) suggested that the Warren Court was out of step with history in ignoring originalism, but the Warren Court did not in fact disregard or abandon originalism. It used originalist sources quite frequently, more so than did previous Courts. Justice Black of the Warren Court has been called the "most influential originalist judge of the last hundred years" (Strauss 2009, 4). Of course, the Warren Court is renowned as an ideologically activist Court. Its apparent reliance on originalism in some cases may simply have been as a rhetorical tool in service to an outcome-oriented agenda. It used originalism especially in cases that aroused public opinion (Friedman & Smith 1998). The Warren Court's use of originalist history has been amply criticized (Kelly 1965). But the Warren Court nonetheless employed originalism as a tool for constitutional interpretation.

Burger Court

Warren Burger was appointed by President Nixon to serve as something of an antidote to Warren Court jurisprudence, but at the time originalism was not yet fully the focus of the attack on the Warren Court. The Burger Court became attacked by Meese and other originalists for following the path of the Warren Court. It is generally considered a disappointment to conservatives, including originalists. Burger Court opinions did contain some reliance on originalism, however.

Commentators have analyzed the Burger Court's devotion to originalism in its separation of powers opinions. The Court reportedly used originalism "selectively" to promote a particular vision of an "apolitical administration" of the government (Claeys 2004, 407). In the very important opinion in *Buckley v. Valeo* (1976), the Court emphasized the original meaning of the appointments clause of the Constitution and cited *The Federalist* and *Farrand's* notes of Madison in support of its ruling. It has been criticized, though, for ignoring portions of *The Federalist* that are directly contrary to its vision (Claeys 2004).

Similarly, the Court's decision invalidating the legislative veto (*INS v. Chadha* 1983) relied on *The Federalist* and *Farrand*. The Court likewise relied on originalism to protect presidential powers in *Bowsher v. Synar* (1986). These opinions, which went to the heart of the original Constitution, emphasized originalist interpretation, though Claeys (2004) maintained that the originalist approach was used only to legitimize a broader view of administration for the government. Another commentator has suggested that the Burger Court followed an originalist approach in cases involving the measure of congressional power but not in controversies involving presidential power (Chemerinsky 1987). Indeed, in an opinion on the authority of executive agreements without congressional approval, the Court clearly rejected originalism and relied on a longstanding historic practice to provide a "gloss" on the powers established by the Constitution (*Dames & Moore v. Regan* 1981).

The Warren Court's opinions often relied on originalist sources for support. The importance of this reliance can certainly be disputed. A scan of these opinions shows that originalism was invoked usually as a paragraph or perhaps a footnote, rather than the basis for an extensive discussion, as found in some later opinions. However, these opinions generally had greater brevity than many of those from subsequent Courts, and this does not disprove the meaning of originalism as a basis for the opinions.

Roe v. Wade, for some the classic antioriginalist opinion, was issued by the Burger Court. It became the basis for a repeated argument that the Court should be limited to the original Constitution and not create its own living Constitution responsive to the times. The originalist criticism of reproductive rights jurisprudence was not limited to outside commentators. Justice White wrote in a dissent that the Court did not subscribe to the "view that constitutional interpretation can possibly be limited to the 'plain meaning' of the Constitution's text or the subjective interpretation of the

Framers" (*Thornburgh v. Am. College of Obstetricians and Gynecologists* 1986, 789). Once again, originalism was prominent in a dissent but disregarded by the majority.

Rehnquist Court

Originalism truly emerged as a conservative priority in the Reagan era, as a response to the Burger Court as well as the Warren Court. Decisions such as *Roe* issued by the Burger Court were more recent and at least as objectionable as older Warren Court holdings. Now Chief Justice Rehnquist had expressed a devotion to originalist interpretation, and he had conservative allies with a possibly similar orientation. Justice Scalia and, later, Justice Thomas gave Chief Justice Rehnquist allies in pursuit of an originalist agenda. Originalism was prominent in a number of decisions issued by the Rehnquist Court, and the era has been summarized as one of a turn to history in constitutional interpretation (Bhargava 2006).

Originalism was central to a decision on whether a federal statute could reopen judicial judgments in actions that had been time barred and dismissed (*Plaut v. Spendthrift Farm* 1995). Justice Scalia cited *The Federalist*, old court cases, and secondary sources to find that the approach violated the separation of powers. A dissent from Justice Stevens also used originalism and argued that the majority was inconsistent with both history and precedent. He did not dispute the originalist evidence of the majority but simply contended that an original meaning that the legislature could not review the results of specific cases did not settle the legislature's rights to review broad classes of cases. Contrary to the typical dispute, this did not pit one originalist source against another but instead involved the degree to which originalist evidence on a given question could be extrapolated to a somewhat different contemporary case before the Court.

For *Printz v. United States* (1997), originalism was central and highly contested. Scalia's majority opinion held that the federal government could not "commandeer" state governments to enforce its gun control laws. He had to confront the fact that statutes of the very First Congress put requirements on state courts. Justice Scalia distinguished these as applying only to judges, not state executive officers. Combined with the recent holding in

Plaut, though, the opinion illustrates a problem with originalism. In *Plaut*, Justice Scalia took evidence from the framing era that was not identical to the current controversy and found it analogous. In *Printz*, Justice Scalia took evidence from the framing era that was not identical to the current controversy and distinguished it.

The most aggressive use of originalist evidence in *Printz* was found in Justice Souter's dissent. He relied extensively on *The Federalist*, which suggested that the national government could employ the states in the execution of federal laws. Justice Scalia responded that the declarations did not explicitly say that the federal government could *compel* state compliance. He also issued criticisms of reliance on *The Federalist* itself, noting that it should not receive conclusive weight and that it "reads with a split personality" on federalism issues (*Printz v. United States* 1997, 915). In the face of a "powerful historical claim," Scalia scrambled to explain "why the lessons of the founding period have nothing to offer" (Nichol 1999, 969). Although he has often cited *The Federalist*, Justice Scalia threw the source overboard in this decision.

The *Printz* dispute over federalism is a revealing one. Originalism was central, but there was considerable disagreement over its direction. Scalia primarily emphasized the *absence* of evidence; the lack of any showing that the federal government of the era had commandeered state executive operations. Yet the absence of evidence is notoriously not evidence of absence, and Justice Scalia has not generally relied on the "absence of originalist evidence" standard in other cases, such as *Plaut* (where there was a similar absence of originalist evidence on the particular issue before the Court). Nor has he questioned the reliability of *The Federalist* in cases where he used the source. Together, the two cases suggest that originalist evidence is not directly applicable to the facts of the case before the Court and can therefore be used by either side of the dispute. Each party can select bits of supportive originalist evidence and claim that any contrary evidence is inapplicable.

Federalism was an area of the law where the Rehnquist Court clearly turned to reliance upon originalism. *Seminole Tribe v. Florida* (1996) and *Alden v. Maine* (1999) included extensive originalist discussion by the justices. The majority's support for states' sovereign immunity rights under the Eleventh Amendment relied heavily on unclear background principles of England, even though the constitutional text itself appeared contrary. While the majority invoked Madison, Hamilton, and Marshall, it dismissed other contrary originalist evidence as "equivocal" (*Alden v. Maine* 1999, 726).

Justice Souter offered extensive dissents in *Seminole Tribe* and *Alden* that were thick with originalism, also relying on the views of Madison, Hamilton, and Marshall. His view appeared "more diligent in following Justice Scalia's admonition to take into account the attitudes and beliefs of the time" (Canja 2000, 536). Indeed, the conservative majority relied more heavily on precedent, while Justice Souter engaged in classical originalism (Kleinhaus 2000). Without taking a position on the correctness of the competing originalisms, it was clear that both positions had originalist support, and the justices divided on lines largely ideological (Canja 2000). All the justices paid tribute to originalism, but the theory did not plainly dictate a result.

An interesting use of originalism can be found in *Atascadero State Hospital v. Scanlon* (1985). In that case, the conservative majority found that there was no waiver of Eleventh Amendment immunity by a state that received funds under the Rehabilitation Act, but the justices provided little originalist analysis. A remarkably lengthy dissent written by Justice Brennan (and joined by Justices Marshall, Blackmun, and Stevens) did not merely cite originalist sources but undertook an extensive originalist analysis, using *The Federalist* and *Farrand*. The dissent relied centrally on the ratification debates that went on for nearly fifteen pages. The dissent followed with a discussion of practice in the First Congress. This was arguably the most originalist opinion written at that time, yet it was issued in dissent and was written by liberals typically considered to be nonoriginalist.

The federalism cases are among those with the greatest reliance on originalism, but the justices have fallen into a pattern on the use of the sources in these cases. They commonly split five to four, with both sides relying substantially on originalist sources (Smith 2004). The conservative majority relies substantially on the Anti-Federalist comments around ratification, while the liberal minority relies on the Federalist response. The justices seem to be selecting originalist evidence that supports their preferences and disregarding contrary evidence.

On separation of powers issues, Claeys (2004) claims that the Rehnquist Court tracked the Burger Court's practice of selective invocation of originalism in pursuit of a theory of apolitical administration. The Court was charged with "veering erratically between originalist and non-originalist interpretive methodologies with barely any explanation" (Claeys 2004, 407). When the justices used originalism, they could not agree. In perhaps the most prominent case, *Morrison v. Olson* (1988) on authority for independent prosecutors, the majority found no originalist support for the claim that the action was unconstitutional, citing *Farrand*, while Justice Scalia dissented and concluded the practice was unconstitutional, also citing *Farrand*. In *U.S. Term Limits v. Thornton* (1995), both the majority and the dissent likewise relied heavily on originalist sources.

An interesting dispute arose in *McIntyre v. Ohio Elections Commission* (1995), which found that a prohibition on distribution of anonymous literature during an election campaign violated the First Amendment. The majority showed some concern for originalism, citing *The Federalist*, but focused on a rather vague reference to the purpose of the First Amendment, but Justice Thomas wrote a strikingly originalist concurrence with considerable analysis of the framers' reliance on anonymity. In dissent, Justice Scalia (joined by Chief Justice Rehnquist) wrote that the evidence of a practice did not establish that it was constitutionally protected. When the original meaning, for Justice Scalia, was "unclear," the "widespread and long-accepted practices of the American people are the best indication of what fundamental beliefs it was intended to enshrine" (*McIntyre v. Ohio Elections Commission* 1995, 378). This could be read as a broad indictment of the value of originalism because original meaning will seldom be truly clear in cases that reach the Supreme Court. But it was an embrace of a broad originalist purposivism.

Although the Rehnquist Court was perceived as relatively originalist, the theory did not pervade the Court's decisions. Some of the most notable originalist opinions came in dissent or concurrence, not the majority opinion. Thus, when Justice Thomas took a strong originalist position on the Establishment Clause, the Court's majority agreed with the outcome but not the originalist reasoning, forcing him into a separate concurrence (*Zelman v. Simmons-Harris* 2002). A vigorous originalist opinion on the negative Commerce Clause was found only in the dissent of Justice Thomas (*Camps Newfound/Owatonna, Inc. v. Town of Harrison* 1997).

On other occasions, originalism was largely ignored. In the negative commerce clause action of *West Lynn Creamery, Inc. v. Healy* (1994), the majority very briefly referenced Madison in support of the existence of its requirements, but the dissent of Justices Scalia and Thomas in criticism of the negative commerce clause offers no originalist sources. Indeed, in the negative commerce clause cases, it is normal for defenders to cite a letter of Madison issued decades after the Constitution's passage and critics to cite nothing originalist. Perhaps originalist sources offer little or nothing on this issue, but it is a very important one.

One logical candidate for an originalist interpretation was *Bush v. Gore* (2000), which functionally decided the 2000 presidential election. The decision could have been based on evidence from the original framing period of the Constitution, based on Article II, and some justices did adopt this rationale, but they offered no real originalist justification for their position. The absence of originalism from such a crucial opinion is significant.

Originalism was also used in Rehnquist Court establishment clause decisions. In *Van Orden v. Perry* (2005), the majority emphasized that the challenged display of the Ten Commandments was typical of a history of government action dating back to the founding era. While the majority opinion was at best very weakly originalist, Justice Scalia had a more originalist concurrence. However, even this reliance on original meaning had little actual support from the time. The most originalist opinion of the case was rendered in dissent by Justice Stevens, who relied on evidence from the Constitutional convention and letters written by Thomas Jefferson and James Madison. Of course, he also noted that the original intent of the establishment clause was really limited to Christian groups and would have excluded protection of Jews, among others. An authentic originalism, he argued, would substantially eviscerate the protections that had developed from the establishment clause. The majority did not take issue with the latter historical analysis.

The Rehnquist Court is generally regarded as being more originalist than prior courts. This era saw the first explicit reference to "originalism" as a method of constitutional interpretation. Commentators have noted an apparent dramatic increase in use of *The Federalist* during the Rehnquist Court (Durschlag 2005).

While the increased use of *The Federalist* might be seen as an increased dedication to originalist theory at the Rehnquist Court, there are some reasons to doubt this. The lack of a similar increase in use of certain other originalist sources may indicate that the citations to *The Federalist* are "for show" or legitimization rather than an attempt to find true original meaning. Moreover, the frequency of dueling references to *The Federalist* in both majority and dissent, typically decided along ideological lines, also gives reason to doubt its controlling influence on decisions of the period.

However, my research also shows a dramatic increase in the use of early dictionaries for interpretation. Prior to 1987, the Johnson and Sheridan dictionaries, presumably available to the justices, were cited in only four cases in opinions commanding only thirteen justice-votes (over nearly 200 years of opinions). In the next twenty years, though, these dictionaries were cited in twenty cases in opinions joined by seventy-three justices. The dictionaries do not have the same iconic status as *The Federalist*, and their greater usage might well reflect an increased commitment to original meaning originalism. Still, this was a selective originalism without any justification offered for why some sources were useful while others were not.

Roberts Court

The Roberts Court is in its nascence as I write, and its devotion to originalism is uncertain. The confirmation hearings preceding the Court were instructive. Justice Roberts, under questions, expressly disclaimed originalism, at least as anything like an exclusive philosophy for constitutional interpretation. Justice Alito said only that originalism was one of many considerations for judicial decisionmaking, seemingly adopting a pluralist approach to constitutional interpretation. Expressed devotees of originalism, such as Justices Scalia and Thomas, remain on the Court, but the new justices have made efforts to distance themselves from their originalism (Amar 2009). However, some recent opinions of the Roberts Court evidence considerable commitment to originalist interpretation, so the status of originalism remains somewhat unclear.

The opinion in *District of Columbia v. Heller* (2008) has been lauded as the epitome of contemporary originalism at the Supreme Court (Solum 2009). The majority opinion of Justice Scalia relied very heavily on originalist materials, including the ratification debates, dictionary definitions, comments of the era, and other materials. In dissent, Justice Stevens also relied heavily on originalist materials, including comments from the ratifying conventions and James Madison. The opinion might be considered evidence of the triumph of originalism. The majority opinion contains the Court's closest clear expression of reliance on original public meaning (*District of Columbia v. Heller* 2008, 576–577). The dissent's particular originalist theory is more obscure, and some have considered it reliance on original intent rather than original meaning.

A closer look at *Heller*, though, might give one pause. The dueling reliance on originalist materials appears to suggest that the theory is indeterminate rather than constraining. The votes in *Heller* tracked not originalism per se but the ideological proclivities of the justices. Either the originalism behind the opinions was insincere, or it was so indeterminate that it could not be sincerely applied. The opinion is an interesting illustration of originalism at the Supreme Court, but it does not clearly commend the practice, as it resulted in a court divided along ideological lines. Originalist sources did not move any of the justices from their presumed policy preferences on the law.

Nor is it clear that the majority got the originalist resolution of the case right. Historian Saul Cornell (2009, 1106) claims that "Scalia's new originalism interprets the meaning of the Second Amendment from a post-Founding-era perspective and substitutes that later interpretation for the Amendment's original meaning." Judge J. Harvie Wilkinson (2009, 270) similarly complained about this usage and observed that it made it easy for judges to cherry-pick evidence to support their preferred position "choosing from a vast array of materials those that appear to support the preferred result." The individual rights opinion of the Court has been characterized as the product of shabby "law office history" found in law reviews (Spitzer 2008).

Moreover, the true originalism of the opinion is seriously disputed even by proponents of individual gun rights. Lund (2009) contends that the Court's reasoning was in respects very nonoriginalist and even an embarrassment for the justices of the majority. He notes that the application of the Second Amendment to handguns did not even purport to be a historical analysis but was based on present-day attitudes. More significantly, Justice Scalia provides in the opinion a laundry list of gun regulations that would be constitutional, but he provides zero originalist basis for these conclusions. Lund (2009, 1376) concludes that, judging from the opinion, "not a single member of the current Court takes originalism, or the purpose of the Second Amendment, quite that seriously."

Originalists, notwithstanding Lund, commonly take a stand with the opinion in *Heller*. But that opinion provides weak support for the theory. Many believe the opinion got the history wrong. As Lund (2009) notes, a crucial part of the opinion was wholly divorced from originalism. Even if the ultimate holding of the opinion was correct, it fundamentally illustrates the manipulability of originalism, given the division of the justices. Had the Court a different ideological composition, one suspects that a highly originalist majority opinion, written perhaps by Justice Stevens, would have reached the opposite result. Commentators would have criticized its originalist analysis, perhaps, but the Court would have still reached that opposite result.

The controversial corporate free speech opinion in *Citizens United v. Federal Election Commission* (2009) is also instructive on the role of originalism in the current Court. In dissent, Justice Stevens undertook an extensive discussion of original meaning to show that corporations were not entitled to such rights as a person. Justice Kennedy's majority opinion relied heavily on precedent and largely ignored the originalist issues, but Justice Scalia wrote a concurrence (joined by Justices Thomas and Alito) specifically to respond to Stevens on the originalism question.

Justice Scalia provided his own originalist evidence. Interestingly, he observed that even if the framers disliked and would not have given rights to the monopolistic corporations of their time, this attitude should not be applied to modern corporations of the free market. Here, he recognizes that changed circumstances could alter the original intent of the text, though he is unclear on the precise original meaning that implies this outcome. The position carries an implication that the original meaning may not have included corporations of the time but that it reflects a broader principle that would protect today's corporations. Scalia does stress the absence of any explicit rejection of rights for corporations. The latter test, of course, could be used in the vast majority of controversies to reject any originalist evidence.

The opinion in *Citizens United* was ideologically very polarizing. The president of the United States criticized it in his State of the Union address, but conservatives rushed to its defense. On examining the positions of the justices, we see liberals opposing the majority on originalist and nonoriginalist grounds, conservatives supporting the majority on originalist grounds, and conservatives supporting the majority on nonoriginalist grounds. There is no indication that originalism, though used, played any role in the outcome. Rather, the votes lined up as expected ideologically, and assorted justifications, such as originalism, were given for the preferred outcomes of the justices.

In the important holding in *Boumediene v. Bush* (2008), involving the availability of a habeas corpus challenge to detention at Guantanamo, the Court eschewed reliance on originalism. The Court extensively surveyed the historical record of habeas both before and at the time of the Constitution. However, it found that the record was incomplete and that there was no analogous law involving use of the doctrine on foreign soil leased by the United States (*Boumediene v. Bush* 2008, 746–752). Originalism was considered but could not inform the outcome. Justice Scalia's dissent showed relatively less concern for original meaning.

The Roberts Court has already seen opinions steeped in originalism. But like its predecessors, the use of originalism was not uniform. While *Heller* relied heavily on originalism to apply the Second Amendment, the Court decided other Bill of Rights cases in the same term, with no mention of original meaning or use of originalist materials. This selective usage calls the Court's commitment to originalism into question. Perhaps the absence of originalist citations in these cases testifies only to their limited value in resolving the dispute before the Court. This is a more modest critique of originalism, simply suggesting that the method is unhelpful for many current constitutional controversies. More cynically, one might suggest that these were less controversial decisions for which the justices found rhetorical use of originalism unnecessary (though *Bush v. Gore* would be contrary to this hypothesis).

The recent history of originalism demonstrates its significance to the Court. Reliance is frequent in at least some areas of the law. This testifies to the usefulness of the theory. The practical significance of the theory remains uncertain, though. Debates over the application of originalism commonly involve its invocation by both majority and dissent. The usefulness of originalism may simply be the public legitimization of the justices' ideologically preferred outcomes, though this is yet unproved. It is suggested that the originalist position is rhetorical more than true decisional (Greene 2009). The reality of this claim is evaluated later in the book.

SIX

Evaluating the Supreme Court's Use of History

Correct originalism calls for at least some skills of historical analysis in which justices are typically untrained. Justice Scalia has remarked that originalism is "better suited to the historian than the lawyer." Yet it is lawyers, not historians, who are appointed to the Court, and, when doing originalism, the justice acts to some degree as a historian. The historical research of a leading originalist, Robert Bork, has been characterized as "too often sloppy, superficial, and sometimes inaccurate," relying only on "stock citations from the Federalist Papers" (Farber & Sherry 2002, 17). He was critiqued for writing a lengthy book on originalism without citing Madison's Convention notes. Of course, Bork was not trained as a historian, and this could possibly explain shortcomings.

Judges also may operate under severe time constraints that limit their ability to do a full historical analysis of a question. A circuit court opinion declared that "judges do not have either the leisure or the training to conduct *responsible* historical research or *competently* umpire historical controversies" (*Velasquez v. Frapwell* 1998, 393). Judges typically "lack the expertise, let alone the time" to get history right (Sutton 2009, 1184). Because judges are untrained in the field, "they routinely botch history when they set their hands to it" (Bassham 1992, 97). A commitment to originalism as an interpretive theory seems to imply confidence in the capacity of judges to correctly find and apply historical materials.

Under true original meaning originalism, historians may not be the best judges as they may often look to original purpose or intent. Original meaning is truly a linguistic exercise. Of course, lawyers and judges are not skilled linguists, either. And some understanding of history should be necessary to put language into the times and ascertain its original public meaning.

However, this lack of training need not doom originalism. Lawyers and judges constantly address questions from other fields in which they lack training. Opinions commonly involve scientific matters, or technological ones, in which lawyers are not directly trained and for which they may lack the ability to resolve "competently." Some have criticized this more general tendency as the "lawyer as astrophysicist" assumption that lawyers can master any discipline. Yet these matters must often be resolved to decide a case. One can't simply throw up one's hands in hopelessness. Judges appear to do reasonably well at resolving questions beyond their training.

Judges don't have the luxury of not deciding. While a historian may declare a question open and uncertain, judges must resolve cases. Robert Bork has recognized the difficulties of assessing history and warned that originalists should not expect too much, just best efforts, or "we must abandon the enterprise of law and, most especially, that of judicial review" (Bork 1990, 163). The judicial process is imperfect for resolution of factual truth in many ways but still essential for the functioning of our legal system. This is not a complete exoneration, though. If judges were especially bad at evaluating history, that could be grounds to call originalism into doubt as an interpretive method, in comparison with other methods at which judges may be more skilled.

The previous chapters summarized instances in which the Supreme Court has used some originalist history in its decisions. In various cases, I questioned the reliability of the originalist conclusions of the justices. This chapter will more broadly review the accuracy of those determinations, according to historians and other academics. Historians and others have written critically about the past practice. An early review suggested that the Court commonly relied on archaic, outdated works, nonhistorians, or its own flawed assessment of the historical record (Murphy 1963).

Originalism implicitly presumes that there is some authentic, objective original meaning of the text to be found (Festa 2008). But this notion of objective historical fact has been disputed. Historians typically concede that there is no single objective history to be found. Thus, "the belief in a hard core of historical facts existing objectively and independently of the interpretation is a preposterous fallacy" (Carr 1961, 6). William Leuchtenberg (1992, 11) suggests that the use of history in court is the best evidence against the "impression that historians are objective scholars who can certify the facts of the past much like scientists reporting on the contents of a test tube." Most historians of today admit that "historical truth is elusive if not impossible to obtain" and that historical facts carry "a great deal of the inherent subjective baggage of the person doing the interpreting" (Richards 1997, 817). Historical claims are said to be "by definition, interpretations, and eventually any analytic consensus will be replaced by another" (Hurewitz 2004, 211). This does not suggest that historical truth can be found to govern constitutional interpretation by establishing the original public meaning.

The historical record is necessarily incomplete, requiring that choices and judgments be made about the sources on which to rely. All historians are prisoners of their own experience who bring to the task the preconceptions of their personalities and their age (Schlesinger 2007, A19). Schlesinger suggests that the quest for objectivity in history is a doomed enterprise. The search for historical facts has been called "illusive and intangible" (Becker 1955, 330). Thus, the "same series of vanished events is differently imagined in each succeeding generation" (Becker 1955, 336). None of those generations, not even the most recent, necessarily got the answer right; they each made historical interpretations grounded in their own backgrounds and beliefs. The "first-year graduate student in history" learns that the field is not a matter of clear fact but one of interpretation, influenced by the historians' own biases (Wiecek 1988).

Historians have intermittently aspired to objectivity, and for a time it was a professional norm. But this has proved "psychologically and sociologically naïve" (Novick 1988, 6). He pointed to a tradition of historians using the past for advocacy reasons rather than searching for objective truth.

By the 1960s, an ideological polarization among historians, with all claiming objectivity, made the thesis difficult to sustain. A historian's viewpoint and preferences shape the historical materials he or she consults and how they are interpreted; historians may refer to historical truths only to add weight to their preferred accounts of the past and censor contradictory accounts (Jenkins 1991). Thus, "history is always biased in some way" (Fasolt 2004, xix) and by its nature political.

If historians dispute the existence of objective historical truth, what hope does the procedure offer for lawyers? Professional historians often do not try to answer these questions "because they recognize that history is indeterminate" (Sherry 1995, 441). Objective historical truth may not be ascertainable. But judges cannot escape deciding cases on the grounds of historical indeterminacy, and they too are influenced in their historical findings by their own backgrounds and beliefs.

Some historians have contended more broadly that it is not realistic to apply factual findings about the past to current controversies. By this standard originalism "fails to understand the past on its own terms and maintain a respect for its integrity" (Bernstein 1987, 1568). Such use in the context of originalism may be dismissed as presentism and a misuse of history (Festa 2008). Such a conclusion inevitably condemns any use of history by the Supreme Court, though, and it seems too strong a criticism. The Court cannot render its opinions oblivious to the history of the Constitution, the Court, and the facts of the very case before it.

The challenge to the existence of objective history plainly proves too much for originalist legal purposes. Even as historical truth may not be precisely determinable, historical falsity may sometimes be found (Richards 1997). Some historical facts are known, though. Few would dispute the fact that the Japanese bombed Pearl Harbor, for example. We have a Constitution, and it contains certain words (disputes may remain over punctuation). That Constitution was adopted in the wake of commentary such as that found in *The Federalist*. The meaning of at least some of its words, such as age requirements for office, is clear. While it may be impossible to objectively identify certain past historical events, that does not make it impossible to draw a reasonably confident conclusion about some events. Whittington (1999, 162) claims that while the historical record for originalism is "hardly perfect" there is little basis to hold that it "is generally radically deficient." Jack Rakove (1997, 1588) argues that "skepticism about the limits of judicial reasoning does not require a blanket dismissal of the possibility that historically grounded approaches . . . might yield fruitful results." Of course, Supreme Court decisions rarely involve clear or certain questions, and history may be less plain for those matters. Thus, the practical value of history is uncertain.

Setting aside this question of the possibility of doing objective history, it is unclear whether justices could accurately find objective historical facts, should they exist. Just as "lawyers would not trust historians with their cases," it is argued, "historians shouldn't trust lawyers with the past" (Kozinski & Susman 1997, 1586). Prominent historian John Philip Reid (1993, 195–196) contends that the "crossing of history with law" is a "mixture containing more snares than rewards, as it risks confusing rules of evidence basic to one profession with canons of proof sacrosanct to another." The classic criticism of the Court's use of history was written by Alfred Kelly (1965), who reviewed numerous cases of the Court that relied on historical evidence and found them quite wanting. Alexander Bickel (1962) has shown that historical conclusions in some of the nation's most famous opinions were soon abandoned by professional historians in favor of contrary positions.

For example, Kelly's assessment of Justice Black's use of history in one case found reliance on sources that "were so stale and inadequate that a properly trained historical scholar would hesitate to suggest that an undergraduate student rely on them" (Kelly 1965, 121). In reapportionment cases, Black "mangled constitutional history" (Kelly 1965, 135). Justice Marshall engaged in "historical revelation by judicial fiat, with little if any inquiry into actual history" (Kelly 1965, 123). The *Dred Scott* opinion was characterized as very bad history. He concluded that "from a professional point of view" most of the Court's ventures into history were "very poor indeed" (Kelly 1965, 155). An updated assessment of Kelly's analysis for the modern era of originalism found that it was still apt criticism (Richards 1997). While Kelly evaluates all historical usages, his criticism applies to the Court's application of sources such as *The Federalist* as well (Tillman 2003). Even Kelly did not call for the abandonment of the Court's use of history, however.

A more recent review was comparably critical (Derfner 2005). The author argued that the Court had bungled the history of the equal protection clause and the Eleventh Amendment. Farber (2000) likewise claims that these rulings "reflect a high degree of historical ineptitude." Derfner (2005) also notes the significance of history to gay rights decisions and how the Court in *Lawrence* conceded that it had gotten the history wrong in *Bowers*.

Other legal historians have been similarly critical of the Supreme Court's use of history in its opinions. They are "skeptical about the possibility of knowing the founders' intentions" (Richards 1997, 364–364). They emphasize the disparity between "historians' legal history" and "lawyers' legal history" and find the latter dubious (Bernstein 1987, 1578). Legal arguments from even the "most rigorous theorists" based in history have "habits of poorly supported generalization—which at times fall below even the standards of undergraduate history writing" (Flaherty 1995, 526). The Court has consistently "resorted to suspect, if not invalid, and to inconsistent, if not incompatible, methods" of originalism (Miller 1969, 3). When the Court's historical theory errs, it may not be due to simply getting facts incorrect but is more likely due to a highly selective assembly of historical facts (Miller 1969). It has been suggested that "those with legal training are . . . ill-equipped to understand the rudiments of the process of historical research" (Melton 1998, 384). Academic criticism of Supreme Court history is so common that it is considered to be flogging a dead horse (Wiecek 1988). There are some exceptions, though, who suggest that the justices' use of history is generally accurate (Daly 1954).

It may be that limitations in the Court's past use of history are due to the fact that originalism generally involves "asking questions of history that history cannot answer" (Richards 1997, 886). Modern constitutional disputes may simply be unamenable to originalist historical analysis. There are cases in which the available historical evidence "is either insufficient, or is hopelessly ambiguous, or simply cannot be made germane to our purposes" (Wiecek 1988, 234). There is a tendency for judges to read "eighteenth-century evidence as if it were formulated to meet twentieth-century standards, and hold the record to a measure of accuracy that simply is not there"

(Reid 1993, 202). Circumstances have changed dramatically, and contemporary questions, such as those about the scope of the establishment clause, may simply be irresolvable by reference to history (Kelly 1965).

Whittington (1999, 211) believes that some historical truth can be ascertained for originalism but concedes that "interpretation of the text often falls short of providing clear guidance in making the fine distinctions required to settle contemporary disputes." It is said to be the "rare dispute today that can find a direct answer in the historical record in which originalists seek the original understanding" (Smith 2004, 231). Thus, even perfect historical analysis at the Court may fail. There may be occasional cases, though, where history provides an answer, and they may not be so rare as claimed. When history does not provide a conclusive answer to a legal queston, it may still provide bounds on the breadth of an opinion.

Even when the answer might truly be found in history in theory, legal history has shortcomings. Legal scholars too often "make a fetish of one or two famous primary sources and consider their historical case made" (Flaherty 1995, 553). This is apparent from the Supreme Court's heavy use of *The Federalist*.

Accurate history requires a broader perspective. Quotations must be placed in context, and the full record must be explored. Originalists recognize this in theory, but practice may not have kept up to this standard. Flaherty (1995) applies the standard to legal scholars, not the courts, and finds that they tend to make conclusory assertions about history to support a preferred story. Perhaps "legal academics . . . may never be expected to pursue the often tedious work that keeps historians employed" (Flaherty 1995, 590), though they have more time for a question than the typical judge. Judge Posner (2000, 595) declared that "legal professionals are not competent to umpire historical disputes." If so, that does not commend reliance on history. Others are more optimistic, though, noting the ethical standards of lawyering and arguing that history can be useful, even in adversarial process (Festa 2008).

Court procedures may interfere with historical determinations. While the justices have great resources and multiple clerks, the cases that come to the Court are selected by the litigants, who present their arguments in briefs for their clients' interests, not for the objective truth. This is sometimes described as "law office history." When lawyers use history, it is only selectively, to advance a particular legal argument (Kelly 1965). The lawyer's history may be entirely fictional but "if it produces victory, it has served its purposes" (Miller 1969, 192). Law office history remains pervasive in constitutional arguments (Richards 1997).

If the information presented to the Court by the attorneys is biased, it is more difficult for the justices to find the truth. One might think that they could simply assess the evidence from each side and choose the more compelling, but this may not yield historical truth. There is a possibility that the historical truth lies in between the positions of the two litigants, but neither has an incentive to present evidence for that option, which would not so clearly favor their position.

The nature of advocacy would tend to produce historical interpretations tilted toward the extremes. When the Court sought historical information in *Brown*, the NAACP produced a brief that "manipulated history in the best tradition of American advocacy, carefully marshaling every possible scrap of evidence in favor of the desired interpretation and just as carefully doctoring all the evidence to the contrary, either by suppressing it when that seemed plausible, or by distorting it when suppression was not possible" (Kelly 1965, 144). This was simply pursuing their client's case and should be expected.

Much of the criticism of judicial use of history implies an incompetence of the judiciary. Widespread use of originalism in the Court might help overcome this failing, though. Law schools could expand historical training, amici from historians could be given greater weight, and justices could work on improving their aptitude. If originalism controlled constitutional interpretation, one might expect more scholarship to shed light on contested questions. Academics in both history and law might devote more effort to the discovery of historical truths. Briefs would focus more on the theory, and more experienced judges could apply it better. The push for originalism has already produced this result to some degree (Richards 1997).

A greater risk of reliance on judicial history may be judicial bias. When a justice searches history for the answer to a contemporary question, there is a temptation to find what that justice wants to find in the record. Kelly (1965, 131) concluded that reliance on historical evidence was "an apparent rationale for politically inspired activism" by both liberals and conservatives. Bork "repeatedly ignores or distorts history to reach his own conclusions," such as limiting judicial defense of the Bill of Rights (Farber & Sherry 2002, 17). A historical review of opinions on the religion clause found that the "Court has too often pretended that the dictates of the nation's history, rather than the mandates of its own will, compelled a particular decision" (Howe 1965, 4).

The relative indeterminacy of the historical record, discussed in the preceding pages, enables this manipulation. Justice Blackmun himself has claimed that Justice Scalia simply views history as "a grab-bag of principles, to be adopted where they support the Court's theory, and ignored where they do not" (*Lucas v. South Carolina Coastal Council* 1992). Historians themselves are known to demonstrate ideological biases in their research (Richards 1997). It's been said that whenever one needs evidence from the past to support a proposition, a historian can be found to provide the desired evidence (Sutton 2009, 1185). Historians "have often had their agendas, be they conscious or unconscious results of the times in which they write" (Melton 1998, 386). Thus, the justices cannot simply rely on historical expertise.

Historians have sometimes sought to contribute to the Court's use of history by filing amici briefs, most notably hundreds of historians presenting evidence in support of reproductive rights in *Webster*. While the brief was filed by historians without any direct personal interest in the case, it has been charged with considerable distortion of the historical record (Keown 2006; Finnis 1994). The counsel of record acknowledged that the brief could be inaccurate because of tension between advocacy and truth-telling (Law 1990). Even a signer of the brief stated that he did not "consider the brief to be history" but instead a "political document" (Mohr 1990, 25), and the contents of the brief actually contradicted the findings of his separate scholarly research (Finnis 1994). He eventually declined to sign a subsequent version of the brief filed in *Casey*. Dozens of the historians apparently signed the brief without even having read it (Keown 2006). The open goal of the brief was to support the prochoice position, not to provide the most accurate record of the history of abortion. This experience is not encouraging of hopes that historians can help discover objective truth.

A historian writing nearly five decades ago on the Supreme Court's use of constitutional history suggested that it involved "an approach toward the discovery of historical reality that might generously be called one of philosophic-metaphysical analysis geared to establish the validity of political orthodoxy" (Murphy 1963, 66). When justices use history, it is as "authority, not evidence" that does not "lead the judge to a decision" but is used instead "to support an outcome" (Reid 1993, 204). Originalism has been said to "provide a magnificent smoke screen for the 'real' reasons behind the Court's decisions" (Miller 1969, 4). The effect may be an inevitable one, given the "difficulty and open-endedness of the historical inquiry and the immense historical distance from the founding" (Cunningham 1997, 147). History is thus merely a tool for other ends.

While the use of originalism is supposed to temper this bias in pursuit of historical truth, it may in fact exacerbate it. Kelly (1965, 125) notes that nineteenth-century opinions invoked originalism "as an instrument of extreme political activism" and as a "precedent-breaking instrument, by which the Court could purport to return to the aboriginal meaning of the Constitution." Originalists allegedly manipulate history to reach whatever result they seek (Levy 2000). Prominent originalist Keith Whittington (2004, 599) concedes that judges make use of originalism when "they find it helpful to advancing their position." Cloaking a result with the imprimatur of the framers may be a convenient means of legitimation for ideological judicial activism. Research has shown that justices appear more likely to use originalism when striking a statute than when upholding a statute. The theory may be only a rhetorical cloak for expanding judicial power.

Richard Posner (2008, 103–104) has suggested that originalism inherently conduces to this ideological abuse, writing that:

> The backward orientation [of originalism] actually enlarges a judge's legislative scope, and not only by concealing that he is legislating. A judge or Justice who is out of step with current precedents reaches back to some earlier body of case law (or constitutional text) that he can describe as the bedrock, the authentic Ur text that should guide decision. And the older the bedrock, the greater the scope for manipulation of meaning in the name of historical reconstruction or intellectual archeology.

Given the ambiguities of the historical record of the ratification, justices have ample materials from which to choose their desired supportive evidence. And the hegemony of exclusive originalism means that they can disregard anything contrary, whether precedent or pragmatic effects, in fealty to claimed original meaning. This effect may not be a dishonest one; psychological effects may well drive the decision, as will be discussed later. Nevertheless, "history's great attractiveness for judges occurs when they are indulging in judicial activism" (Reid 1993, 204), as it empowers them to run roughshod over all nonhistorical concerns.

Empirical research provides some confirmation of these concerns. The justices were examined for their commitment to judicial minimalism, which is conceived as a modest and nonactivist approach to the justices' task. The least minimalist (most maximalist) justices were Scalia and Thomas (Anderson 2009). Given the widespread assumption that they are the most originalist justices of the Court, the results suggest that originalism conduces to activism, rather than restraint. Given the consistently conservative pattern of their votes, the results suggest that the approach furthers ideological activism.

Even if the historical originalist record were not obscure, there remains the problem of abstraction or generalization from the text to today's problems. As noted previously, the correct meaning of a constitutional term requires a certain generalization into its meaning. Phrases like *due process* are not specific and do not have a specific historical meaning that is readily translated into modern controversies. Even if all the historical facts were undisputed, justices might well disagree as to the correct application of the original meaning of the text. One justice might take a narrower interpretation of the language, more akin to the original expected application of the text. Another could take a broader interpretation of the language as an expression of general principle and reach the opposite result.

The historians' criticism of the Court's past use of history provides important evidence on the shortcomings of originalism but has its own limitations. The historians' analyses are generally anecdotal in nature and have served only to identify erroneous applications of history, without a comprehensive view of the Court's use of the method. Seldom does a reviewer consider cases where the Court may have gotten history right, which might be expected to happen fairly often, if only by random chance. Moreover, these reviews have not fully considered *why* the Court has sometimes erred in its application of the historical evidence.

In general, the Supreme Court's use of history in past decisions has been derided. Numerous cases have been invoked to show that the justices get history wrong. This may be incompetence, but there is reason to worry that instead it is manipulation; law office history invoked to support and legitimize whatever decision a justice might prefer. A review of opinions from the 1940s (O'Neill 1949, 3) declared:

> . . . my criticism is not that the Justices have interpreted historical facts or phrases in a way that seems to me unjustified from the standpoint of either semantics or history, but that these justices of the Supreme Court apparently do not know the most important facts of our constitutional history which have a bearing on the question they are deciding. The other possibility is that they do know the facts but either callously ignore them, or willfully misrepresent them.

Judicial incompetence at history is potentially surmountable; ideological manipulation less so. While justices may not do well in historical analyses, the ultimate threat to originalism is that they don't care to do well but seek only to legitimize decisions made on other grounds. One historical analysis of the earlier period of our history concludes that "while the United States Supreme Court will use convention debates and proceedings to show that the intention of the framers thus revealed affirms or does not contradict the position of the Court, such intent so discovered will be disregarded when in conflict with the interpretation of the Constitution announced by the Court" (tenBroek 1938, 451). Following chapters will provide some empirical evaluation of this claim.

SEVEN

The Justices of Originalism

In this chapter, I examine the relative fealty of the Supreme Court's recent justices to originalist methods. I adopt a quantitative approach that is grounded in the citation of certain originalist sources by the justices. Some justices have simply made declarations from on high about original intent (Kelly 1965), without documenting their basis. I don't count these claims as originalist, though, absent an effort to support those declarations with actual evidence from the founding period. Instead, I focus on the use of originalist sources to justify a decision.

Even nonoriginalists do not ignore originalist sources, although their position is commonly a pluralist one that places relatively less emphasis on them. But true originalist justices should use originalist sources more often, and pluralists may vary in their reliance on originalism. This chapter seeks to differentiate the justices in their relative reliance on originalist sources of constitutional interpretation.

This chapter considers the relative use of major originalist sources (*The Federalist* is by far the most common) and the historic pattern of such use. Examining the use of originalism throughout the history of the Court's opinions reveals fluctuations with a steady growth in recent decades. The originalist sources used by recent Courts have shifted, however. Although use of originalist sources is higher today than ever, this is essentially due to greater citation of *The Federalist* and not other leading originalist materials.

Some justices are perceived as being strong originalists, while others seem to be openly nonoriginalist, but the evidence of practice does not bear this out so clearly. In the early years of the Court a few justices stood out as being more originalist. In more recent years, use of originalism is common to all justices, and the purported nonoriginalists cite originalist sources about as often as the self-proclaimed originalists.

Coding Approach

Originalism is difficult to measure. In theory, one might read every opinion of the Court and assess its fealty to the originalist method. This approach is unrealistically difficult, though, and also would suffer from the subjective biases of the assessor. I have adopted a more objective approach based on the sources used by the justices in their opinions. Use of an originalist source for interpretation is surely direct evidence of originalism.

My study attempts to count all historic references to *The Federalist*, coverage by *Elliot's Debates* of the ratification materials, and the *Farrand* compilation of Madison's notes on the Constitutional Convention. These are by no means the exclusive sources for originalist interpretation, which often considers other historical materials of the era. However, these are three of the very best sources, as I discussed in Chapter Three. Moreover, they appear to be the three sources most frequently invoked by the Supreme Court in originalist analysis. They also have the virtue of being readily easy to search for and identify in a database of Supreme Court opinions.

To these three primary sources, I also consider the use of dictionaries from the era. While less frequently invoked than the prior three sources, this resource is an obvious one for evaluating original meaning without consideration of original meaning and hence a good source for assessing the contemporary theory of originalism. The two most common dictionaries used for originalist interpretation appear to be those of Samuel Johnson and Thomas Sheridan, and I count references to this source.

Finally, I measure references to the Declaration of Independence. While this is a highly contested source for originalist interpretation, it is a document from the early era of the Constitution's creation that the Court has occasionally cited in support of an opinion. Moreover, it reflects a particular view of natural rights originalism, which is a competing originalist interpretive theory.

As noted in Chapter Three, many other originalist sources are also used by the Court, so my analysis is not a comprehensive one, but I capture the leading sources. The data for the study begin with the Court's first year and run through the end of the Rehnquist Court period. Per curiam opinions using originalism were quite rare and omitted from the results.

These originalist materials are measured by each justice vote. That is, I consider whether a given opinion contained reference to one of the materials and then note which justices wrote or joined that opinion. Each of those justices is coded with a "1" for that originalist source in that opinion. I also examine other opinions of that same decision. If the other opinion also relied on the particular source, it was coded with a "1" also, but if it did not mention that source, it was coded "0." Sometimes, a separate opinion used an originalist source when the majority opinion did not, and these were also counted. The decision to join an opinion with originalist content, rather than a contrary opinion, is a material choice.

For an example of the operation of the coding system, consider *Hamdi v. Rumsfeld* (2004). Justice Souter wrote an opinion concurring in part and dissenting in part, which was joined by Justice Ginsburg, in which he cited *The Federalist*. Justice Scalia wrote a dissenting opinion in which he was joined by Justice Stevens, which also cited *The Federalist* numerous times. Justice Thomas wrote a dissenting opinion, in which he cited *The Federalist* once. The majority opinion, authored by Justice O'Connor and joined by Chief Justice Rehnquist, Justice Kennedy, and Justice Breyer, did not cite to *The Federalist*. Under my coding, Justices Souter, Ginsburg, Scalia, Stevens, and Thomas receive a "1" in the column for this case, for citing *The Federalist*. Justices O'Connor, Rehnquist, Kennedy, and Breyer receive a "0" in this column for this case because some other justice relied on *The Federalist* in an opinion in the case and they did not. The coding does not take into account the fact that the justices cited different *Federalist Papers* or that an opinion may have more citations to the source.

No distinction is drawn for the opinion's author. One might hypothesize that originalism is best tested by evaluating an opinion's author rather than all those joining the opinion because the author ultimately drafts the opinion and the legal materials on which it will rely. The opinion author's control over content is not so absolute, however, as he or she must hold together a coalition of justices. Chief Justice Rehnquist (1992, 270) noted that, in some decisions, the opinion author was "under considerable pressure" to satisfy the demands of other coalition authors. Justices commonly issue bargaining statements, indicating that they will join an opinion if certain changes are made, and authors frequently compromise and add materials to an opinion (Wahlbeck, Spriggs & Maltzman 1998).

The opinion may not even reflect the true views of the author. In *Craig v. Boren* (1976), internal records reveal that authoring Justice Brennan's preferred position was to hold gender discrimination to a strict scrutiny standard (like race discrimination), but he could not accumulate the votes for such an opinion. He therefore adopted an intermediate scrutiny standard, an opinion driven by other justices of the majority coalition (Epstein & Knight 1998). Other internal communications among the justices reveal bargaining over opinion content within the preliminary majority coalition. Thus, the reported author may not truly control the opinion's content.

Some models of political science suggest that the opinion's content, like the result, is driven by the necessary fifth justice vote for achieving the majority. This median voter should be able to command any opinion changes that he or she wishes, on the threat of abandoning the majority, leaving it only with a plurality opinion (Lax & Cameron 2007). Other members of the majority coalition may also have some weight, but losing a sixth voter still leaves the opinion with a majority, so it is the fifth voter who is hypothesized to be critical, though each member of the majority might be that necessary fifth vote, so each must be considered relevant to the opinion's content.

Nevertheless, there is reason to believe that the content of an opinion remains substantially under the control of the assigned opinion author. Drafting an opinion may take considerable time and effort (as may reviewing another's draft and requesting changes). Each of the justices has a material workload of his or her own opinions to draft for the Court. Rejecting a majority opinion because of its content may necessitate that a justice embark on his or her own effort of drafting a separate opinion.

Records of the justices suggest that they do not generally seek substantial changes in draft opinions circulated to them (Maltzman, Spriggs & Wahlbeck 2000). An empirical analysis suggested that both the majority opinion author and the median voter had influence on the majority opinion content, but the author's influence was somewhat greater (Bonneau, Hammond, Maltzman & Wahlbeck 2007).

When it comes to citing originalist sources, one might expect that all the justices joining an opinion could have some influence on its content. If a justice were to suggest that the preliminary draft majority opinion add a reference to *The Federalist*, for example, it seems unlikely that the opinion author would reject such a suggestion. Originalist support can help legitimate an opinion, and we will see that no justices are so adamantly antioriginalist that they would reject in principle the citing of an originalist source. The main limitation on this effect would presumably be the time and effort required for the nonauthoring justice to suggest alteration of the draft majority opinion, but the Supreme Court's relatively small docket allows a committed originalist the time to so act. A commitment to originalism might be seen best by considering both the role of the opinion author and that of the joining justices, and both will be considered in this chapter.

A strong guide to originalism might be seen in the justices authoring separate opinions (dissents or concurrences). While majority opinions are assigned by the chief justice or the senior justice of the Court majority, separate opinions are chosen by each justice who elects to write separately. A separate concurring opinion relying on originalism could thus represent the clearest sign of dedication to originalism by insisting that it form the basis of the result achieved by the majority (or perhaps by arguing that the majority got originalism wrong). A dissenting opinion using originalist sources could well be based on a claim that the majority improperly ignored those sources or got their implications wrong. Thus, authoring separate opinions will be considered as an important guide to a justice's originalism.

No attempt is made to assess the degree to which the originalist source *caused* the decision of the justice. An originalist citation that "decorates" an opinion is substantively different from one that relies heavily on originalist sources as the basis for an opinion. Any attempt to ascribe causation, though, would be subjective and require reading the mind of the justice. Use of the source is considered sufficient tribute to originalist analysis in this analysis. Many constitutional cases include no originalist references whatsoever. A justice's decision to employ such sources is of some meaning. And the need for an objective measure in my analysis precludes subjective evaluations of significance of sources.

Nor do I differentiate cases in which a justice references a source, such as *The Federalist*, and then concludes that it was inapplicable to the facts of the case before the Court. The recognition of and distinguishing of an originalist source is testimony to its importance. And originalist theory recognizes that originalist sources may be misapplied to a controversy and properly distinguished by the Court. Indeed, an authentic originalist would surely distinguish an originalist source in an opinion, rather than simply ignoring its existence.

The coding system is clearly an imperfect measure of originalism. The coding is occasionally unfair to justices' originalism. The majority may cite an originalist source, and the dissent may accept it but disagree with another nonoriginalist part of the opinion. In this case, the majority would be considered originalist and the dissent not, though both were truly in agreement. Such cases are rare, though. A greater flaw of the method is the failure to consider all possible sources of originalism, so the study should be considered limited to those sources analyzed.

In terms of justice-votes, Table 7.1 displays the results of my study over the history of the Supreme Court by the sources I consider. The overwhelming prominence of *The Federalist* is clear from the results. Its references exceed those of all the other studied sources combined. *The Federalist* is especially renowned, which may mean that its greater usage is more to impress the opinion's reader than as a true foundation for the Court's decision. But it is also important to remember that some of the other leading sources were not available for citation for much of the Court's history (though *The Federalist* is also the most common in the modern era when those sources are available). The second most common source, *Elliot's Debates*, does suggest a judicial focus on original meaning for the ratifiers, as *Farrand* (more associated with original intent) is used somewhat less often.

Table 7.1. Frequency of originalist sources.	
Source	Number of reliances
The Federalist	2,870
Elliot's Debates	1,000
Dictionaries	213
Farrand	630
Declaration of Independence	275

Table 7.2. Court consensus for originalist sources.	
Source	Consensus
The Federalist	.612
Elliot's Debates	.525
Dictionaries	.418
Farrand	.621
Declaration of Independence	.480

The counting of the number of reliances on a source can be somewhat misleading. Greater use of *The Federalist* might not be due to its greater respect but instead attributable simply to its greater usefulness for the controversy at hand. As an exposition of the fundamental principles underlying the Constitution, *The Federalist* might simply be more instructive about current controversies than the ratification debates, which were more focused on disputes of the period.

In addition to absolute reliance numbers, it is instructive to consider judicial consensus around sources. If more justices use a given source in a given case that may be testimony not only to its relevance to the case but also to its persuasiveness. The Table 7.2 reports the frequency with which an opinion using a given source commanded more of the justices of the Court. The results mean that when one justice used *The Federalist* as a citation, 61 percent of the voting justices also relied on the source. By contrast, an opinion's use of one of the early dictionaries of the period could command only a minority of justice-votes. The greater consensus might be associated with the precision of the source. Perhaps dictionaries command relatively little consensus because their definitions are very general and lacking the context of the full constitutional text.

The consensus results also require caution in evaluation. Different cases may command greater consensus for reasons unrelated to originalism, such as ideological salience. Different periods of the Court's history had different norms of consensus; dissent was not always so common as it is today. For decisions of earlier times, higher consensus might simply be a reflection of justices' reluctance to dissent. Higher consensus numbers for *The Federalist* could simply be due to its greater use in an earlier time period. Finally, the numbers should logically be influenced by the originalist orientation of the

Court of the time. An aggressively originalist justice might command less consensus simply because the other justices of his time were nonoriginalist.

Qualifications on Evidence

The limited originalist sources measured create another necessary caveat for my findings. While there is no apparent reason that the common sources I study would be used in a systematically different way from other originalist sources (such as Story or letters from prominent framers), such a difference is a possibility. In addition, I use only materials associated with the founding of the original Constitution (though they are also sometimes invoked in the interpretation of the Bill of Rights).

I don't consider originalist interpretations of the Civil War amendments such as the Fourteenth Amendment, though this is also a very important originalist interpretive task for the Court. This omission could skew some of my results, because Justices Thomas and Scalia have been criticized for failure to follow originalism on the Fourteenth Amendment while adhering to the philosophy for the founding period. My findings are limited to the founding era, but they should provide a valuable guide to originalist practice at the Supreme Court. To the extent that some justices are more reliably originalist only with respect to the original constitution, that fact would only bolster my findings.

Through this study, I can assess the relative devotion of Supreme Court justices to originalist methods. Steve Griffin (2008, 1191) has questioned "whether any federal judge, alive or dead, has ever followed as a matter of consistent judicial philosophy what new originalists recommend." Even a casual evaluation of Supreme Court opinions validates this conclusion. But some justices may be much more committed to originalism than others, even if they are imperfect in their commitment. The remainder of this chapter explores the relative devotion of the justices to originalist sources.

Perceived Originalist Justices

This section considers the conventional wisdom about the justices who are dedicated to originalist interpretation. A justice's commitment to originalism may be evaluated by his or her public statements. When confirmation testimony was analyzed in one study, the authors found that Justices O'Connor and Breyer were more expressly committed to originalism than Justices Scalia and Thomas (Czarnezki, Ford & Ringhand 2007). Few would argue that this confirmation testimony provides a reliable clue to their judicial practice, however, so this finding is questionable

Some justices have written about originalism outside their opinions. Justice Scalia is the most prominent of this group. He was an early published proponent of original meaning (Scalia 1997). He emphasized that he consulted the writings of those such as Hamilton and Madison, not because they were drafters of the Constitution but because their writing displayed how the text was originally understood. He had previously acknowledged difficulties of originalism and conceded that his devotion to the theory was fainthearted (Scalia 1989). Justice Thomas has written that originalism reduces discretion and maintains judicial impartiality by tethering holdings to the "understanding of those who ratified the test" (Thomas 1996, 7). Justice Rehnquist also has written on originalism. He criticized the notion of a "living Constitution" (Rehnquist 1976) in favor of judicial restraint. This forms the basis for impressions of relative originalism of these justices, but the actual decisions of the Court should be more reliable evidence of originalism in practice.

Originalism was less discussed in the early era of the Court. John Marshall appeared an originalist in some opinions, but this doesn't carry a great deal of meaning because his opinions were nearly concurrent with the time of the founding. He and the other justices of the era did not have to grapple with applying the fixed constitutional text to dramatically changed circumstances.

Philip Kissam (2006) has compared and contrasted three prominent nineteenth-century justices—Joseph Story, Roger Taney, and Stephen Field. On reviewing the opinions, he found that Story used common law methods to resolve constitutional disputes. Taney was more of a true originalist, in *Dred Scott* and other opinions. Field had more of a Lockean, natural rights–based approach to constitutional interpretation, such as might be found in Declaration-based originalism. This is a rare assessment of interpretive theories of the earlier justices and suggests that Taney was a leading originalist of the era.

As I observed in Chapter Four, reliance on originalism apparently waned in the progressive and New Deal eras, but it was not entirely absent. Justice Sutherland is often lauded as a classical originalist, thanks to his dissents. Other than a couple of prominent dissents, though, he showed little commitment to originalism. The most famous justices of this era, such as Holmes and Brandeis, appeared to be leery of originalism.

In the Warren Court era, Justice Black is renowned for his devotion to originalism, even before the theory was widely accepted and explicated. He reportedly "tried to interpret constitutional phrases in accordance with the intent of the Framers and the history of the clause or amendment" (Ball & Cooper 1992, 318–319). Segal and Spaeth (1993, 57) contend that the "justice who most consistently argued for interpretation bound to the text and history of the Constitution was Hugo Black."

However, the quality of Justice Black's originalism is commonly criticized. While he argued that the "Framers were emphatic defenders of free political speech" or "committed partisans of legislative reapportionment," no "serious historian would support such extravagances" (Ackerman 2007, 1799). Kelly's (1965) attack on the Supreme Court's use of originalism focused largely on Justice Black's efforts.

Justice Brennan is commonly regarded as antioriginalist, based in part on a speech he made to the Federalist Society (1986). He there maintained that originalism was "arrogance cloaked as humility." Brennan argued that the historical record provided little helpful evidence and that typically "all that can be gleaned is that the Framers themselves did not agree about the application or meaning of particular constitutional provisions" (Brennan 1986, 58). He questioned whether there could be an original intention for the collectively drafted Constitution and emphasized that any purportedly originalist interpretation was in fact refracted through a prism of contemporaneous thought. He also worried that originalism contained a substantive bias against claims of individual rights.

These views have been summarized in a lengthy concurrence he wrote in *School District of Abington v. Schempp* (1963) on the First Amendment's establishment clause. In that opinion, he argued that the record was ambiguous and could support either side of the case. He also argued that America had changed greatly since the time of the framing. A substantial increase in religious diversity changed the context for application of the establishment clause. Yet, as I shall show, Brennan was not averse to use of originalism in other opinions.

Justice Rehnquist may be considered an originalist of the time, in opposition to Brennan. He wrote a law journal article on the necessity for originalism and stressed that judges "should not change the meaning of the Constitution" (Rehnquist 1976, 129). Rehnquist's article actually did not speak much of originalism or how it should be implemented but instead primarily rejected any notion of a "living Constitution." Some maintain, though, that Justice Rehnquist "was not a focal or consistent defender of originalism, particularly in his later years" (Greene 2009b, 15).

The apparently stark contrast between Justices Brennan and Rehnquist has been evaluated with content analysis of their opinions. Although they apparently differed dramatically on interpretive theories, including originalism, their opinions were surprisingly similar (Phelps & Gates 1991). While Rehnquist employed more historical (originalist) language, it was not at a statistically significant level. For both justices, doctrinal (precedent-based) content overwhelmed historical argument. The authors found no substantial differences in the opinions of the two justices.

Justice Scalia is commonly regarded as a particularly ardent proponent of originalist interpretation. His "uniqueness stems from his notable role as the Court's most consistent, forceful advocate of constitutional interpretation according to the original meaning intended by the framers" (Schultz & Smith 1996, 80). Scalia is reputedly the "most well known advocate" of originalism today (Ryan 2006, 1628). Only Justice Thomas might be considered a better originalist than Justice Scalia.

Justice Scalia's commitment to originalism has been much criticized, however. Some say that what "is notably absent from Scalia's major opinions is any sense that his rulings were initially motivated by a study of the historical record" (Farber & Sherry 2002, 44). When originalist evidence is "inconvenient" to Justice Scalia, he is said to simply ignore it (Nichol 1999, 969). He is said to use originalism "selectively when it leads to the conservative results he wants," but he "ignores [it] when it does not generate the outcome he desires" (Chemerinsky 2000, 385).

Others have criticized Justice Scalia for undue reliance on original expectations rather than textual original meaning (Colby & Smith 2009). It is argued that an "originalist would have to take very different positions than Justice Scalia on regulatory takings, affirmative action, the unitary executive, and campaign finance, among other issues" (Neuman 2006, 181). Justice Scalia himself has conceded that he is but a fainthearted originalist, and he may be regarded more as a devotee of original expected applications than contemporary original meaning originalism (Chapman, 9), despite his profession to the contrary.

One of the most prominent current academic originalists has argued that Justice Scalia is "simply not an originalist" (Barnett 2006, 13). Barnett complained that Scalia ignored the obvious original meaning of the Ninth Amendment. He noted that Scalia has shunned joining strongly originalist concurrences of Justice Thomas in cases such as *United States v. Lopez* (1995). Barnett concludes that Scalia is pursuing a certain vision of "law" that does not correspond to true originalism.

Justice Thomas may have surpassed Justice Scalia as the leading originalist on the Court, and he finds greater embrace from some major academic originalists. Some of his opinions have been called the "most uncompromising originalist opinions in decades" (Levinson 1996, 501). His opinions are said to be "replete with references to the primacy of the Framers' intentions," which he treats as "compelling directives that dictate the outcomes and reasoning in cases" (Smith 1997, 9). A reading of his opinions found no more "consistent originalism and dedication to founding principles and documents" in the Court's jurisprudence (Holzer 2007, 155).

Even Justice Thomas's commitment to originalism has been disputed, however. One examination found that Justice Thomas "is less a consistent originalist than he is a consistent conservative" (Telman 2009, 401). Another review found that Justice Thomas switched from strict public meaning originalism to natural law–based originalism in cases. His choices appeared "results-driven" reflecting his "policy preferences" (Book Note 2008, 1435). Thus, he appears selective in his use of abstraction of original meaning.

Mark Graber (2003) has provided an extensive examination of Justice Thomas in the Rehnquist Court. He observed that when authoring a majority opinion he rarely uses an originalist approach. He typically reached a conservative result, often minimalist in nature. He was more likely to produce a liberal result, Graber suggested, when he used originalist rhetoric. The concurring and dissenting opinions of Justice Thomas, though, displayed "a justice entirely different from the one who crafts his majority opinions" (Graber 2003, 77). Of course, this may be partly due to the opinions that he was assigned to write. The vast majority of these take conservative positions, and many rely on an originalist approach. Graber suggests that the Thomas opinions cannot commend originalism. He is not an advocate of judicial restraint in these opinions. His results could not be distinguished from those of a conservative who was not an originalist, and he was inconsistent in his use of originalism.

Justice Stevens is not commonly regarded as an originalist like Justices Scalia and Thomas, but his *Heller* dissent relied on the method. Yet he is generally regarded as "no fan of originalism" (Strang 2009, 928). He has written that "our understanding of the Constitution does change from time to time" (*Roper v. Simmons* 2005, 587). In *Georgia v. Randolph* (2006) he urged that an originalist approach should "recognize the relevance of changes in our society." In other cases, though, Stevens has chastised justices for failing to follow originalist principles.

The role of originalism in the opinions of Justice Stevens is unclear. While he has criticized an unyielding adherence to originalism, he sometimes bases opinions on the method. Justice Stevens occasionally authors vigorous dissents that rely heavily on originalist interpretation (*Granholm v. Heald* 2005). While Justice Stevens often used originalism in his opinions, it appeared that the invocations performed only a "ceremonial function" (Durschlag 2005, 308). Maybe he invokes originalism simply to give a persuasive effect to his conclusions. Eastman (1999, 430) suggests that "use of originalist history is more likely to be mere lip service when utilized by critics of originalism, such as Justice Stevens."

On today's Court, Justice Breyer is particularly known as a nonoriginalist (Smith 2009). His book emphasizes the role of democracy in interpretation and describes originalism as an unsatisfactory decision rule. He criticizes originalism on various grounds, including the indeterminacy and subjectivity of the process and the potentially harmful consequences of reliance on the theory (Breyer 2006). The latter concern about bad results may be a major motivator of Breyer's concerns about the method.

Breyer is generally seen as a pragmatist justice, trying to identify the most sensible outcome of a dispute, considering the practical consequences of the decision, rather than the result commanded by originalism or other conventional legal command. Breyer is called the only justice "who writes openly consequentialist opinions of the living Constitution variety" (Calabresi & Fine 2009, 701).

Breyer's opinions sometimes use originalist sources, but one review found that he cited the *Federalist* in a few cases but only as a "bit player" of the opinion (Durschlag 2005, 311). This is consistent with a strategic rhetorical use of originalist materials. Even in his book, he suggested that the Establishment Clause should be interpreted "to implement the basic value that the Framers wrote the clause to protect" (Breyer 2006, 121), evidencing a dedication to broader principles-based originalism. Thus, Ryan (2006) contends that Breyer's theory uses originalism with a higher level of generality.

Other current justices are not typically regarded as strong originalists. In confirmation hearings, Justice Kennedy declared that the "doctrine of original intent does not tell us how to decide a case." His occasional use of foreign judicial doctrine has been said to make him an "antioriginalist" who "feels that the present day Americans have a better understanding of the meaning of the Constitution than the Framers themselves did" (Ghoshray 2006, 712).

Justice Souter is not clearly in the originalist or antioriginalist camp, though he has certainly engaged in originalism and dueled tightly with Scalia in *Printz v. United States* (2007) over the proper reliance on *The Federalist*. He has challenged the practice of originalism on the grounds that the "Framers simply did not share a common understanding" on important matters and that "they, like other politicians, could raise constitutional ideals one day and turn their backs on them the next" (*Lee v. Weisman* 1992, 626). Perhaps more than any other justice, Souter is likely to find the originalist record inconclusive. This is not an intrinsic attack on the theory, though, but simply a recognition of its limitations. When he engages in originalist analysis, his efforts "appear to be unusually extensive and scholarly" (Davies 2002, 246).

Justice Ginsburg is not considered an originalist but rather a devotee of the living Constitution. She believes that the text belongs "to a global 21st century, not as fixed forever by 18th century understandings" (Ghoshray 2006, 73). Yet this could simply be an originalism that takes account of changed circumstances. Monaghan (2004, 38) suggests that Justice Ginsburg "looks for the central purposes of the relevant constitutional provision and tries to apply it in a vastly different world." She has written that the Constitution has "evolved" and did not mean what it did in "the beginning" but also paid respect to the "constitutional legacy, shaped and bequeathed to us by the framers" (Ginsburg 2001, xii). For some, this may not qualify as true originalism, however, but rather sounds as interpreting a living Constitution. Yet she has declared: "I count myself an originalist" (Ginsburg 2004, 330).

Of the current Court, Justices Roberts and Alito did not self-identify as originalists in confirmation hearings. Nor did Justices Kagan and Sotomayor. The time on the Court of these justices is still small, though, and originalism has remained a significant feature of several of the opinions of the Roberts Court.

Ascriptions of individual justice's devotion to originalism vary. From casual observation, there appears to be uncertainty over which justices are originalist. Monaghan (2004) suggests that four members of the then contemporaneous Court were serious about originalism—Justices Ginsburg, Souter, Thomas, and Scalia. Yet Slobogin (2009, 868, 1477) suggests that "Justice Ginsburg was considered the Justice who was least committed to originalism theories." Eastman (2006) suggests that "Justices Stevens, Souter, and Ginsburg" were "not known for their devotion to the originalism enterprise." Commentators differ in their evaluations, but Justices Scalia and Thomas are commonly considered more originalist than the other justices of today's Court.

The frequency of any justice's reliance on originalism, though, is not so great. Cass Sunstein (2008, 249) has argued that originalism was "not a significant theme on either the Rehnquist Court or the Roberts Court." Fallon (2001, 3) argues that the "originalist model departs radically from actual Supreme Court practice." Shaman (2010, 90) contends that "originalism has not been a significant theme on either the Rehnquist Court or the Roberts Court." The typical Court opinion relies primarily on precedent, though occasionally a decision appears to turn on originalist sources. Some justices appear to depend more on those originalist sources than others.

One past study examined the use of *The Federalist* in opinions issued between 1986 and 2007 (Festa 2007). He found considerable variance in usage among the justices, though the results were not as predicted. Justices Stevens and Brennan used the source a great deal. While Justices Scalia and

Powell were frequent users, so was Justice O'Connor, but Justice Thomas was not. Yet Justice Thomas is perceived as a devoted originalist.

There may be no true originalists on the Court of the stronger variety. Richard Fallon (2008, 1130–1131) has thus written:

> Indeed, all of the current Justices, including the self-proclaimed originalist Justices Scalia and Thomas, have self-consciously accepted the authority of precedents that could not themselves have been justified under originalist principles. It is also pertinent that all of the Justices, again including the originalists, apparently converge in recognizing as currently valid a number of past decisions that many scholars think would be difficult if not impossible to justify on originalist grounds. These include decisions establishing that paper money is constitutional, as is Social Security; that the Equal Protection Clause bars race discrimination in the public schools; that Congress has broad power under the Commerce Clause to regulate the national economy; that the Due Process Clause of the Fifth Amendment . . . restrains the federal government from employing racial or gender-base classifications; and that the Equal Protection Clause requires the distribution of voting rights on a one-person, one-vote basis.

The numerous constitutional opinions that do not rely on any originalist materials surely confirm this conclusion. But imperfection in application does not doom the theory. Some justices may be relatively more originalist than others, and this greater originalism may be defended as improving constitutional interpretation.

Historic Use of Originalist Sources

There is no existing rigorous study of the degree to which the Court has used originalist sources in their constitutional decisions. Mere casual observation has not resolved the question of relative devotion to originalism, as commentators disagree. In this analysis, I provide some new data on this use. I begin with a Court-wide analysis of the use of these sources in opinions, based on justice-votes using such an originalist source.

The relative use of originalist sources over time is to some degree dependent on the Court's docket. Some courts have taken many more cases to decide per year than others (Epstein, Segal, Spaeth & Walker 2003). More cases mean more opportunities to cite any legal authority, including originalist sources that I examine. Moreover, the particular cases chosen for decision in a given year will influence the relevance of originalist sources. While cases involving statutory interpretation or common law will seldom call for use of originalism, my originalist sources will be relevant to constitutional cases involving the original constitutional text.

This qualification on use of originalism is not so significant as it might initially seem, however. The Court has control over its docket through the *certiorari* process. While the Court is somewhat limited by the nature of the cases for which *certiorari* is sought, it takes only a small fraction of the possible cases, and constitutional cases are especially prominent. One might expect a Court devoted to originalism to take more cases where it is relevant to correct constitutional jurisprudence. In addition, justices functionally can summon cases to be presented by signaling to litigants (Baird 2007). Committed originalists should be more interested in deciding more cases where originalism governed, and constitutional decisions are common throughout the years of the Court's docket.

I begin by examining the use of originalist sources in the early era of the Court, up to 1900. In this period, the only source used of those that I studied was *The Federalist*, although the ratification records were theoretically available to the justices. Figure 7.1 displays the number of justice-votes relying on this source for five-year periods of the era. Thus, the year 1795 displays usages from 1795 through 1799. For most of this period, *The Federalist* saw only very limited use. The first five years saw nineteen justices join opinions using the source, representing only three cases in which it was invoked. The next fifteen years saw no references to the source. Use of *The Federalist* was much greater from 1840 to 1850. The years from 1865 to 1869 saw a burst of reliance on the source, as did 1875 through 1879. Many other years of the century, though, saw much less use of the resource.

Figure 7.2 replicates the same compilation of justice-votes using *The Federalist* for the twentieth century. The scale here is very different. As expected, the justices of the progressive era made relatively little use of *The Federalist*, even less than in the preceding century. Use began to expand, though, in the New Deal era, but still only at levels comparable to those of the nineteenth century.

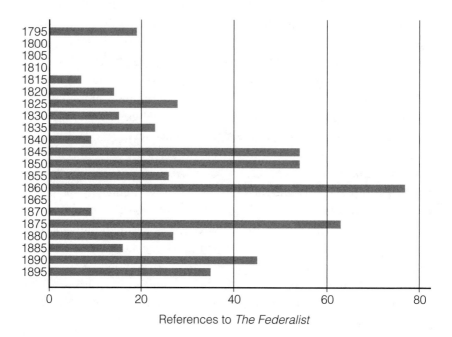

Figure 7.1. Use of *The Federalist* up to 1900.

Although the Warren Court is commonly considered antioriginalist, it used *The Federalist* extensively in its opinions, at a level higher than in any preceding years. The latter Warren Court years used the source more than any previous Court of American history. Usage of *The Federalist* truly exploded, however, in the final years of the Burger Court and the ensuing Rehnquist Court. Justice-votes in support of opinions citing *The Federalist* were more than ten times higher than for most periods of the nineteenth and early twentieth centuries and more than twice as high as the peak years of Warren Court citations. These findings are consistent with those of Lupu (1998) through the period of his study.

This record appears to testify to the ascendance of originalism in recent decades. The growth in citations to *The Federalist* throughout the twentieth century is quite dramatic. While usage in the Warren Court was quite significant, the more recent Courts have cited the source at vastly higher rates than at any time in our prior history. This appears to reveal a considerable increase in concern for originalism at the Court.

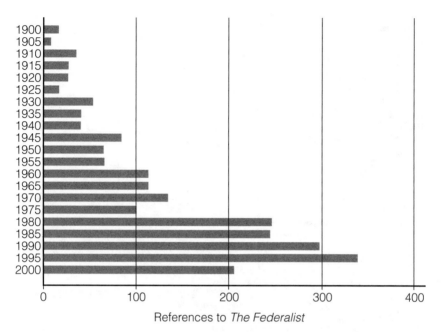

Figure 7.2. Use of *The Federalist* in the twentieth century.

But *The Federalist* is just one relevant originalist source and not necessarily the best one. *Elliot's Debates* is arguably the best evidence of ratifier understanding of actual meaning because it reports the declarations of the ratifiers themselves. This source became available midway through the nineteenth century and saw its first reference in a Court opinion after the Civil War. Figure 7.3 displays the justice-votes joining opinions citing *Elliot's Debates* from this time forward. *Elliot's Debates* saw occasional usage in the second half of the nineteenth century, a rate that declined in the first part of the twentieth century but that then grew considerably in the Warren Court era. The Warren Court relied on this source a great deal, as did the Burger Court. Both cited *Elliot's Debates* more than any other Court of history, including the succeeding Rehnquist Court. Use remained fairly high in the Rehnquist Court by historical standards, but citations were still much lower than during the immediately preceding years. Although not used so often as *The Federalist*, *Elliot's Debates* is obviously an originalist

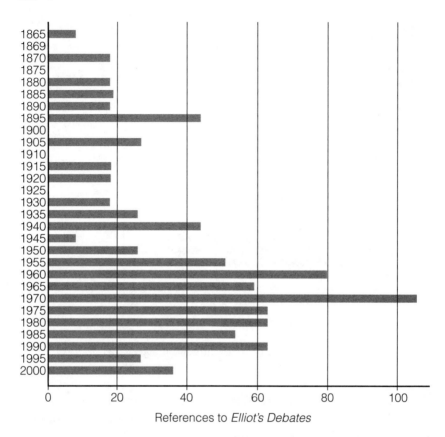

Figure 7.3. Use of *Elliot's Debates.*

source invoked often by the Court, with a rate that blossomed during the 1960s through the 1980s.

Madison's notes as presented by *Farrand* became available only in the twentieth century, so they could not be cited by earlier Courts. Once they became available, though, the Court promptly started citing them. Figure 7.4 displays the frequency of references to this originalist source over time. *Farrand* found considerable use in the Warren Court, with citations growing over time. The Burger Court appears to be the epitome of originalism as judged by the use of *Farrand*. Although the source is used less than *The Federalist*, the Burger Court had more justice-votes citing *Farrand* than any previous Court had for any originalist source checked, including *The*

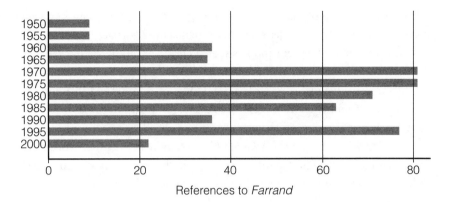

Figure 7.4. Use of *Farrand.*

Federalist. While the Rehnquist Court cited *Farrand* with reasonable frequency, they never reached the citation level of the 1970s. Madison's notes compiled in *Farrand* appear to be the third most frequently cited source of originalist history, which is increasingly used in more recent years.

The two other originalist sources I examined, early dictionaries and the Declaration of Independence, have far fewer citations than *The Federalist*, *Elliot's Debates*, and *Farrand*. The first use of either dictionary was in 1870, and they were again used in 1886 and 1903. After another usage in 1952, the dictionaries began to see much greater attention in 1988. Within a decade, they were found in more opinions than in the entire prior history of the Court, and they have steadily been used in succeeding years.

The Declaration of Independence was first cited by the Court in 1857, and it saw some more limited use in the remainder of the century. The Declaration was rarely cited, though, until the 1970s, when it was used in several cases. After receiving no citations for several years, the Declaration began receiving additional citations in the 1990s. Like dictionaries, the Declaration has been used in more opinions in recent decades than in the entire prior history of the Court.

The Rehnquist Court has cited more originalist sources than any prior Court, but this effect is due solely to reliance on *The Federalist*. It made less use of *Elliot's Debates* or *Farrand* than did the Warren and Burger Courts. The Rehnquist Court also dramatically increased reliance on early dictionaries, though the absolute number of such references remained quite small, only a couple of cases per year. The growth of originalism in recent years is basically attributable to greater reliance on *The Federalist*.

Constitutional interpretation has seen a clear turn to increased reliance on many originalist sources in the second half of the twentieth century. But this process began with the Warren Court and continued through the Burger Court and the Rehnquist Court. Originalism is not, as often depicted, a conservative reaction attributable to the Reagan administration. Its use burgeoned during the Warren Court, against which early originalism was a backlash. The Rehnquist-era originalism is really a turn to *The Federalist* specifically (and to a lesser degree dictionaries) than it is to originalism generally.

The Justices of Originalism (Early Period)

I first consider the justices in the early part of our history, before the Warren Court. At this time, only *The Federalist* saw some use, among the sources I study. The figures presented earlier in the chapter reveal the relatively infrequent use of this source in the Court's decisionmaking. Still, there are differences among the justices in their reliance on originalist materials. Table 7.3 displays the number of times a justice joined or authored an opinion that relied in part on *The Federalist*. I include the "top twelve" justices (and their years of service) based on total number of usages. The justices with the most citations to *The Federalist* served in the post–Civil War period. The early years of the Court are largely unrepresented. Citations in the early twentieth century are fewer, though Justices Stone, Van Devanter, and McReynolds make the list. While Justice Sutherland has occasionally been noted as a prominent originalist, this was based on only a couple of opinions; his overall usage was not high. Interestingly, New Deal justices Black, Douglas, and Frankfurter nearly made the "top twelve" list, even though their service at the Court had only just begun by 1950.

This list of justices using *The Federalist* is not the most auspicious grouping. While the first Justice Harlan and Justice Field are typically highly regarded, Justices Taney, Van Devanter, and McReynolds are commonly considered some of history's worst justices. Some of those on the list are basically obscurities. Others, commonly regarded greats of the era, including Marshall, Story, Brandeis, Hughes, and Cardozo, do not approach the

Table 7.3. Justices using The Federalist before 1950.

Justice	The Federalist
Field (1863–1897)	28
Nelson (1845–1872)	24
Miller (1862–1890)	23
Grier (1845–1870)	23
Harlan (1877–1911)	22
Wayne (1835–1867)	22
McLean (1829–1861)	22
Stone (1925–1946)	21
Taney (1836–1864)	20
Van Devanter (1911–1937)	18
McReynolds (1914–1941)	18
Catron (1837–1865)	18

Table 7.4. Opinion authors using The Federalist before 1950.

Justice	The Federalist
Taney (1836–1864)	6
Bradley (1870–1892)	6
Brown (1891–1906)	5
Hughes (1910–1916)	4
McLean (1829–1861)	4
Miller (1862–1890)	4
Wayne (1835–1867)	4
Marshall (1801–1835)	4

"top twelve." Originalism, though, was simply a less prominent theory of the court for this era. The numbers of usages are less than for later years.

Perhaps opinion authorship using an originalist source is a better guide to an originalist commitment for a particular justice. Table 7.4 displays the justices who authored opinions during the period that cited *The Federalist*. I include all justices who authored at least four opinions using the source during this period. There is only partial overlap between usage and authorship. Only Justices Taney, McLean, and Wayne appear on both lists. An even stronger cue to originalist commitment, though, might be authoring a separate opinion. Here a justice self-selects him- or herself to write an opinion contrasting with that of the Court's majority. Such separate opinions are therefore more likely to reflect the author's commitment to its content. They also may better display justices' interpretive philosophies. Justice Scalia is well known for concurring in statutory interpretation opinions but writing separately to disavow reliance on legislative history. Hence, separate opinions could be quite revealing on originalist commitment. Of course, these numbers could be skewed by different judicial norms over time. Some periods saw many more separate opinions than other periods. Table 7.5 displays the frequency with which a separate opinion author cited *The Federalist*, during this period before 1950, listing the top ten justices (with over four such opinions). Only Justices Taney and McLean appear on all three lists, and they might be fairly considered leading originalists of the early period. Justice Field appears atop two of the lists, so he should be considered especially originalist, and Justice Stone stands out for use of

Table 7.5. Separate opinion authors using
The Federalist before 1950.

Justice	*The Federalist*
Field (1863–1897)	12
McLean (1829–1861)	9
Daniel (1842–1860)	9
Thompson (1823–1843)	9
Catron (1837–1865)	8
Campbell (1853–1861)	6
Stone (1925–1946)	6
Gray (1882–1902)	5
Holmes (1902–1932)	5
Taney (1836–1864)	5

The Federalist during a time period when this reliance appeared to be out of fashion.

Simply counting references to *The Federalist* is a crude tool for comparing justices who served for different time periods. The legitimate opportunities to rely on originalist sources will vary according to the cases heard by the Court. Moreover, merely counting references will advantage justices who served for a longer time period on the Court. Hearing more cases provides more opportunities to use any legal materials. One can gain some idea of this effect by examining the years of service. Justice Hughes, authoring four majority opinions citing *The Federalist* in only six years on the Court, displays a remarkably high ratio, but this could be an artifact of the particular cases heard in those years. I will perform some adjustment for this effect in the following section, involving the more recent era of the Warren, Burger, and Rehnquist Courts.

The Justices of Originalism (Recent Period)

As shown in Figures 7.1 through 7.4, originalism has increased considerably since the beginning of the Warren Court era. The recent period has also seen the political and academic controversy over the validity of originalism as a primary means for constitutional interpretation. This is the time frame in which the relative validity of the method was debated and in which the Court first referred explicitly to the theory in opinions.

Table 7.6. Justices using *The Federalist* and *Elliot's Debates.*

Justice	The Federalist	Median	Elliot's	Median
Black	19	.452	11	.379
Blackmun	63	.557	13	.351
Brennan	67	.545	26	.490
Breyer	43	.605	8	.667
Burger	41	.641	12	.400
Clark	12	.375	8	.348
Douglas	30	.508	12	.343
Frankfurter	13	.722	8	.667
Ginsburg	50	.641	10	.770
Harlan	23	.639	12	.429
Kennedy	70	.614	9	.450
Marshall	58	.552	16	.444
O'Connor	85	.574	12	.387
Powell	50	.756	12	.480
Rehnquist	105	.597	22	.500
Scalia	81	.664	12	.522
Souter	57	.600	10	.589
Stevens	97	.577	21	.552
Stewart	38	.594	18	.474
Thomas	60	.706	9	.600
Warren	14	.424	9	.474
White	76	.598	22	.454

As with the prior period, I begin with consideration of justice usages. As already noted, the absolute number of justice usages of a source is but a limited guide to reliance, influenced by citation opportunities. Given the greater frequency of usages for this period, I supplement the count by considering the number of cases in which a justice did not use an originalist source while some other justice did use such a source in an opinion of the same decision.

Ignoring an originalist source used in a separate opinion should be considered evidence that a justice was not committed to originalism. It is certainly possible that a highly originalist justice would not rely on an originalist source, while another did, simply because that source was inapposite to the case at hand. But one would expect that an originalist justice would at least explain why the originalist source was not relevant.

Table 7.6 displays the absolute number of usages for the major justices of the era for *The Federalist* and *Elliot's Debates*, arguably the two primary sources of original meaning for ratifiers and those most commonly used by the Court. The right-hand column in the table, labeled "Median," shows the probability that the justice joined an opinion using the source, when some justice of the court used it. A median of 50 percent would mean that, of all the cases where at least one opinion referred to the source, the justice joined an opinion referring to the source half the time. This adjusts for cases when the originalist source was clearly "in play" in the opinions of the Court. These results reveal the significance of originalist sources. I believe the median figures are more revealing than the absolute numbers because they were cases where an originalist source was "in play" and are less biased by judicial tenure. Justice Rehnquist joined more opinions using *The Federalist* than any other justice of the era, but this appears attributable to his lengthier service on the Court. His relatively middling median score reveals that he was not especially likely to use the source when used in some opinion of the Court.

One interesting finding from these results is the relative lack of difference among the justices in their simple use of originalism. Absolute usage is frequent for all the justices, save perhaps for Chief Justice Warren. Median usage is also relatively high, with most of the justices having scores over 50 percent for *The Federalist*, but this score has considerable variance. Justice Thomas is relatively high for both sources, as are Justices Frankfurter, Scalia, and Souter, while Justice Powell is high for *The Federalist* and low for *Elliot's Debates*. Justice Breyer is relatively high, especially for *Elliot's Debates*. Interestingly, Justice Black is quite low for both sources.

Some results of the usage count are not as expected. The self-proclaimed antioriginalist, Justice Brennan, uses originalist sources with some frequency, much more than Justice Black, who is commonly regarded as an early originalist. Reputations of the justices may poorly reflect reality.

The results are also revealing for the significance of the different sources. Among the justices, *The Federalist* was not only used more often than *Elliot's Debates* in absolute terms, it also has consistently higher median scores (with Justices Breyer and Warren the only exceptions). Perhaps *The Federalist* is regarded as a more helpful or conclusive originalist source, though this result may instead simply testify to its relatively iconic status as a source of legitimating an opinion.

The next analysis replicates this approach but for citations of Madison's notes in *Farrand*, the third most common originalist source identified for Court usage. This source is more associated with original intent of the framers than original meaning for the ratifiers, but it is also a relevant source of

Table 7.7. Justices using *Farrand.*

Justice	Farrand	Median
Black	9	.409
Blackmun	23	.639
Brennan	28	.571
Breyer	0	0
Burger	21	.808
Clark	7	.500
Douglas	11	.379
Frankfurter	5	.714
Ginsburg	10	.667
Harlan	14	.778
Kennedy	14	.636
Marshall	21	.538
O'Connor	24	.750
Powell	18	.720
Rehnquist	33	.702
Scalia	18	.720
Souter	11	.647
Stevens	26	.634
Stewart	18	.563
Thomas	11	.733
Warren	7	.438
White	32	.653

evidence for the latter (Kesavan & Paulsen 2003). Table 7.7 reports absolute usages for each recent justice and the median score, measuring frequency of use when some other justice referenced the source. Justice Rehnquist joined the most opinions citing *Farrand,* followed by Justices White, Brennan, and Stevens. The median score is probably the best measure for fealty to originalism, and, by that standard, the most devoted to *Farrand* are Justices Burger, Harlan, O'Connor, Thomas, Powell, and Scalia. In general, though, the median scores are high as compared to other originalist sources. Perhaps this resource is especially useful to the justices. Still, there is not a great deal of differences among the justices, save for Breyer, who appears to resist using this source.

Use of Originalism by Opinion Authors

The next data involve opinion authorship on recent Courts. As already noted, the author has some control over the content of an opinion, especially a separate opinion, and greater use of an originalist source is some

Table 7.8. Opinion authors citing *The Federalist.*

Justice	Majority opinion	Dissenting opinion	Concurring opinion
Black	6	4	3
Blackmun	4	9	5
Brennan	7	11	3
Breyer	2	11	5
Burger	10	4	0
Clark	0	0	0
Douglas	5	11	4
Frankfurter	3	7	3
Ginsburg	2	4	6
Harlan	3	6	3
Kennedy	9	4	10
Marshall	5	6	1
O'Connor	13	6	9
Powell	7	5	5
Rehnquist	14	9	1
Scalia	10	19	9
Souter	6	10	4
Stevens	14	22	11
Stewart	2	3	0
Thomas	3	11	11
Warren	5	0	0
White	4	10	7

testimony to the justice's devotion to the theory. Of course, the separate opinion numbers are influenced by other factors, such as the given justice's willingness to author a separate opinion and not agree with the majority. Table 7.8 presents the results of this analysis for each category of opinion. While some of the results for majority opinion authors are as expected (Justices Scalia and Rehnquist with larger numbers), others are quite unexpected (Justice Stevens with very high numbers and Justice Thomas with very low numbers for majority opinions). This may simply be an artifact of opinion assignment, however. Perhaps *The Federalist* is more relevant to major constitutional cases and those cases are more likely to have opinions written by a chief justice (for example, Burger or Rehnquist) or to a swing justice (such as O'Connor or Kennedy), which would tend to increase their citation numbers for majority opinions. Such cases may simply not be assigned to Justice Thomas, who tends to be toward the ideological extreme of the Court.

This might be controlled somewhat by considering the number of cases in which a justice was a majority author and did not use *The Federalist*, though some separate opinion did. This was a common event for our highest scorers on the authorship measure. While Justice Rehnquist authored thirteen opinions citing *The Federalist*, he authored twelve majority opinions that did not cite this source, though some separate opinion did. Justice Scalia authored eight majority opinions in cases where another justice used *The Federalist* but his majority opinion did not. This shows some limitations of the originalism of these justices. The one majority opinion author who used this source in virtually every case where any justice used it was Justice Kennedy. Of all the justices, he was the least likely to ignore *The Federalist* in a majority opinion.

Separate opinions may be revealing regarding commitment to originalism and, as expected, the numbers for Justice Thomas increase dramatically when including dissenting and concurring opinions. Justice Scalia, who had a significant number of majority opinions, also has an unusually high number of separate opinions using *The Federalist*. Less expectedly, we see a similar tendency for liberal Warren-era justices (Brennan and Douglas) and subsequent relatively liberal justices (Blackmun, Breyer, and especially Stevens). Although members of the latter group are not generally regarded as dedicated originalists, they frequently author separate opinions that rely on *The Federalist*.

Surprisingly, of all the justices of history, the one most likely to author an opinion citing *The Federalist* is Justice Stevens. He is tied for first in majority opinions authored, tied for first in concurring opinions authored, and a clear first in dissenting opinions authored. This could be partially attributed to his long tenure at the Court. For the period that I studied, he had twice the years of service of Justice Thomas. This cannot entirely explain the results, though. He had nearly twice the number of opinions authored using *The Federalist* as Justice Thomas. By this scale, Stevens is a leading originalist on the Court.

The next analysis analyzes opinion authors citing *Elliot's Debates*, the second most used originalist source of the Court. Table 7.9 displays the justices' authorship of opinions that cited to this source. The numbers of opinions authored using *Elliot's Debates* are much less than for *The Federalist*, and some relative differences in justice usage appear. Some high users of *The Federalist*, such as Justices Burger, Powell, and O'Connor, largely eschew use of *Elliot's Debates*. Chief Justice Rehnquist is remarkable in that

Table 7.9. Opinion authors citing *Elliot's Debates.*

Justice	Majority opinion	Dissenting opinion	Concurring opinion
Black	6	3	0
Blackmun	0	2	2
Brennan	5	5	1
Breyer	0	3	0
Burger	0	0	1
Clark	0	0	0
Douglas	2	1	2
Frankfurter	3	1	2
Ginsburg	0	1	0
Harlan	2	5	2
Kennedy	1	0	1
Marshall	0	0	1
O'Connor	0	0	0
Powell	3	2	1
Rehnquist	2	2	0
Scalia	3	2	0
Souter	1	4	1
Stevens	5	5	1
Stewart	2	0	0
Thomas	0	2	1
Warren	3	0	0
White	0	3	0

he authored eight majority opinions in cases in which *Elliot's Debates* was cited by some justice, but he himself cited the source only twice in these cases. One would expect a sincere originalist to use sources such as *Elliot's Debates* with some frequency and not rely entirely on *The Federalist.* Justice Rehnquist's high disregard for this originalist source is curious. Justice Black showed the more originalist pattern here, with a significant number of references to *Elliot's Debates.*

On today's Court, Justices Thomas and Scalia, along with Justice Souter, seem most inclined to refer to *Elliot's Debates.* Historically, high-frequency users of *Elliot's Debates* were Justices Brennan and Harlan. And once again Justice Stevens stands out as an unusually high user of this originalist source, far beyond that of the justices considered originalist in nature. In terms of opinion authorship for *The Federalist* and *Elliot's Debates,* Justice Stevens may be the most originalist member of the recent Court.

Farrand is cited less frequently and hence has fewer authoring opinions, but there are enough to be revealing about the justices' usage of this originalist source. Table 7.10 displays the usages by opinion authors. Chief Jus-

Table 7.10. Opinion authors citing *Farrand.*

Justice	Majority opinion	Dissenting opinion	Concurring opinion
Black	3	2	0
Blackmun	2	1	1
Brennan	5	1	4
Breyer	1	1	1
Burger	7	0	2
Clark	1	1	2
Douglas	1	1	3
Frankfurter	0	1	1
Ginsburg	0	0	2
Harlan	2	3	2
Kennedy	1	1	1
Marshall	1	0	0
O'Connor	0	1	3
Powell	3	1	3
Rehnquist	3	2	2
Scalia	3	3	2
Souter	2	1	1
Stevens	4	2	1
Stewart	0	2	2
Thomas	1	4	0
Warren	2	0	0
White	1	4	3

tice Burger was the most likely to cite the source in a majority opinion. Justices Brennan and Stevens are relatively high users of this source, as is Justice Scalia. Justices Thomas and White commonly employed it in dissenting opinions that they authored. *Farrand* is a relatively important originalist source but not one that clearly commands the Court's devotion. It has a remarkably high percentage of its citations in concurrence or dissent.

Dictionaries and the Declaration of Independence

The two remaining sources that I investigated were early dictionaries and the Declaration of Independence. As illustrated by Table 7.1, these sources are used much less by the Court than the other sources I studied, with less than 10 percent of the usage received by *The Federalist.* The pattern of their use by the Court is interesting and revealing.

The historical use of early dictionaries as an originalist source is quite uneven. They have been infrequently used for interpretation, with traditional historic usage quite rare, and some sign of current slightly greater consideration. Use of early dictionaries is largely the province of the contemporary conservatives regarded as originalist. Justice Thomas has joined fifteen opinions using the dictionaries, and Justice Scalia has joined twelve such opinions. The next most usages are O'Connor, Rehnquist, and Stevens, with seven.

The pattern is repeated by opinion authorship. Justices Scalia and Thomas are far more likely to author opinions using one of these dictionaries than is any other justice. However, the overwhelming majority of opinions they authored using the dictionaries were dissenting opinions. Even Justices Scalia and Thomas have rarely cited the dictionaries in majority opinions that they authored. Dictionaries still play only a small supporting role in originalism at the Court.

The justice who joined far more opinions citing the Declaration than any other justice is Justice Stevens, with eleven. He is followed by Justice Brennan (eight opinions), Justices Rehnquist and Marshall (seven opinions) and Justices Ginsburg and Douglas (six opinions). Justice Thomas has joined five opinions using the Declaration, a high number given his briefer period of service on the Court to date.

The Declaration is often used in dissent. No justice cited the Declaration in more than a single majority opinion that he or she authored. However, Justice Douglas authored four dissenting opinions using the Declaration. Justices Brennan, Scalia, and Stevens each authored three dissents that used the Declaration of Independence.

The proper role of the Declaration of Independence in constitutional interpretation, even under originalism, is quite disputed. The practice seems consistent with the theory in which the Declaration is viewed as providing fundamental animating principles that underlie the Constitution. It is invoked only at a very high level of generality as a clue to the underlying purpose of the text, as a device of construction more than one of true original public meaning interpretation.

Summary of Justices and Originalism

The association of the justices with originalism is far more complicated than normally portrayed. Justices Thomas and Scalia are clearly originalists to some degree with relatively high levels of use of some originalist sources. However, they are not clearly more originalist than Justice Stevens or even Justice Brennan, who also made heavy use of originalist sources in their opinions. Stevens and Brennan had more overall uses of originalist sources and, adjusted for time on the Court, nearly so many on an annualized basis, notwithstanding their reputation as somewhat hostile to originalism.

Perhaps the most significant finding is the relative lack of difference among the justices in using originalist sources. Justices Warren and Clark appear nonoriginalist by comparison with their colleagues, but all of the other justices made substantial use of the originalist materials. Moreover, there appear to be no pure originalists. Considering the median scores, even Justice Thomas ignored an originalist source about 30 percent of the time when some other justice used such a source. None of the justices, even those openly devoted to originalist interpretation of the Constitution, truly appears to be a fully faithful devotee of the method. Nor do any justices plainly reject the use of originalism.

One might question whether originalist sources are a true measure of reliance on originalism. Some justices may invoke originalist sources insincerely. Others may do so erroneously. Still other justices may rely heavily on originalist sources as evidence of original intent, rather than the prevailing theory of original public meaning. But none of these questions are truly relevant to my analysis. When a judge invokes originalist sources, that judge is "doing" originalism. If the judge is doing originalism falsely or badly, that too is significant for the theory.

Brennan used originalist sources a great deal. Yet Howard and Segal (2002, 118) suggested that it would be "fanciful" to claim that he was truly influenced by originalism. Perhaps he and others, such as Justice Stevens, simply invoked originalist sources to lend credibility to decisions they reached on other grounds. But if one believes those two justices had this insincere practice, why not generalize it to all justices? While there is no way to test a justice's sincerity, the power of originalism might be seen if its principles cause justices to reach decisions they otherwise would not. The succeeding chapters examine this question.

EIGHT

Ideology and Supreme Court Decisions

This chapter reviews evidence on the determinants of the justices' votes in the cases before them. While the justices are supposed to simply apply the law to make decisions, they are commonly criticized for judging ideologically. This chapter examines the evidence underlying the criticism and possible reasons for patterns of judicial voting. This dispute is vital to appreciating the relevance of originalism. For originalism to be meaningful, it must overcome any tendencies for the justices to vote based on their ideological preferences or any other extralegal reasons.

The Supreme Court, like all other courts, is expected to make decisions based on the facts of the case and the relevant materials of the law. However, the very existence of an appeal to the Supreme Court suggests that the law may not clearly resolve the dispute. Oftentimes, lower courts have differed over how the law should be applied. Both sides of the case will present factual and legal arguments, and both may have convincing arguments. In a majority of cases, the justices disagree about who should prevail. The fact that the Court's justices often divide in these cases, with dissenters, also reveals that the requirements of the law are uncertain. The divisions could simply reflect cases where the legal question is a very close call, with justices simply coming to different conclusions about its requirements. This would be entirely consistent with reasonable legal decisionmaking.

The Court's divisions may be explained by extralegal factors, however. Confronted by debatable legal questions, the justices may be influenced, consciously or subconsciously, by some other factors, such as elements of the justice's background. The role of these outside factors became prominent with the growth of legal realism in the early twentieth century. The realists argued that justices were making decisions based on their personal preferences, not the law. The concerns of legal realism have since been carefully studied, and researchers find that divisions among the justices are quite predictable. Most can be explained by apparent ideological differences among the justices, with conservatives consistently deciding cases differently from liberals. Perhaps the law is too uncertain to provide a resolution, or perhaps the justices' preferences outweigh their commitment to the law. Either scenario presents a challenge to interpretive methods such as originalism. This chapter examines the evidence and the reasons why such differences may arise, with implications for use of originalism.

Legal Realism

The standard story in legal history is that historic lawyers and judges were formalists who believed that legal materials could be applied to the facts of cases in a scientific way, to yield an objectively correct resolution. Under this story, judges were not so much individuals but instead vessels for transmitting the law. The story did not depend on a belief that every decision was the correct one, though it typically sought to justify nearly all of them. But if a judge got one wrong, it was due to application error, not bias. In the progressive era, though, this view was challenged in a movement commonly known as legal realism.

Jerome Frank (1930), an experienced lawyer, federal judge, and perhaps the leading realist, argued that judges could not engage in truly correct legal decisionmaking. He believed that, as a psychological matter, a judge would dwell on the facts of a particular dispute and try to reach the "best" resolution for the particular case independent of what the law might demand. The judge would then seek to find legal materials that would provide a rationalization for this predetermined decision. But those materials were simply a cover-up of the true reason for the decision. Apparent reliance on the law was hypocritical.

Frank appeared to believe that judicial decisionmaking was largely idiosyncratic based on the personality of the individual judge and could vary depending on what the judge had for breakfast the morning of the decision. The "sociological" branch of legal realism disagreed and argued that the judge's decisions were predictable based on individual characteristics (just not according to the law). This wing suggested that the facts of the individual case were not so significant as some overarching view of the law or justice held by the particular individual judge, and that view was socially determined.

Like any theory, the strength of the claims of legal realism varied. While some appeared to suggest that the law was intrinsically meaningless, others suggested that it could matter to some degree. Perhaps the law mattered in some cases but not others. Karl Llewellyn did not suggest that the law was immaterial but simply argued that its power could not be presumed (Tamanaha 2010). An opinion's analysis was not necessarily the determinant for the outcome reached but might merely be a post hoc justification.

Brian Tamanaha (2010) argues that the realists were not truly such a break with history and that it was long recognized that law was not purely scientific or formalistic. He points to nineteenth-century jurists who ridiculed the view that the law perfectly controlled judges' rulings. Some notion of legal realism, he maintains, was always with us, even if it did not obtain a name until the 1930s. While Tamanaha makes a strong case that there never was an era of classical formalism, he overly downplays the rise of realism. Were the limits of the law always recognized, the writings of Frank and others would not have been regarded as so exceptional, but they were. Moreover, some of the strongest realist claims rejecting the significance of law were something new.

The legal realists did not dwell on judicial politics as a basis for decisions, but it was always lurking in the background. The idiosyncratic branch of realism did not directly ascribe much to ideology. The sociological realists, though, suggested that judges had some solidarity in pursuing rules that conformed to business culture and practice. These realists suggested that judicial decisions were driven by factors such as class and legal experience but also ideological preferences (O'Neill 2005). The realists argued that judicial decisions were "opinions as to policy which merely embody the preferences of a given body in a given time and place" (Robertson 1998, 7).

Significantly, the realists were generally not judicial nihilists but sought to improve the operation of the legal system. Karl Llewellyn believed that most decisions were in accordance with traditional, more formalistic legal approaches; he just suggested that a substantial number were not (Tamanaha 2010). While the realists were attacking a simplistic formalism, that "did not mean that they embraced the polar opposite: the notion that legal rules and principles do not have a significant role in judges' decisions" (Tamanaha 2010, 96). Even the realists acknowledged that law was part of a judge's decision; they merely argued that it was not the only part and not always the most important part.

This left important questions open. The first question was whether as a society we wished the law to play an important role in judicial decisions, if not the only role. To this question, the answer is almost uniformly yes. The rule of law has great value to a society, and the alternative rule of judges' political preferences in particular cases is typically regarded as unfairly arbitrary. Judges are not elected and have no obvious authority for using their ideological discretion to resolve disputes. The neutral law seems fair and allows parties to arrange their actions in accordance with an expected decision of a court. Parties want clearly defined contracts, so they can make enforceable contracts. They want clearly defined criminal laws, so they can steer clear of legal violations.

Assuming that we want judges' decisions to be grounded in law insofar as possible, the second question was about how to achieve this objective. The debate over achieving more law-based decisions revolves mainly around interpretive methods. The theory is that some methods of legal interpretation are more binding and leave justices with less discretion to exercise their personal preferences. As already noted, originalists have promoted their method for precisely this reason—that it was more constraining on judges. Yet others have argued the opposite, that originalism is highly indeterminate, and the relative constraint of originalism is largely untested in any rigorous manner.

The legal realists had a deeply positivistic and scientific view of law. The practice of law should be evaluated by empirical testing, not what judges asserted that they were doing. The claims of justices could not be taken at face value but had to be investigated. The realists were not themselves empiricists, however, and their critique was nearly so anecdotal as those who propounded formalism.

Thus, legal realism, while always lurking as a background suspicion, never really took hold as a general jurisprudential belief. The realists never truly proved their case about judicial decisionmaking. Realism was largely displaced by the process school, which emphasized internal legal procedure and reasoned decisionmaking. Duxbury (1995) argues that the shortcoming of realism was that it never was truly a theory, but just a "mood." In the latter half of the twentieth century, though, political scientists took up the challenge of propounding a nonlegal theory for judicial decisionmaking. Moreover, they embarked on the empirical measurement of decisions to test this theory and prove its claims.

Political Science and the Attitudinal Model

Political scientists took up the challenge of measuring the degree to which judicial decisions are based in the law, as opposed to the judges' political preferences. The pioneers in this research, such as C. Herman Pritchett, found patterns in the decisions of Supreme Court justices of the New Deal Court. Glendon Schubert found that justices' ideologies appeared to determine their decisions. Some justices tended consistently to vote for parties pushing a liberal legal position on the Court, while others voted against those parties. These patterns could commonly be predicted by the ideology of the president who had appointed the justice to the Court.

Jeff Segal and Howard Spaeth (1993, 2002) expanded on the claims of ideological decisionmaking in what they called an attitudinal model. They dismissed the traditional legal model of judicial decisionmaking, noting that precedent did not reduce judicial discretion because precedents could support either side in the typical appellate case and justices used the same precedents to produce different outcomes. They claimed, therefore, that precedent "provides no guide to the justices' decisions" (Segal & Spaeth

1993, 48). Their theory was that justices resolved cases according to their political predilections, not precedents or other accepted materials of the law.

Segal and Spaeth likewise criticized reliance on originalism. They questioned whether any meaning from a term could be gleaned from such a broad group of people as the ratifiers. They objected that Madison's notes were incomplete and that *The Federalist* should be considered "political propaganda" (Segal & Spaeth 1993, 59). Disagreements even among supporters of the Constitution or its amendments were common. Segal and Spaeth also note that the very broad and indeterminate wording of constitutional provisions, such as due process, do not enable justices to find a clear original meaning. Originalism, therefore, could not constrain the justices. They argue that all forms of the legal model, including originalism, are meaningless for the Supreme Court.

Segal and Spaeth's attitudinal model says that justices vote for their ideologically preferred outcome. The ideologies of the justices could often be characterized by the ideology of the president who appointed them or the perceptions of their ideology as recognized by the media at the time of their appointment. Segal and Spaeth used the latter measure and found that they could predict about three-fourths of the justices' decisions based on their perceived ideology. This could well underestimate the role of ideology because perceptions at the time of appointment may be inaccurate. Moreover, some conservative outcomes may simply be *too* conservative for even conservative justices, who would therefore cast a vote for the other side, so ideological decisionmaking could actually be obscured and underestimated by the empirical method. Yet it showed significant results. Most of the justices in recent history showed considerable ideological consistency in outcomes, regardless of precedent.

The persistence over time of ideological outcomes associated with individual justices, despite wholly different cases each year, further suggests the power of ideology. The attitudinal model appears to predict Supreme Court decisions better than does any legal model (Cross 1997). One study compared computer predictions grounded largely in the attitudinal model with predictions of legal experts for the 2002 term and found the computer did somewhat better (Ruger, Kim, Martin & Quinn 2004), getting 75 percent of the outcomes right, while the experts got about 60 percent correct.

Although the realists generally did not dismiss the role of law entirely in judicial decisionmaking, some political scientists, such as Segal and Spaeth, have come close to this extreme position. The basic theme of this attitudinal model theory is that justices "first arrive at their desired conclusion and only then develop a legal rationale that buttresses their decision" (Wahlbeck 1997, 780). The claim that the justices decide cases according to law has been called a myth, much like that of St. George and the dragon (Brisbin 1996). This echoed the conservative criticism of the Warren Court's decisions but suggested that it was common to other Courts and to conservative justices as well.

Segal and Spaeth provided ample empirical evidence of ideological voting by the justices, but some aspects of their empirics have come into question. Their outcome depended on the accuracy of their coding of particular outcomes as conservative or liberal in their nature. Shapiro (2010) challenges this coding, noting that many cases could be characterized either way, depending on the dimension considered. For example, Segal and Spaeth characterize a decision in favor of plaintiffs in voting rights cases as liberal, but what if those plaintiffs are conservative Republicans? Decisions in favor of First Amendment rights are considered liberal, but such decisions are more recently pressed by conservatives in support of the speech rights of businesses. Harvey and Woodruff (2009) suggest that subjectivity in coding the direction has skewed the database. Moreover, there are groups of cases in which ideological direction is aligned with a particular legal variable, so it is impossible to differentiate the effect of the two (Cross 1997).

While there are undoubtedly flaws in the Segal and Spaeth database, as with any research project, the criticisms do not truly undercut their results. There simply is no doubt among legal commentators that the justices reach ideologically different outcomes in a systematic way. One can expect Justices Thomas and Scalia to produce results desired by conservatives in most cases, while other justices disagree with those results. There clearly is an ideological component, though the precise amount estimated by Segal and Spaeth could be questioned. However, errors in the database potentially could mean that the ideological results were understated and its role more powerful even than as estimated by Segal and Spaeth (Cross 1997).

Segal and Spaeth's research on the attitudinal model has seen ample confirmation in other studies. A study that predates Segal and Spaeth based ideology on appointing president and found statistically significant differences

in the Court's voting in certain areas (Nagel 1961). Dan Pinello (1999) conducted a meta-analysis of over 100 studies of the attitudinal model counting
hundreds of thousands of judicial votes. He found that virtually every study
found an association. The role of ideology differed by level of the judicial
hierarchy, with the Supreme Court clearly the most ideological, though its
influence was found at all levels. Many believe the attitudinal model is *the*
determinant of Supreme Court decisions. There is little remaining doubt
that judicial ideology explains some decisions.

In contrast to the attitudinal model, some research suggests that legal
variables may influence the justices' votes. Edelman, Klein, and Lindquist
(2008) noted that justices' votes frequently fail to fall precisely along predicted ideological lines. For most of the Courts they studied, a majority of
justices' decisions did not do so. While this did not disprove the existence
of any ideological decisionmaking in these cases, the "disordered voting"
called its extent into question.

Another study examined Supreme Court decisions in cases where the
lower courts were in conflict over the results and added potentially legal
variables to the model (Lindquist & Klein 2006). They considered whether
the justices were influenced by whether the majority of circuits found a
particular result, the presence of lower court dissents and concurrences,
and the effect of particularly prestigious circuit court judges. They found
that these effects mattered and often appeared to trump the role of ideology. While this study did not directly measure the effect of law, its findings
suggested a role.

Law was more directly studied by Richards and Kritzer (2002), who
examined opinion content. They hypothesized that opinions created certain "jurisprudential regimes" that structured the outcomes of subsequent
cases. After the Court changed the standards for evaluating government
restrictions on speech, subsequent decisions appeared to rely on the new
standards. This study is a rather indirect attack on Segal and Spaeth, who
considered only decision outcomes. Richards and Kritzer consider opinion
content, with a true legal variable, and their research also recognizes the
role of case selection by the Court itself. The authors confirmed their results in other legal areas as well, such as search and seizure law (Kritzer &
Richards 2005).

Others have also found some role for law, or at least precedent, in Supreme Court decisions. Wahlbeck (1997) finds that the justices are less

likely to change a legal rule when more consistent precedents accumulate to support that rule. Epstein and Kobylka (1992) closely examined death penalty and abortion decisions and found that they were substantially influenced by legal arguments. Bartels (2009) considers opinions on different levels of scrutiny and finds that the law shapes the degree to which the justices' ideologies are influential.

In addition, while Segal and Spaeth presented strong evidence that different ideologies had some influence on Supreme Court decisionmaking. Their study left a large number of votes, apparently contrary to a justice's ideology, unexplained (Cross 1997). The many unanimous decisions of the Court also call into question the universality of ideological decisionmaking. These decisions may simply suggest that we are unable to precisely estimate a justice's ideological preferences. However, it is very possible that unanimous decisions are due to the effect of the law. Their frequency suggests this effect. Perhaps the law does control at least a certain subset of cases at the Court. Perhaps certain interpretive theories, when available and used, have a more constraining effect. Because the empirical research of Segal and Spaeth had no variable for legal effects, they were criticized for ignoring the law and its possible role in the Court's holdings.

Given the challenge to study the effect of law on political decisionmaking, political scientists have struggled to capture a quantitative measure for the law, so that its influence may be compared with that of the justices' ideologies. The defenders of the role of law stress that both sides present legal arguments but have no way to measure the relative legal validity of those arguments. Both sides have legal support, but one side has stronger legal support, which the justices may identify and follow. Some political scientists have begun to try to study the role of law with research on legal precedent.

Studies of Precedent

Precedent is by far the leading legal resource used by the Supreme Court. It is used far more often than originalism (Phelps & Gates 1991) or any other interpretive method. Indeed, citations to precedent considerably exceed citations to all other forms of legal authority (Knight & Epstein 1996). Stare decisis, or deciding according to precedent, appears to govern the Court (though some think originalism should trump precedent in certain constitutional matters). Reliance on prior precedents, as evidenced by citations to prior opinions, is commonly considered the prime determinant of the Court's decisions (Cross, Spriggs, Johnson & Wahlbeck 2010).

Some argue, however, that precedent does not truly drive the Court's decisions. Instead, justices cite precedents only to lend legitimacy to results they reached on other grounds. Even when confronted with an identical body of preexisting precedent, justices differ in its application to a case. It is not uncommon to see one opinion of the Court follow a precedent, while a separate opinion distinguishes it to reach the opposite result. Much like the criticism of originalism, academics have argued that stare decisis developed to lend credibility to judicial decisions, as being grounded in the law and not the will of judges (Knight & Epstein 1996), though this was not truly the case. The practice of relying on precedent may have been created for the very reason of legitimizing the Court's opinions (Cross, Spriggs, Johnson & Wahlbeck 2010).

Supposedly, one can find a precedent to support any desired outcome, so the justices are unconstrained and simply pick and choose the citations that suit their preferred outcome. This is the position taken by legal realists and devotees of the attitudinal model of Supreme Court decisionmaking. Precedent may be simply a "mask hiding other considerations" (Monaghan 1988). Any precedent contrary to a desired outcome, it is said, may be distinguished away. If the precedent cannot be distinguished, Justice Rehnquist has noted that stare decisis "is not an inexorable command" (*Payne v. Tennessee* 1991, 828), and undesirable precedents can be ignored or overruled. As the highest court in the land, no precedents truly bind the Supreme Court, even in theory.

It is undoubtedly true that precedent is imperfectly constraining on the justices, but "a large leap is required" to reach the "conclusion that the law provides *no* important guidance to judges in the decisionmaking process" (Lindquist & Klein 2006, 138). Even when precedent may allow different results, "some will frequently be more plausible than others—not because the law *mandates* a particular conclusion, but because the methodological and professional conventions of judging make some arguments more persuasive than others" (Lindquist & Klein 2006, 138). Thus, it is plausible that precedent matters, but this still must be tested.

The effect of precedent as a constraint has been much more studied than that of originalism or other methods of decisionmaking. These studies of precedent provide the best evidence available on the role of law at the Court. The best known of these studies, conducted by Spaeth and Segal (1999), tested whether justices changed their votes in response to precedents that they opposed in the first instance. Their research strategy began by identifying cases that involved dissenting opinions as their landmark cases. Then they identified the precedential "progeny" of those opinions, based on citations. Then the authors considered how the dissenters from the original opinion voted in the progeny cases.

Spaeth and Segal's theory was that, if precedent was controlling, the dissenters in the original opinion would flip the direction of their votes from the progeny cases because that original opinion set a controlling precedent that they were bound to follow. This behavior characterized only about 12 percent of the justice-votes examined, however. In the vast majority of instances, the justices who dissented from the original decision continued to reject it in deciding the progeny cases. They concluded that the predictions of the attitudinal model overwhelmed precedent as a determinant of voting on the Supreme Court. Although the Supreme Court has the authority to override or ignore its own opinions, it generally respects prior opinions and failure to do so undermines stare decisis.

The Spaeth and Segal study of the effect of precedent at the Court promptly saw various criticisms, however. The authors considered as progeny only major cases that received oral argument. The Court's more straightforward summary dispositions, though, are likely to be the cases most governed by precedent (and therefore requiring no formal legal argument before the justices). When summary dispositions were included in the study, the justices followed precedent, rather than their preferences, about 75 percent of the time (Songer & Lindquist 1996). The cases examined by Segal and Spaeth were therefore the ones in which the landmark precedent was not clearly governing.

The coding method of Spaeth and Segal was also dubious. They decided that a subsequent progeny opinion that limited the scope of the original precedent was attitudinal in nature and not legal. Yet this is simply a misunderstanding of the meaning of stare decisis. When a case arises before the Court seeking to expand on the scope of the ruling of a prior case, the earlier opinion is instructive but does not truly govern the progeny case. Nothing about the earlier opinion means that a later opinion must expand its scope. A dissenter's choice to vote against expansion of the earlier opinion may show an attitudinal influence but is not a rejection of precedent. Indeed, a reexamination of the authors' progeny cases indicated that the Court's opinion typically "explicitly reaffirms the doctrine announced in the landmark case" (Songer & Lindquist 1996, 1054).

Another problem with the Spaeth and Segal study was the failure to consider the effects of the landmark precedent opinion on the Court's agenda and the cases to be litigated. A precedent-following Court would not take for discretionary review cases that were plainly governed by earlier opinions. That would be an unnecessary waste of their time, as the lower courts are fully able to apply the precedent where it plainly controls. Instead, the Court would take cases on the margins, where the original precedent is indeterminate in deciding the case. If this were true, constraint might not show up in the opinions of the justices, even though it was a powerfully controlling effect on the law. The observed attitudinal effect would be limited to cases that precedent did not govern, which is not much of an indictment of the power of stare decisis.

Indeed, other research suggests that precedent does have an effect on the Court's decisions. One study considered responses of the Rehnquist Court to precedential opinions, considering ideology and other factors (Lim 2000). The existence of an underlying precedent was statistically significant in various different models with different variables considered. Justices departed from an earlier dissent to adopt the precedent created by a case with material frequency.

Political scientists who believe that precedent's function is primarily that of legitimation of the Court's processes have also suggested that this legitimation function nevertheless imposes constraints on the justices' decisions. While suggesting that the justices are primarily "policy seekers," Epstein and Knight (1998, 45) find that the need to legitimate policies based on the law prevents the justices from fully effecting their preferences. The fact that justices regularly invoke precedents in nonpublic arguments among themselves testifies to their relevance. If precedent were only a mask to legitimate cases to the general public, there is no reason why the justices would vigorously argue precedent among themselves in private conferences—yet they do.

The best study of precedent is probably that of Hansford and Spriggs (2006). While they did not directly test the constraining effect of ideology on the justices, they carefully examined citation practices at the Court and how they were influenced by the justices' ideologies. The authors found that the more a precedent was cited, the more powerful it became and the more likely it was to be cited as a determinant of future decisions. The ideology of the justices also mattered. Liberal justices were more likely to follow a strong existing liberal precedent but distinguish a strong existing conservative precedent (and vice versa). But this effect was only a marginal one, not a typical one. Hansford and Spriggs (2006, 11) concluded that "the Court's prior interpretation of a precedent, the need to legitimize policy choices, and the legal arguments put forward by organized interests influence the law."

Perhaps the greatest testament to the influence of precedent is found in the decisions that did not occur. Despite the loud conservative protests against Warren Court liberal decisions and the conservative ascendency on the Court in subsequent years, those decisions largely survived. The later Courts may have trimmed them back, creating exceptions or distinguishing the original holding for new facts, but they have not overturned them. *Miranda* may be weakened, but it remains the law. When new justices join the Court, they appear to accept the control of existing precedent, at least for the most part.

Precedent is often cast in opposition to originalism. If precedent is but a mask and does not constrain the justices' decisions, that fact might argue for greater dedication to originalism. Unless the evidence showed that precedent was utterly meaningless, though, this would not necessarily follow. The evidence, even that of Spaeth and Segal, does not indicate that precedent is utterly meaningless. It suggests that precedent is somewhat manipulable but nevertheless exercises some control over the opinions that the Court renders. The true question is the relative constraint of the two methodologies: That is, is originalism more constraining than stare decisis, or vice versa? Before considering this question, though, I explore why the justices' decisions seem ideological and why this pattern need not be a sign of dishonesty on their part.

Motivated Reasoning

While the evidence of some constraining effect of precedent suggests a role for the law in the Court's decisions, the remaining powerful evidence of attitudinal determination of decisions may seem troubling. One might infer that the justices are judging willfully, that they are disregarding the law to make policy, contrary to their constitutional authorization. Such judging would involve the justices taking advantage of their position, with life tenure, to take illegal actions, even as they served as the law itself. Yet such conscious disregard for judicial responsibility is not demonstrated by the evidence.

The leading attitudinalists have recognized this fact and are famously agnostic about whether their discovery reflects any conscious action. It is quite cynical to suggest that judges are intentionally violating legal requirements, and this doesn't fit with their self-perceptions. Judges are aware of the risk of inappropriate motivations and make some effort to resist them (Braman & Nelson 2007). Judges typically strive to make impartial decisions, and most judges "expend significant energy and thought consciously avoiding personal biases and prejudices in the decision-making process" (Irwin & Real 2010, 1–2). Yet countless studies have shown that the justices' decisions fall into patterns that trace contemporary ideological differences (biases and prejudices).

Claims of ideological or willful judging are commonly accompanied by claims of judicial dishonesty. Such intentional disregard of duty need not be presumed, though, and is probably inaccurate. Instead, the apparent ideological decisionmaking of the Court is perfectly consistent with justices sincerely trying to apply the law. The justices are just influenced by what psychologists consider "motivated reasoning," which produces an ideological pattern even among sincere and honest justices.

Another term used by psychology to describe this motivated reasoning effect is confirmation bias (Nickerson 1998). This is a natural tendency of people to favor information that confirms their preexisting beliefs. Famously, 90 percent of us believe we are "above average" at tasks such as driving, though this would be impossible. This confirmation bias can manifest itself in several ways. First, there is the biased search for information. People have a preference for discovering information that confirms their perspective and avoiding dissonant information.

The adversary process helps control the biased search for information to some degree. Each side of a case before the Supreme Court typically has skilled lawyers who assemble the best legal argument for their side. Justices will therefore be confronted by data contrary to their preferred outcome and may not hide from discomforting information. However, this does not dispel the bias, because people are also biased in their interpretation of the data.

Even if the audience has the exact same information, confirmation bias arises from the interpretation of that information. People can view the same thing with very different interpretations. Studies show that "people tend to overweight positive confirmatory evidence or underweight negative confirmatory evidence" (Nickerson 1998, 180). Thus, individuals tend to selectively credit information that is congenial to their preferences (Kahan, Braman, Slovic, Gastil & Cohen 2009). Supreme Court justices thus may be inclined to view the facts in a biased manner or choose a legal interpretive method that yielded their preferred conclusions.

This effect was strikingly illustrated by a Supreme Court case that included a video of a fleeing suspect to help address the question of whether the suspect presented a risk to the public (*Scott v. Harris* 2007). To some justices, the threat seemed quite obvious, though Justice Stevens dissented from this conclusion. A subsequent study of the video found that responses differed sharply among different groups of the American public (Kahan, Hoffman & Braman 2009). Sociodemographic differences among members of the audience colored their perceptions of the facts. What seemed obvious to some did not to others. And this was a pure factual question, not a matter of law.

A follow-up study made the effect even clearer. The authors showed students a demonstration. Half the students thought the demonstration was outside an abortion clinic, and the other half thought it was outside a military recruitment facility (Kahan, Hoffman, Braman, Evans & Rachlinski 2011). A key legal question is whether certain actions are constitutionally protected speech or are intimidating actions that may be constitutionally regulated by the government. The authors found that the subjects' likelihood to characterize actions as constitutionally protected depended significantly on whether the protestors conformed to their cultural worldview. Liberals tended to find the protest of the military more protected than protests of abortion clinics, while conservatives showed the opposite tendency.

What people *see* appears to "turn on who they *are*" (Kahan, Hoffman, Braman, Evans & Rachlinski 2011, 34).

Judges, of course, are expected to combat these natural human tendencies. Yet the implicit biases derive from "the fundamental mechanics of the human thought process" (Irwin & Real 2010, 3) and hence may be difficult to overcome. There is some evidence that judges sometimes do better than laypersons at counteracting their own biases (Guthrie, Rachlinski & Wistrich 2007). However, there is ample evidence of perhaps inevitable failures by judges who "report seeing different things" even when confronted with the same evidence (Kahan, Hoffman, Braman, Evans & Rachlinski 2011, 35).

The tendency toward motivated reasoning is not unlimited, however, and it does not doom all efforts to constrain the ideological impulses of judges. The seminal article on motivated reasoning demonstrated that it did not always govern human decisions and that steps could be taken to demotivate decisionmaking (Kunda 1990). There are "accuracy" goals and "directional" goals of decisionmakers. The concern for the Supreme Court is when the directional motivation surpasses the accuracy motivation (Boiney, Kennedy & Nye 1997). The directional goals tend to cause people to adopt strategies most likely to yield a desired conclusion.

Kunda (1990) found a lessening of motivated reasoning when a decision had greater stakes, when the decision had to be justified, and when the decision would be made public. These circumstances are common features of judicial decisionmaking, which should reduce the risks of motivated reasoning at the Court. Conversely, though, the Supreme Court is likely to take on the toughest cases, less clearly resolved by legal methods, for which motivational biases may be more available (Baum 2010).

Tetlock (1985) has also shown how accountability concerns can mitigate motivated decisionmaking. He finds that accountable decisionmakers use cognitively more complex decisionmaking procedures, show greater consistency of judgment, process information in more detail, and are more discriminating in response to evidence (Tetlock 1985, 229). Although justices are not fully accountable, they do have some accountability to the very expert groups that are most likely to evaluate them on true legal decisionmaking issues. Judges may be criticized, even embarrassed, by the commentary of these groups on their decisions.

Of course, with judicial independence and life tenure, courts are often viewed as unaccountable. They cannot be removed from office for transgressions, as elected officials can be. This view is overly simplistic. Judges care how they are perceived, especially by professional audiences (Baum 2006). Surely their fellow justices are among the audiences they care about. Judges are held accountable for their opinions, even if they cannot be punished financially, and they care about their reputation, with lawyers, politicians, the media, professors, and other groups. Justices' "desire to court, appease, or satisfy any one of these audiences can act as a real constraint on their decisional behavior" (Braman 2010, 215). In addition, justices may be constrained by public opinion.

There is also evidence that the presence of stronger arguments contrary to the preexisting preferences will reduce the influence of motivations (Jain & Maheswaran 2000). Even a "highly motivated decision maker will resist severely distorting information to support a desired conclusion" (Boiney, Kennedy & Nye 1997, 4). Braman and Nelson (2007, 941) suggest that "the judicial context may be one of the least hospitable environments for such biases to flourish." Professional norms help counteract such biases. There is ample evidence that judges intrinsically value accuracy goals of correct legal decisionmaking (Baum 2010) as well as their directional goals.

Heterogeneity in preferences also may help combat motivated reasoning. A Court with different perspectives will produce a dialectic of arguments and perhaps a published dissent. Some psychological research shows that diversity and dissent serve to improve decisionmaking by a group (Schulz-Hardt, Brodbeck, Mojzisch, Kerschreiter & Frey 2006). Decisions of a majority may be influenced by persistent advocates for a majority position, at least when their arguments must be addressed by the majority (Sinaceur, Thomas-Hunt, Neale, O'Neill & Haag 2010). Motivated reasoning does not doom efforts to promote legal decisionmaking at the Court. Instead, it counsels for interpretive methods that may be constraining, such as, perhaps, originalism.

The issue of motivated reasoning has been directly studied in the context of the judiciary. Guthrie, Rachlinski, and Wistrich (2007) have examined judicial decisionmaking broadly at the trial court level. They noted the tendency of individuals to make intuitive "snap" judgments before even examining the relevant evidence, consistent with the expectations of motivated reasoning. Judges are also subject to this tendency. The authors submitted a general test to judges and found a strong tendency toward intuitive decisionmaking. However, judges may sometimes override their snap judgment through cognitive reflection on the evidence. The authors found that some conditions of the judicial system encouraged deliberation but recommended additional steps to do so to a greater degree. Addressing trial courts, they suggested increasing the time available to render decisions and requiring more opinion writing. Time and publication are characteristics of Supreme Court decisions, of course, which might therefore be expected to be more reflective.

Braman and Nelson (2007) studied motivated reasoning with an experiment using students evaluating a discrimination case. They found strong evidence that prior ideological opinions influenced decisions about the applicability of precedent, by both undergraduates and law students. They also found that objective facts could restrain the effects of motivated perceptions and that the law students showed less bias than the undergraduates. Legal training could thus reduce motivated reasoning, so we might expect judges to be less susceptible to the effect.

Research on role theory could support this conclusion. Judges are trained in the law as students and imbued in a judicial role on the bench (Cross 1997). This role might help them fight tendencies to engage in motivated reasoning. Political scientists have studied the judicial role and found that it does have some effect on judges (Gibson 1978). Most "judges hold deeply internalized role constraints and believe that judgment is not politics" (Sullivan 1992). The judicial role may thus help combat the biases of motivated reasoning.

Motivated reasoning is an inevitable feature of human reasoning. However, its power may be influenced by circumstances. Some groups, such as the legally trained, may be less susceptible to motivated reasoning on certain issues. Some features, such as the need to justify decisions, may also limit motivated reasoning. While extirpation of motivated reasoning is an unrealistic goal, it would be reasonable to try to limit its influence insofar as possible. Interpretive theories may be the tool for such limiting. Some theories may be more constraining on judicial preferences.

Relative determinacy of law would be an important factor in combating the justices' inevitable tendency to motivated reasoning. Clear legal commands should restrict motivational biases. However much a given justice might like to see a teenager elected president, the clear age qualifications of the Constitution surely would preclude him or her from ruling to allow it. Judges are human, with human foibles, and an interpretive theory must work within that context. Motivated reasoning is constrained by a person's inability to justify the reasonableness of a preferred conclusion (Kunda 1990). The more indeterminate the governing materials, the easier it is to make that preferred conclusion seem reasonable (Baum 2010). Precedent has been criticized for great indeterminacy, with cases to be found in support of either side. Originalism, though, with its murky historical record and need for abstraction, might be even more indeterminate and subject to manipulation.

Originalist Sources and Ideology

Ideological decisionmaking is a central issue for originalism. A key argument for originalism is its ability to restrain willful judging. If originalism can do so, that fact alone would not validate the theory, but such restraint would provide a powerful argument for reliance on originalism. Conversely, however, if originalism cannot restrain judges, the theory would be invalidated as a practical matter. If justices can use originalism to reach any result they wish, the theory is functionally meaningless.

Richard Posner (2000, 593) suggests that "history provides a useful mask for decisions reached on other grounds." He contends that originalist history is "simply not verifiable" as a practical matter (Posner 2000, 594). This is because of both the indeterminacy of the historical record and the judgment required in abstracting from it to resolve today's problems. Given the disagreements among the framers themselves, originalism can be subjective and manipulable by the justices (Somin 2006). If so, originalism may be unconstraining and therefore fairly meaningless as an interpretive approach. Of course, it would be too strong to suggest that *every* constitutional provision was so contestable. Some have a straightforward original meaning. It seems likely, though, that the important and controversial Supreme Court opinions will commonly have originalist evidence for both sides.

Justice Scalia is one of the leading proponents of originalism on the grounds that it serves to constrain justices. Yet he has written that there "is plenty of room for disagreement as to what original meaning was, and even more as to how that original meaning applies to the situation before the Court" (Scalia 1997, 45). Yet this room for disagreement obviously undermines the constraining effect of originalism. With unbiased judges who are totally committed to originalism, the theory might have a true impact, but history does not suggest that the existence of such unbiased judges committed to originalism is likely to be common.

Matthew Festa (2007) has illustrated this problem by examining cases where originalism was invoked by both sides. He identifies as a fairly frequent recent phenomenon "the citation by different Justices to the same historical source (such as *The Federalist*) to support divergent or opposing historical interpretations of legal meaning" (Festa 2007, 75). While not infrequent, this phenomenon of both sides citing the same originalist materials existed in only a relatively small minority of cases and hence does not itself invalidate the constraining effect of originalism.

It is unrealistic to expect that any legal theory would be perfectly restraining on judges. The Supreme Court justices commonly disagree over the meaning of particular statutory language or a particular precedential decision. The law and language itself are simply too imprecise to provide perfectly determinate answers. Different theories may provide relatively different degrees of constraint, though (and some might provide little or no constraint). If we presume that the apparent ideological orientation of the justices is due to motivated reasoning, we could seek out a theory that tends to limit the practice insofar as possible.

The prevailing alternative to originalism is a pluralist system in which justices may choose different interpretive methods in different cases. This might seem especially susceptible to motivated reasoning biases, because justices may pick and choose among interpretive theories. They can simply select the interpretive approach that best suits their biases. As a practical matter, though, precedent overwhelms all alternative approaches at the Court. Consequently, the true issue may be a comparison of originalism with precedent, which is the leading contrary method for interpretation of the Constitution.

Daniel Farber and Suzanna Sherry (2010, 287) contend that originalism fares worse by this standard, writing:

> Given that professional historians themselves disagree about such issues, and that judges are not trained in historical analysis, originalism cannot effectively constrain judicial discretion. Indeed, it is likely to prove less effective in constraining discretion than the common law method with which judges have years of professional training and experience to guide them.

Judge Posner (2001, 165) similarly claims that "history provides a mask for decisions reached on other grounds," and its use is "almost always a mask, because of the indeterminacy of most historical inquiries of the sort that might be thought to bear on legal decisionmaking." Because of its public political effect of legitimizing decisions, originalism would be a particularly attractive mask.

This is a plausible critique of originalism, but it remains unproven. Any interpretive theory will be subject to manipulation, whether intentional or as a mere product of motivated reasoning. Different theories may be compared, though, and some may be more malleable than others. Originalists maintain the historical record is sufficiently determinate to constrain the justices, at least relatively speaking. I will attempt to study this contention in the following chapter.

NINE

The Intersection of Ideology and Originalism

As the prior chapter has indicated, judging is both a political and a legal activity. Most American citizens want to reduce the political component of judging as much as possible and maximize the legal component, at least in theory. If the Constitution is to have governing meaning for society, it should be applied according to the law and not the preferences of the justices who happen to be sitting on the Court at the time.

The case for originalism was substantially grounded in the desire to restrain ideological decisions by the justices, replacing such "willful judging" with decisions according to law. The evidence of ideological influence at the Supreme Court is considerable, but the results do not show that ideology inevitably overwhelms all other legal considerations. The law constrains the justices to a degree but does so imperfectly. Presumably, justices fail to follow the law in cases where it is relatively indeterminate, in which cases they have freedom to act on their ideological preferences, or their motivated reasoning produces such action. The key to a constraining legal methodology could thus be in its relative determinacy in application. When the law is clear, justices are more likely to follow the law even at the expense of their ideological preferences.

Sunstein (2005) argues that there is no separation of legal interpretation from ideology. If originalism produces certain requirements, it is therefore associated with the ideology of those requirements. The choice of originalism is a political one, he maintains. While this is understandable, it does not necessarily follow. Suppose government officers were to be selected by a coin flip, and the resulting flips, by chance, favored conservatives. One would not say as a result that flipping a coin is a conservative method for selection of officers.

Originalism is different from coin flipping because the original text has a substantive ideological content of its own. Perhaps that text is substantively conservative, at least by modern standards. If so, originalism could be said to be an ideological, conservative approach to legal interpretation and the decision to be an originalist a political decision. This is certainly disputed, as originalism could shift the law in a liberal direction in some areas, such as the power of the presidency.

Defenders of originalism would probably say that this really does not matter. They assert that the rule of law is more important than particular ideological policy consequences. One should favor following the rule of law (if originalism is indeed central to that value) over particular ideological consequences. Because the Constitution can be amended, the undesirable policy implications of its terms may be corrected. Abandoning the rule of law, though, has its own bad consequences that by definition cannot be corrected by changing the law.

This chapter begins by considering whether originalism is truly an ideological conservative approach to constitutional interpretation and if that is the true reason the theory is embraced by conservatives. While often asserted, this claim is rarely substantiated. This book has noted that some prominent liberal academics have embraced originalism, and the history shows that originalist sources have commonly been used by liberals as well as by conservatives. The association of originalism with conservatism may simply be an artifact of the Reagan administration origins of a different approach to originalism.

If originalism were intrinsically conservative that could complicate the debate over the method, but, if not, originalism seems more appealing. If originalism were intrinsically conservative, it might seem simply a stalking horse for political conservative objectives. Perhaps the "campaign for a jurisprudence of original intention should be seen for what it is: a quest for political results" (Fischman & Law 2009, 139–140).

Sasha Volokh (2008) has suggested that judges might choose an interpretive method specifically because it produces ideologically attractive results. This generally implies a conscious decision, though it could be a subconscious attraction to a method based on the outcomes it produces. Under this theory, of course, the interpretive theory is constraining of results. If it were not, the judge wouldn't have to worry about choosing an approach that produced his or her desired results. Or perhaps the judge would choose a theory that is not constraining (in contrast to others that were) because it would not interfere with preferred case outcomes.

The central issue of this chapter is the extent to which originalism truly furthers the rule of law by constraining ideological judging. James Wilson (1985, 72) claims that whenever the Court found that "history presented views contrary to its planned holding, the Court rejected, ignored, or distorted that history." This suggests that historical orientation simply yields manipulable law. Others have made similar claims, but the assertion has not been rigorously tested.

The issue thus is as follows: "If it turns out, for example, that Justice Scalia only relies on originalism when it plausibly supports a politically conservative outcome, we have reason to be skeptical when he does rely on history, because he has already demonstrated a disposition to be results oriented" (Ryan 2009, 1632). As discussed in Chapter Seven, many make this claim. Originalism is sufficiently flexible that conservative originalists are said to reach conclusions at odds with their political preferences "between very rarely and never" (Eisgruber 2007, 40). Originalists allegedly manipulate the rules of construction to achieve whatever result they wish (Levy 2000). If a justice decides, "I happen to like originalist arguments when the weight of the evidence seems to support the constitutional outcomes I favor" (Rakove 1996, xv), the justice is not truly an originalist.

Because we cannot see inside the minds of the justices, the constraining effect of originalism cannot be directly tested. Even if we could see inside their minds, we would still have to identify the existence of motivated reasoning. Looking at the pattern of justices using originalist sources and vote outcomes, though, can provide indirect evidence of the constraining power of originalism or lack thereof. I examine two possibilities. First, I consider whether originalism is intrinsically conservative in ideological effect. Second, I consider whether the use of originalist sources tends to push justices away from the ideological outcomes that they presumably would prefer.

The Conservatism of Originalism?

It is sometimes thought that originalism systematically produces politically conservative results. The theory gained association with conservatives in the Reagan era with backlash against Warren Court decisions. Originalism was propounded to prevent the issuance of future liberal decisions. Some suggest that originalism is a tool "to serve a conservative political agenda" (Goldford 2005, 43), especially in light of the Reagan administration promoting it as an antidote to Warren Court liberalism. Existing research indicates that conservative justices have been somewhat more likely to cite *The Federalist* than were liberals (Corley, Howard & Nixon 2005). Barkow (2006, 1073) suggests that "it is likely that a Justice chooses originalism as his or her preferred methodology because it will, in the vast majority of cases, produce a conservative outcome that accords with his or her preferences."

Conservatives have gone to some effort to dispel this presumption, however. They commonly claim that originalism is not intrinsically conservative. Indeed, the political implications of interpretive methods have become unclear. While originalism was initially presented as a backlash to the Warren Court, it has been embraced by some liberals, traditional conservatives, and strong libertarians. Festa (2008, 497) argues that "the use of history in deciding legal issues cannot be tied to or dismissed as the tactic of those of any one political persuasion."

Even if originalism were innately conservative, that would not actually defeat the case for originalist reliance. From a legal perspective, an interpretive method should rise or fall on its rationale, not its results. If originalism were the theoretically correct standard for constitutional interpretation, the fact it produces conservative political outcomes would show nothing

Table 9.1.   Originalist sources
          and ideology.

Source	Conservative votes	Liberal votes
Federalist	939	910
Elliot's Debates	320	318
Farrand	258	257
Declaration of Independence	84	112
Dictionaries	77	67

Table 9.2.   Originalist sources and
          ideology in dissents.

Source	Conservative votes	Liberal votes
Federalist	202	268
Elliot's Debates	53	108
Farrand	59	48
Declaration of Independence	24	34
Dictionaries	27	7

more than that the conservative outcomes were the legally correct ones. Intrinsic ideology, though, can make the argument more difficult to win.

However, it is not so clear that originalism is in fact conservative by nature. As already observed, strong liberals like Jack Balkin make a case for originalism with more politically liberal results. To analyze the association between originalism and ideology, I consider cases that used originalist sources and the ideological direction of their outcomes.

For ideology, I use the well-established Segal and Spaeth U.S. Supreme Court database, which codes each Supreme Court outcome as either liberal or conservative in direction. These data do not cover the entire history of the Court but begin in 1952. Obviously, a number of cases lack an obvious ideological valence, and the database has been criticized for its coding of outcomes. However, it remains the best resource for research in this area, and the constitutional cases using originalism that I study tend to be more ideologically plain. In Table 9.1, I report the absolute number of justice-votes using each originalist source that were cast for a conservative or liberal outcome. The reliance on originalist sources does not appear to have a distinct ideological effect, as the difference between conservative votes and liberal votes is quite slight. The proportionally greatest difference is for the Declaration of Independence, which is used more in decisions producing liberal outcomes. Other sources tended to be associated with conservative results, but only to a very small degree.

I repeat this analysis for votes cast in dissent (see Table 9.2). The decision to join a majority opinion is inevitably more of a compromise for a justice. While I have noted the evidence suggests that nonwriting members of a majority coalition may influence the opinion, it is likely that much of the

Table 9.3.   The Federalist and ideology.

	Conservative votes	Liberal votes
No use of *The Federalist*	361	398
Use of *The Federalist*	578	512

control of opinion content rests with the author. Dissenting opinions have no real legal authority and may therefore be a more accurate depiction of the role of originalist sources. They may expose a lack of originalism in the majority opinion, and dissents require additional effort by a justice. The ideological differences for originalist sources here are more profound and somewhat surprising. The classical sources for original meaning (*The Federalist* and *Elliot's Debates*) are clearly more associated with liberal dissents than conservative ones. Originalism looks rather liberal by this scale.

These results may show the ideological neutrality or nonconservatism of originalism, but this may simply be due to its great manipulability. If a theory can be molded to suit any outcome, its usage is likely to appear neutral. And the Supreme Court justices may ignore sources that they find inconvenient. A better test would consider whether a justice ignored an originalist resource when other justices employed it. Table 9.3 reports the relative justice usages in this circumstance for *The Federalist*, which is by far the most common originalist source used by the Court. Here we see a slightly larger ideological disparity, with *The Federalist* appearing more conservative as a resource. When *The Federalist* was "in play," conservative outcome voters were about 10 percent more likely to cite it, while liberal voters were about 10 percent more likely not to cite it. This suggests some conservatism for the use of the source but not a great deal.

All these general statistics may be distorted though by the interests of particular justices of the Court. Suppose one particular justice has an affinity for citing *The Federalist* and is also quite conservative. The resulting pattern of citations could make *The Federalist* appear to be a conservative source, when this was not truly the case. It simply happened that a conservative justice liked invoking the source for conservative opinions. The much higher use of dictionaries in conservative dissents may simply be due to the affinity of Justice Thomas for use of this resource. The role of individual justices in ideological use of originalism is considered later in this chapter.

Existing Research on Ideology and Originalism

Despite the prominence of originalism as an interpretive theory, there has been a paucity of research on its operation. Robert Howard and Jeff Segal (2002) directly examined its use and whether it appeared to drive decisions of the Supreme Court or whether it was a cover for ideological decision-making. The "correct" originalist outcome cannot be objectively measured, so the authors examined the briefs submitted to the Court. They looked to see if the briefs for one or both sides emphasized the plain meaning of the text or referred to evidence of intent. The study was not limited to constitutional cases but also included statutory interpretation (with originalism associated with reliance on legislative intent). The study found that the ideology of the justices overwhelmed the nature of the legal arguments as an explanation of the decisions of a majority of the justices.

While providing some evidence, there are great limits to the implications of the research. Howard and Segal (2002) recognize that there may be systematic differences among litigants in their own commitment to present originalist arguments. More seriously, the combination of constitutional and statutory claims limits the findings. The justices reputed to be most committed to original meaning originalism are also opposed to use of legislative history in statutory cases. By combining the two in a single category, the authors may have confounded true results for constitutional cases. The study does not directly test for constitutional originalism.

Relying on briefs is also problematic. Contrary to the authors' suggestion, the briefs are not an overwhelming source of materials on which the Court relies. Although the lawyers are highly competent, the Court frequently ignores the briefs and relies on its own *sua sponte* investigation. Research reveals that the briefs submitted to the Court are not a good cue for the sources on which the Court relies. A study of precedent found many cases cited in the briefs for *both* sides that the Court opinion ignored, while it cited many cases that were found in neither brief (Cross 2008).

Benesh and Czarnezki (2009) studied decisions made by judges of the Seventh Circuit Court of Appeals, based on evidence of the judges' historic usage of particular interpretive theories, including originalism. Judges using originalism produced more conservative results. The most intriguing finding of the study was that conservative originalist judges produced more conservative results and liberal originalists produced more liberal out-comes, both with statistical significance. This was true even controlling for their career ideological votes. Originalism did not constrain; it apparently liberated judges to be even more ideological in this study. However, the study did not consider the use of originalism in the particular cases pro-ducing ideological results, just the judge's general pattern. It suggests that judges committed to originalism may be relatively more ideological in their decisions, but this may be due to other characteristics of the judges, rather than the use of originalism itself, as it didn't isolate the use of originalism in those decisions.

Peter Smith (2004) examined the use of originalism in federalism cases decided by the Court since 1970. He divided framing-era statements into nationalist claims of Federalists, Anti-Federalist claims, and more moderate nationalist positions taken by Federalists in response to Anti-Federalist ar-guments. His survey found the justices to be selective in their use of period evidence. The conservatives would rely on Anti-Federalist "hopes" for a weaker national government but ignore Anti-Federalist "fears" of a power-ful national government, while liberals took the opposite position (Smith 2004, 257). The conservative majority commonly disregarded the national-ist statements of the prevailing Federalists. Selective citation enabled both sides to justify their position with originalism. Smith (2004, 217) concluded that "judges seeking the original understanding are largely unconstrained in their ability to mold the historical record to serve instrumentalist goals."

Corley, Howard, and Nixon (2005) provide some additional evidence in their assessment of cases citing *The Federalist*. They found that citation to the source was most common when the Court faced a potential legitimacy challenge to its decision, such as in a decision involving an alteration of precedent or expansion of judicial power. The authors concluded that the source was used strategically to gain support for the opinion, but they did not directly measure for the potential ideological use of the source. Their findings are potentially consistent with perfectly sincere use of originalism.

Evidence on Ideology and Originalism

While the common claim of originalists regards the constraining effect of the doctrine, many argue that originalism is utterly unconstraining. This is an authentic problem and a much more severe challenge to the doctrine than the claim it is inherently conservative. If originalism is so malleable it can be used for any desired end, it is functionally dejustified as an interpretive standard. To have any value, such a standard must be controlling. Even if originalism were the *theoretically* best approach to constitutional interpretation, it still would be worthless as a practical matter if it could not be accurately operationalized. The *Heller* opinions, sometimes considered the apotheosis of originalism, may truly undermine the theory because of the ideological division of the justices, all of whom (save the separate views of Justice Breyer) relied on originalism.

Given the limited empirical evidence, the manipulability of originalism for ideological ends is typically based on anecdotal evidence. Commentators point to particular opinions where originalism seemed in furtherance of ideology. Many now claim that originalism is but a beard to hide whatever outcome the justice prefers. As noted in the previous chapter, this effect need not be a conscious one but may simply be the product of motivated reasoning when evaluating the originalist evidence. A study of federalism decisions found that it was "not uncommon for the majority and the dissent to rely on the same founding-era statement to support competing views of the original understanding" (Smith 2004, 254). This tendency would seem to seriously undermine claims that originalism was constraining.

Scalia's commitment to prodefendant rulings under the Sixth Amendment "lends an air of plausibility to his self-proclaimed originalism" (Howard & Segal 2002, 120). As a conservative, Justice Scalia is presumed to be for limiting constitutional criminal defendants' rights, and he in fact has done so in other contexts. But on issues involving jury trials and the confrontation clause, he has been a strong supporter of defendants based on his interpretation of original constitutional meaning. This has been said to validate his authentic commitment to originalism over ideology.

Anecdotal exceptions to a rule cannot disprove that rule, of course. Moreover, the constraining evidence of this particular set of decisions is unclear. In *Melendez-Diaz v. Massachusetts* (2009), Justice Scalia found that the government could not introduce affidavits about chemical analyses of illegal drugs without affording the defendant some opportunity to cross-examine. The opinion was grounded clearly in originalism (and precedents relying themselves on originalism). The case appears to demonstrate Justice Scalia's commitment to originalism over ideological outcomes. The results supposedly challenge the attitudinal model and evidence the constraint of originalism (Barkow 2006).

Justice Kennedy's dissent in this case also relied heavily on originalism. He noted that the Sixth Amendment was not phrased so broadly as interpreted by Scalia and was meant to be limited to witnesses such as eyewitnesses. He specifically noted that, at the time of the founding, the courts allowed affidavits of "copyists" who were not subject to cross-examination. The dispute over the meaning of the word *witness* saw material originalist evidence supporting both sides.

A review of the case (Chenoweth 2009, 258) suggested that Justice Scalia downplayed "contrary historical evidence" and that the decision exceeded "the reasonable limit of what constitutional principle can be inferred from the text and supported by the limited historical record available here to determine original meaning." The indeterminate record permitted originalism to support either side of the case. Justice Scalia's choice suggests that he might in fact be ideologically inclined to support criminal defendants on this issue. Even if he were not driven by a motive relating to ideology, the case doesn't truly demonstrate the constraint of originalism. Original public meaning originalism did not clearly compel his vote.

Occasional examples of counterintuitive results, even assuming their existence, though, do not demonstrate much about the constraining effect of originalism. Even the most conservative justices cast an occasional vote for apparently liberal ends in cases where originalism is not an issue (whether statutory decisions or constitutional ones without originalist sources). While we stereotype justices as conservative or liberal based on the broad pattern of their decisions, we have no direct evidence of their ideological preferences on particular controversies, and no justices are single-mindedly liberal or conservative in their votes.

Moreover, numerous counterexamples exist as to originalism's constraint. Chapter Seven contained numerous critiques of the failings of originalist justices when originalism was at stake, and many more exist. Smith (2004) demonstrated great bias in the justices' selectivity of Federalist or Anti-Federalist sources in interpretation. But just as anecdotes cannot prove originalism's constraining effect, neither can they disprove it.

The best evaluation of originalism and ideology requires a more systematic analysis. There are reasons to suspect that originalism is not constraining. The indeterminacy of the historical record and the highly indeterminate assessment of the level of abstraction to modern circumstances appear to grant a justice considerable discretion in applying originalism. However, it is possible that a sincere originalist could find materials that bind his or her discretion in deciding particular cases. The following section reports my research into this question.

Originalist Sources and Ideological Decisions

To assess the interaction of originalism and ideology, I simply examine the sources cited by the justices in support of their decisions and the nature of those decisions. Thus, I consider the votes of a particular justice who relies on originalist materials in a case and whether that justice reaches a conservative or liberal result. If the originalist theory were constraining, one would expect to see more liberal results from conservative justices when using originalism (and vice versa). If this pattern exists for some justices, but not all, that might reveal justices who use originalism sincerely while others may not.

Justices Scalia and Thomas are self-declared originalists who frequently invoke originalism in their opinions. Justices Stevens and, especially, Brennan have publicly criticized originalism, but they too commonly invoke originalism in their opinions. If the latter justices tend to reach liberal results, one might be tempted to ascribe their citations to insincere window dressing, a post hoc rationalization of decisions made on other grounds.

Suppose that Justices Stevens and Brennan were insincere in their use of originalism. That to a degree undermines the interpretive theory, as it demonstrates its ideological malleability. But if Justices Scalia and Thomas were sincere in their use of originalism, that fact would hold out hope that the correct use of the theory could possibly produce legitimate legal results, unbiased by politics. We would simply need to appoint committed sincere originalists to the Court. However, even if Justices Scalia and Thomas were sincere in their originalism, tendencies to motivated reasoning could mean that they too were unconstrained by the interpretive theory. Rose, Reagan, and Pollock (2010, 464) suggest that the conservative originalist justices "smuggle their own values into the Constitution by conveniently attributing them to the Framers."

The originalist defender may concede the existence of some insincerity in application but argue that other theories are even more manipulable than originalism. This seems very plausible for broad normative theories of constitutional interpretation but much less plausible for reliance on precedent. The problem is that insincerity cannot be readily detected, so the relative effect of interpretive methods cannot be compared. There is no objective standard for correct originalism, and, if there were, a justice who got it wrong may have simply sincerely erred in his or her interpretation and not have been insincere. Given the clear existence of motivated reasoning, such errors would naturally appear as ideological insincerity.

While one cannot directly test the internal beliefs and motivations of the justices, one can look at their decisions. If originalism is generally constraining, it should yield decisions that do not consistently conform to the preferences of the justices. This permits a simple test. When the justices rely on originalist sources, do they tend to reach results consistent with their ideological preferences, or are they frequently driven away from such results? Table 9.4 reports the results for each of the justices analyzed (again using the Segal and Spaeth database) for justices with at least thirty cases available. It reports the percentage of votes for the more liberal party for each justice in three sets of cases—those in which any justice cited one of the materials of originalism, those in which the particular justice cited one of the originalist sources, and the overall votes in all cases (including nonconstitutional questions where originalism was legally irrelevant). If originalism were constraining, one would expect to see a material difference between at least the second and third columns. There is relatively little evidence of much constraint from the reliance on originalist sources by comparison of liberalism in all cases (third column) with liberalism when a justice uses originalism (second column). For Justices Black and Marshall, votes using originalist sources were more conservative than in other cases, but those votes were still quite liberal. For Justice Breyer, originalism votes were distinctly more liberal. Other justices showed relatively small variations, in both directions. For no justice did originalism appear to cause ideology to dissipate. Moreover, these votes overlapped considerably in similar cases. Breyer's 82.8 percent liberal voting record in these cases with

Table 9.4. Ideological justice voting in cases using originalism.

Justice	Percentage liberal/ any originalism	Percentage liberal/ justice originalism	Percentage liberal/ overall
Black	67.9%	62.2%	81.7%
Blackmun	53.7	56.9	50.8
Brennan	74.4	72.1	83.5
Breyer	81.1	82.8	62.8
Burger	21.2	21.1	26.5
Douglas	82.9	95.7	88.7
Ginsburg	70.5	73.6	68.8
Harlan	36.1	31.0	37.2
Kennedy	36.6	41.0	35.3
Marshall	73.2	70.0	88.9
O'Connor	34.2	31.0	32.0
Powell	29.9	31.3	32.3
Rehnquist	25.0	21.5	18.5
Scalia	22.1	24.1	24.3
Souter	72.0	73.1	62.6
Stevens	65.1	66.9	63.9
Stewart	39.6	35.0	44.5
Thomas	21.4	22.1	17.8
Warren	79.7	81.5	79.2
White	41.1	37.7	44.4

originalist sources largely overlapped with Thomas's 22.1 percent liberal voting pattern.

Slight differences found for most of the justices are likely to be attributable to random variation. Justices Thomas and Rehnquist are slightly more liberal when using originalism but still extremely conservative. Justice Scalia is virtually identical in the ideological pattern of his voting. Differences for other recent justices are also relatively slight, with the greatest effect apparently being a tendency to push Justices Souter and Breyer toward more liberal results. Rather than a tendency to drive results, though, use of originalism may be strategically used only for their legitimization.

More evidence of constraint is seen for the Warren Court. Justices Black, Brennan, and Marshall produced more conservative results when using originalism (though Justice Douglas showed the opposite effect). Perhaps this may be due to somewhat less use of originalism in this period, limited to cases when the originalist evidence was clearer and less amenable to manipulation.

A difference between the first two columns would imply that the originalist sources might not be so manipulable but that the justices simply ignored them when inconvenient to their preferred result. Thus, if a liberal justice had a distinctly higher percentage in the first column, that fact would suggest that he or she was ignoring relevant originalism that would suggest a conservative outcome. This would reveal the purportedly biasing effect of pluralism, allowing justices to pick and choose the legal theories that suit their preferred outcomes.

If this were so, a greater and unavoidable commitment to originalism might produce greater constraint, as justices were forced to confront those sources. However, the differences between these columns tend to be quite small. The results suggest that originalism, at least as measured by use of originalist sources, has failed to constrain the justices, not because justices ignore it but instead because the originalist sources can be employed for either a liberal or a conservative result in the closely contested cases before the Court.

Consider the voting pattern of Justice Thomas, known as perhaps the leading originalist of the Court but also quite conservative. He is also particularly inclined to the use of early dictionaries to extract an original meaning from the constitutional text. In the cases where he joined an opinion using the originalist dictionaries I studied, he reached a conservative decision 91 percent of the time. In the only case in which another justice relied on one of the dictionaries, but he did not, he also reached a conservative outcome. This is a small sample, and the vast majority of decisions did not use a dictionary, but it does not provide evidence for originalism's constraint.

Even the departures from conservative or liberal ideology may not show originalism's constraint. Justices occasionally vote against their presumed ideological preferences in a variety of cases, including statutory interpretation decisions, that do not involve originalism's theorized constraint. The classic examples of purported originalist contrapreferential voting are those of Justice Scalia in the Sixth Amendment cases. Yet, as already noted, there was a strong, perhaps stronger, originalist case for the government's conservative position in these cases.

Scalia's originalism in these cases sometimes relied on the effect of changed circumstances and some generalization of purpose from the text, which are plainly ways to manipulate the originalist evidence. Perhaps strong confrontation clause and jury trial rights are Justice Scalia's extralegal preference. He has "occasionally shown a libertarian, pro-defendant streak" in his views (Bibas 2005, 184). In some other cases, Justice Scalia has reached a similar result, even though "originalism was not the driving force" (Bibas 2005, 201). Thus, it is not clear that originalism constrained even in these cases.

Because we do not know the justices' internal ideological preferences for particular case outcomes, we cannot be certain about the constraining effects of an interpretive method for given sets of cases. Perhaps *every* justice votes his or her preference in *every* case, and Justices Scalia and Thomas happen to prefer the liberal outcome about 20 percent of the time. Or it may be that Justices Scalia and Thomas always prefer the conservative outcome for every case, but about 20 percent of the time they are constrained by the legal materials to instead reach the liberal outcome.

In the former scenario of no legal constraint, neither originalism nor any other interpretive method truly has meaning. Assuming there is some legally constraining effect of interpretive methods, the results still can tell us about the effect of originalism. It appears that originalism may be about as constraining as any other method, in the second scenario. The ideological results in justices' opinions using originalism trace fairly closely the ideological results in opinions not using originalism.

Judge Douglas Ginsburg vigorously argues that originalism does limit the range of plausible outcomes, by restricting the acceptable bases of a decision (Ginsburg 2010). He argues that originalism is constraining because, if it were not, the justices "would fashion original-meaning arguments to bolster their position in every case and thereby preclude the charge that in some cases they are departing opportunistically from the original meaning of the Constitution" (Ginsburg 2010, 236). The fact that they do not do so shows that originalism constrains, in his argument. Of course, this theory is too simplistic in that there are many cases where both the majority and the dissent cite no originalism, and surely both are not departing opportunistically from the original meaning. The fact that they do not do so could be explained by plenty of other reasons, and it is noteworthy that devoted originalists commonly do not cite originalist sources.

Perhaps, in an extreme originalism that considers no other legal sources to ever be valid, the theory could offer more constraint. This imagined world is remote from that of the present and not generally adopted by even fervent originalists, who accept the authority of precedent at some level. But, in realistic practice, all the justices pick and choose when to use originalism, and none are faithful acolytes to the method. The evidence indicates that shifting to relatively more originalism does not appear to add constraint. Moreover, Ginsburg's theory runs afoul of cases like *Heller* or *Printz*, where originalism was paramount for both the majority and dissent, not a sign of any constraining effect. Finally, the necessity to choose some level of abstraction for the original language meaning introduces a great deal of opportunity for ideological discretion.

The dedicated originalist would argue that my study has not truly captured his or her originalism. They would concede that originalism could be manipulated in its different forms but claim that a justice sincerely committed to his or her particular theory, say original public meaning, would not do so. Perhaps this is theoretically possible, but the argument has no apparent real-world meaning. No justice ever has conclusively professed or displayed allegiance to original public meaning originalism. There is no reason to expect this to change. There is no incentive for presidents to appoint and Senates to confirm such justices. Even if they did, even such truly dedicated justices would still fall prey to inevitable motivated reasoning, the incomplete record, and the difficulty of generalizing to today's changed circumstances.

The fact that originalism does not constrain ideological voting need not be evidence of any bad faith of the justices; it may simply be the effect of their inevitable motivated reasoning. There are numerous cases in which one or more justices employed originalist sources in a dissenting opinion, and those sources were ignored by purported originalists writing for the majority. Other cases (notably *Heller*) saw originalism used by both sides. Perhaps this is due to the indeterminacy of the historical record or due to different choices of the level of generality to ascribe to the language or even due to different theories of originalism. In any event, the close association between justice ideology and results in cases using originalism makes the theory appear scarcely constraining.

One plausible hypothesis is that originalist sources are simply used to "decorate" opinions reached on other grounds. Because originalism has great appeal to the public generally and various legal constituencies, the justices may better legitimize and give credibility to their decisions by citing originalist sources. As originalism becomes more prominent to the public, the justices would have relatively greater impetus to add legitimizing originalist sources to their opinions. The predominant use of the iconic *Federalist*, as opposed to other originalist sources, would be consistent with this theory. Whatever legal constraint existed in these cases using originalism may have arisen not from originalism but from other sources such as precedent. In short, the data suggest that reliance on originalist sources is not a particularly constraining, so justices exercise their ideological preferences in cases using originalism as much as in other decisions. Perhaps an imaginary sincere originalist might be constrained, but there is no evidence that such a person has ever served on the Court or is likely to be appointed to the Court.

Epilogue

Originalism is a very appealing interpretive theory for the justices, a theory which they all intermittently invoke in support of their opinions. My analysis indicates, however, that this invocation is very selective and not particularly constraining on the decisions or opinions of the justices. The justices are able to manipulate (or ignore) originalist materials to produce the results they desire to reach on ideological or other grounds. Given the nature of the originalist record, this should not be too surprising. Originalist sources are highly incomplete and address circumstances far different from those confronting today's Court, not to mention the discretion associated with generalizing from the original meaning. Yet their citation adds a certain imprimatur to an opinion, legitimizing it for the public. Originalism does not generally explain decisions, but it is used to make them more appealing.

The study of the results of cases decided using the most prominent originalist sources suggests that the theory is not a meaningful one in the sense of determining case outcomes. The justices all appear to fit those originalist sources to the support of their preferred resolution of the case. Originalism is commonly manipulated. However, my results must come with some caveats. The fact that originalism does not appear to constrain Supreme Court outcomes does not mean that it is meaningless in the law.

Much of the significance of a Supreme Court decision lies in the specifics of the opinion. *Miranda* was significant not just because the defendant prevailed but because the Court laid out specific standards that had to be met for warnings given to criminal suspects. It was the opinion, not just the outcome, that mattered most. The use of originalist sources obviously changes the content of opinions somewhat because they contain the originalist reference. Perhaps the originalist sources have other effects on the opinion, such as limiting (or expanding) its scope. Although originalism is sometimes associated with judicial restraint, Sunstein (2005) suggests that it tends to yield unnecessarily expansive commands from the Court. This is a possible effect in opinions to be examined. Research has shown that originalism appears to be associated with judicial activism. Perhaps the true effect of originalism appears in the content of opinions, not the outcome.

My study is confined to Supreme Court decisions, which typically involve the most closely contested legal questions. Perhaps originalism doesn't drive the results at the Supreme Court but does directly influence the decisions of lower federal courts. Although most of the public and even legal academic commentary addresses the decisions of the Supreme Court, lower court decisions are extremely important; most legal issues do not reach the Supreme Court. If the use of originalism had an influence on these decisions, that fact would be quite significant and would be worthy of study.

While originalism may have an important legal effect unidentified in my study, the absence of any observable material effect on Supreme Court outcomes should at least shift the burden of proof. No longer should one assume that originalism has an important constraining effect on the judiciary. Those who argue for originalism should be called on to demonstrate its effect in practice, not just in theory. The dispute over the importance of the theory of originalism may be an interesting matter of jurisprudence, but the real-world importance lies in its application.

Ultimately, the ongoing dispute over originalism may truly lie in its perceived practical consequences. While the critics of originalism speak of analytical shortcomings of the theory, they may truly be motivated by a "parade of horribles" that supposedly would ensue if the Court were truly originalist.

Cass Sunstein (2005) has been open about this concern. He declares that authentic originalism would eliminate constitutional protection against sex discrimination (and much racial discrimination), eliminate the right to privacy, eliminate the requirement that states' actions comply with the Bill of Rights, and vastly limit federal regulation, among other adverse consequences.

Steve Calabresi (2007), one of the most prominent originalist scholars, has directly taken on Sunstein's list and disputed that many of his "horribles" would actually result from reliance on originalism. In some cases, he concedes the specific originalist argument made by Sunstein but argues that the same outcome should result from a correct originalist approach to other constitutional provisions. For example, he would use originalism to expand application of the privileges and immunities clause to produce the preferred results. Of course, this is a Calabresian originalism, which the Supreme Court has historically rejected. Assuming he is correct in his originalist interpretation, that truth offers little if the Court won't adopt his position, and there is little basis for assurance that it would.

The more interesting aspect of Calabresi's response, though, is where he is in fuller agreement with Sunstein's interpretation. He thinks that authentic originalism would truly eliminate constitutional protection for reproductive rights, restore school prayer, and eliminate the exclusionary rule, but he does not seem to consider these particularly bad outcomes. While originalism would not produce the true horribles, it would yield some changes in judicial outcomes.

It appears that Calabresi, a conservative, believes that originalism would yield those conservative policies that he accepts but not more extreme conservative policies that are incompatible with his own preferences. Manipulation of originalism may not be limited to the justices of the Supreme Court. Friedman (2009b, 311) thus suggests that "originalism somehow magically invalidated conservatives wanted to eliminate, but not those they felt the need to keep." Anyone can force originalism into a set of policies appealing to him or her. Fortunately, this fact reduces the likelihood that originalism will produce a "horrible."

Academic originalists appear to fall prey to the same factors that influence the justices. Prominent originalist Randy Barnett believes the theory is highly libertarian, but prominent originalist Steve Calabresi disagrees. It appears that both find support for their personal policy preferences in the originalist materials, a fact that does not provide much evidence that the theory offers a great deal of constraint. But this result is probably inevitable. The originalist record is obscure, circumstances and legal controversies have changed greatly since the time of the founding, and the proper degree of generalization of original language is highly indeterminate. It should not be surprising that the theory has little controlling legal power and that advocates see in those materials what they want to see.

This research cannot show that originalism never controls the results of any Supreme Court decision. Perhaps an occasional case has clear and binding originalist evidence. Maybe the justices do not have strong ideological preferences in a particular case. But the disparate outcomes, based on ideology, make clear that such cases are quite rare and that originalism is no more constraining than alternative theories of interpretation. Of course, the opposite is true as well—originalism appears no less constraining than other theories.

It appears that originalism has relatively little real effect as a legal theory driving Court outcomes, but that does not necessarily counsel against its use. A powerful and independent judiciary is important to the success of the United States. Insofar as reliance on originalism in opinions strengthens the acceptability of the judiciary's opinions, it has value. Political scientists have suggested that reliance on originalist sources is largely for the purpose of legitimating the Court's decisions (Corley, Howard & Nixon 2005), but this is not a bad thing. Respect for the decisions of the Supreme Court has value. If use of originalism enhances the respect for such decisions (because of the public appeal of the approach), then such use offers value. And the obvious malleability of originalist interpretation should dispel Sunstein's concerns about reliance on the theory producing highly undesirable results.

A great deal has been written about originalism. This writing is overwhelmingly theoretical, and empirical analysis of the theory's application is largely absent. To the extent the application is analyzed, it is only in a case-specific anecdotal fashion. Of course, theory has its own merits, and it is perfectly legitimate for theorists to argue for an approach independent of practice. It is fair for commentators to criticize opinions as wrong in terms of originalism (though one may suspect that those commentator opinions may be shaped by their own ideological preferences and motivated reasoning). But arguing that the Supreme Court *should* rely on a particular version of originalism as a consistent legal determinant appears to be a futile endeavor. There is no reason to think the Court would ever do so.

Dred Scott was presented as a highly originalist opinion. Most originalists now argue that the Court got the originalism wrong in this opinion. Perhaps they are correct. But the salient point is that the Court used its version of originalism and got it wrong. If the Court can't get the theory right (whether due to insincerity or not), the broad theory offers little pragmatic promise. The version of originalism used in *Dred Scott* was quite arguably not that of contemporary original public meaning originalism. But this does not respond to the pragmatic question, which is, "How likely is it that justices will sincerely conform to this or any other originalist theory?" Perhaps the justices of that era might be excused because the original public meaning theory had not been clearly explicated. But there is no evidence that modern justices do any better.

My evidence does not demonstrate that originalism cannot possibly succeed as a ruling theory of interpretation. It might be possible that if some future hypothetical justices coalesced around one particular theory of originalism and were authentically devoted to it above all else, they might overcome their ideological biases. However, given the underdeterminate historic record and unavoidable implicit biases of motivated reasoning, this event seems quite unlikely, as the empirical results of this book confirm. Moreover, there is no obvious reason why presidents and Senates would choose to appoint and confirm such individuals (if they exist) committed to a theory, given the ideological inclinations of the selecting politicians.

This book is meant to provide at least a first step toward the empirical study of originalism in practice. However compelling the theoretical case for some form of originalism might be, the theory still offers relatively little if it cannot be formally realized in practice. Without such evidence, all that has been written about the theory seems much less important. We simply cannot just assume that our optimal approach to the use of originalism will be sincerely and accurately applied by the justices. While such an academic may criticize opinions that do not conform to this approach, such criticism is unlikely to change a justice's decisions. Advocates of originalism should move to demonstrate the practical value of their theory. Perhaps the theory could be modified so as to give it more practical effect. Or they should accept that originalism's function is not one of being a constraining legal theory but merely one of legitimizing decisions reached on other grounds. In any event, it is time to shift at least a portion of the debate from abstract theory to the study of practice.

Cases Cited

Alden v. Maine. 1999. 527 U.S. 706.

Atascadero State Hospital v. Scanlon. 1985. 473 U.S. 234.

Benton v. Maryland. 1969. 395 U.S. 784.

Boumediene v. Bush. 2008. 553 U.S. 723.

Bowsher v. Synar. 1986. 478 U.S. 714.

Brown v. Board of Education. 1954. 347 U.S. 483.

Buckley v. Valeo. 1976. 424 U.S. 1.

Burnham v. Superior Court. 1990. 495 U.S. 604.

Bush v. Gore. 2000. 531 U.S. 98.

Calder v. Bull. 1798. 3 U.S. (3 Dall.) 386.

California v. Acevedo. 1991. 500 U.S. 565.

Camps Newfound/Owatonna, Inc. v. Town of Harrison. 1997. 520 U.S. 564.

Carter v. Carter Coal Co. 1936. 298 U.S. 238.

Citizens United v. Federal Election Commission. 2010. 558 U.S. 50.

Cohens v. Virginia, 1821. 19 U.S. 264.

Craig v. Boren. 1976. 429 U.S. 190.

Dames & Moore v. Regan. 1981. 453 U.S. 654.

District of Columbia v. Heller. 2008. 554 U.S. 570.

Dred Scott v. Sanford. 1857. 60 U.S. 393.

Duncan v. Louisiana. 1968. 391 U.S. 145.

Engel v. Vitale. 1962. 370 U.S. 421.

Ex Parte Bain. 1887. 121 U.S. 1.

Ex Parte Grossman. 1925. 267 U.S. 87.

Ex Parte Wells. 1856. 59 U.S. (18 How.) 307.

Georgia v. Randolph. 2006. 547 U.S. 103.

Gompers v. United States. 1914. 233 U.S. 604.

Granholm v. Heald. 2005. 544 U.S. 460.

Griswold v. Connecticut. 1965. 381 U.S. 479.

Hamdi v. Rumsfeld. 2004. 542 U.S. 507.

Hepburn v. Griswold. 1870. 75 U.S. 603.

Home Bldg. & Loan Ass'n v. Blaisdell. 1934. 290 U.S. 398.

Hunter v. Martin's Lessee. 1816. 14 US 304.

INS v. Chadha. 1983. 462 U.S. 919.

Kyllo v. United States. 2001. 533 U.S. 27.

Lee v. Weisman. 1992. 505 U.S. 577.

The Legal Tender Cases. 1870. 79 U.S. 457.

The License Cases. 1848. 46 U.S. (5 Howard) 504.

Lochner v. New York. 1905. 198 U.S. 45.

Lucas v. South Carolina Coastal Council. 1992. 505 U.S. 1003.

Marbury v. Madison. 1803. 5 U.S. (1 Cranch) 137.

Marsh v. Chambers. 1983. 463 U.S. 783.

McCulloch v. Maryland. 1819. 17 U.S. (4 Wheat.) 316.

McIntyre v. Ohio Elections Commission. 1995. 514 U.S. 334.

McPherson v. Blacker. 1892. 146 U.S. 1.

Melendez-Dias v. Massachusetts. 2009. 129 S.Ct. 2527.

Miranda v. Arizona. 1966. 384 U.S. 436.

Missouri v. Holland. 1920. 252 U.S. 416.

Morrison v. Olson. 1988. 487 U.S. 654.

Myers v. United States. 1926. 272 U.S. 52.

Olmstead v. United States. 1937. 486 U.S. 1009.

Ogden v. Saunders. 1827. 25 U.S. (12 Wheat.) 213.

Payne v. Tennessee. 1991. 501 U.S. 808.

Pennsylvania Coal Company v. Mahon. 1922. 260 U.S. 393.

Plaut v. Spendthrift Farm. 1995. 514 U.S. 211.

Pollock v. Farmers' Loan & Trust Co. 1895. 157 U.S. 429.

Prigg v. Pennsylvania. 1842. 41 U.S. (16 Pet.) 539.

Printz v. United States. 1997. 521 U.S. 898.

Roe v. Wade. 1973. 401 U.S. 113.

Roper v. Simmons. 2005. 543 U.S. 551.

School District of Abington v. Schempp. 1963. 374 U.S. 203.

Scott v. Harris. 2007. 550 U.S. 372.

Seminole Tribe of Florida v. Florida. 1996. 517 U.S. 44.

South Carolina v. United States. 1905. 199 U.S. 437.

Sparf v. United States. 1895. 156 U.S. 51.

Stanford v. Kentucky, 1989. 492 U.S. 361.

Stuart v. Laird. 1803. 5 U.S. (1 Cranch) 299.

Tennessee v. Garner. 1985. 471 U.S. 1.

Thornburgh v. Am. College of Obstetricians and Gynecologists. 1986. 476 U.S. 747.

Towne v. Eisner, 1918. 254 U.S. 418.

United States v. Curtiss-Wright Export Corporation. 1936. 299 U.S. 304.

United States v. Flores. 1933. 289 U.S. 137.

United States v. Lopez. 1995. 514 U.S. 549.
U.S. Term Limits, Inc. v. Thornton. 1995. 514 U.S. 779.
Van Orden v. Perry. 2005. 545 U.S. 677.
Velasquez v. Frapwell. 1998. 160 F.3d 389.
Weems v. United States. 1910. 217 U.S. 349.
Wesberry v. Sanders. 1964. 376 U.S. 1.
West Coast Hotel v. Parrish. 1937. 300 U.S. 379.
West Lynn Creamery v. Healy. 1994. 512 U.S. 186.
Youngstown Sheet & Tube Co. v. Sawyer. 1952. 343 U.S. 579.
Zelman v. Simmons-Harris. 2002. 536 U.S. 639.

References

Ackerman, Bruce. 2007. The Living Constitution. *Harvard Law Review*. 120: 1737–1812.

Aleinikoff, T. Alexander. 1988. Updating Statutory Interpretation. *Michigan Law Review*. 87: 20–66.

Alexander, Roberta Sue. 1986. A Historical Perspective on the Constitution. *University of Dayton Law Review*. 12: 321–330.

Amar, Akhil Reed. 2000. Foreword: The Document and the Doctrine. *Harvard Law Review*. 114: 26–134.

———. 1999. Intratextualism. *Harvard Law Review*. 112: 747–827.

———. 1987. Of Sovereignty and Federalism. *Yale Law Journal*. 96: 1425–1520.

Amar, Vikram David. 2009. Business and Constitutional Originalism in the Roberts Court. *Santa Clara Law Review*. 49: 979–998.

Anderson, Robert IV. 2009. Measuring Meta-Doctrine: An Empirical Assessment of Judicial Minimalism in the Supreme Court. *Harvard Journal of Law & Public Policy*. 32: 1045–1092.

Aprill, Ellen P. 1998. The Law of the Word: Dictionary Shopping in the Supreme Court. *Arizona State Law Journal*. 30: 275–336.

Arkes, Hadley. 1990. *Beyond the Constitution*. Princeton, NJ: Princeton University Press.

Austen-Smith, David, and William H. Riker. 1987. Asymmetric Information and the Coherence of Legislation. *American Political Science Review*. 81: 897–918.

Baade, Hans. 1991. "Original Intent" in Historical Perspective: Some Critical Glosses. *Texas Law Review*. 69: 1001–1008.

Baird, Vanessa A. 2007. *Answering the Call of the Court: How Justices and Litigants Set the Supreme Court Agenda*. Charlottesville: University of Virginia Press.

Balkin, Jack M. 2009. Framework Originalism and the Living Constitution. *Northwestern Law Review*. 103: 549–614.

———. 2007. Original Meaning and Constitutional Redemption. *Constitutional Commentary*, 20: 427–-532.

Ball, Howard and Phillip J. Cooper. 1992. *Of Power and Right.* New York: Oxford University Press.

Barber, Sotirios A., and James E. Fleming. 2007. *Constitutional Interpretation: The Basic Questions.* New York: Oxford University Press.

Barkow, Rachel E. 2006. Originalists, Politics, and Criminal Law on the Rehnquist Court. *George Washington Law Review.* 74: 1043–1077.

Barnett, Randy E. 2009. Original Ideas on Originalism: The Misconceived Assumption about Constitutional Assumptions. *Northwestern University Law Review* 615: 103.

———. 2006. Scalia's Infidelity: A Critique of Faint-Hearted Originalism. *University of Cincinnati Law Review.* 75: 7–24.

———. 2005. Trumping Precedent with Original Meaning: Not as Radical as It Sounds. *Constitutional Commentary.* 22: 257–270.

———. 2004. *Restoring the Lost Constitution.* Princeton, NJ: Princeton University Press.

———. 2001. The Original Meaning of the Commerce Clause. *University of Chicago Law Review.* 68: 101–148.

———. 1999. Originalism for Nonoriginalists. *Loyola Law Review.* 45: 611–654.

Bartels, Brandon L. 2009. The Constraining Capacity of Legal Doctrine on the U.S. Supreme Court. *American Political Science Review.* 103: 474–495.

Bassham, Gregory. 1992. *Original Intent and the Constitution: A Philosophical Study.* Lanham, MD: Rowman & Littlefield Publishers.

Baum, Lawrence. 2010. Motivation and Judicial Behavior: Expanding the Scope of Inquiry. In *The Psychology of Judicial Decisionmaking*, David Klein and Gregory Mitchell, eds. New York: Oxford University Press.

———. 2006. *Judges and Their Audiences.* Princeton, NJ: Princeton University Press.

Beatty, David M. 2004. *The Ultimate Rule of Law.* New York: Oxford University Press.

Becker, Carl L. 1955. What Are Historical Facts? *Western Political Quarterly.* 8: 327–340.

Benesh, Sara C., and Jason J. Czarnezki. 2009. The Ideology of Legal Interpretation. *Washington University Journal of Law and Policy.* 29: 113–131.

Berger, Raoul. 1990. Original Intent and Boris Bittker. *Indiana Law Journal.* 66: 723–756.

———. 1983. Insulation of Judicial Usurpation: A Comment on Lawrence Sager's "Court-Stripping" Polemic. *Ohio State Law Journal.* 44: 611–648.

———. 1977. *Government by Judiciary: The Transformation of the Fourteenth Amendment.* Indianapolis, IN: Liberty Fund.

Berman, Mitchell N. 2009. Originalism Is Bunk. *New York University Law Review.* 84: 1–96.

Bernstein, Richard. 1987. Charting the Bicentennial. *Columbia Law Review.* 87: 1565–1624.

Bevier, Lillian R. 1996. The Integrity and Impersonality of Originalism. *Harvard Journal of Law & Public Policy.* 19: 283–292.

Bhargava, Michael. 2006. The First Congress Canon and the Supreme Court's Use of History. *California Law Review.* 94: 1745–1790.

Bibas, Sephanos. 2005. Originalism and Formalism in Criminal Procedure: The Triumph of Justice Scalia, the Unlikely Friend of Criminal Defendants? *Georgetown Law Journal.* 94: 183–204.

Bickel, Alexander M. 1962. *The Least Dangerous Branch.* Binghamton, NY: Vail-Ballou Press.

Bittker, Boris. 1989. The Bicentennial of the Jurisprudence of Original Intent: The Recent Past. *California Law Review.* 77: 235–282.

Boiney, Lindsley G., Jane Kennedy, and Pete Nye. 1997. Instrumental Bias in Motivated Reasoning: More when More Is Needed. *Organizational Behavior & Human Decision Processes.* 71: 1–24.

Bonneau, Chris W., Thomas H. Hammond, Forrest Maltzman, and Paul J. Wahlbeck. 2007. Agenda Control, the Median Justice, and the Majority Opinion on the U.S. Supreme Court. *American Journal of Political Science.* 51: 890–905.

Book Note. 2008. Justice Thomas's Inconsistent Originalism. *Harvard Law Review.* 121: 1431–1437.

Bork, Robert H. 1990. *The Tempting of America: The Political Seduction of the Law.* New York: Free Press.

———. 1986. The Constitution, Original Intent, and Economic Rights. *San Diego Law Review.* 23: 823–832.

Braman, Eileen. 2010. Searching for Constraint in Legal Decision Making. In *The Psychology of Judicial Decisionmaking*, David Klein and Gregory Mitchell, eds. New York: Oxford University Press.

Braman, Eileen, and Thomas E. Nelson. 2007. Mechanism of Motivated Reasoning? Analogical Perception in Discrimination Disputes. *American Journal of Political Science.* 51:940–956.

Brennan, William J. 1986. Remarks of Justice William J. Brennan, Jr. at "The Great Debate." Washington, DC: Federalist Society. (Steven G. Calabresi ed.) *Originalism: A Quarter Century of Debate.* Washington, DC: Regnery Publishing.

Brest, Paul. 1980. The Misconceived Quest for the Original Understanding. *Boston University Law Review.* 60: 204–238.

Breyer, Stephen 2006. *Active Liberty.* New York: Alfred A. Knopf.

Brisbin, Richard A. Jr. 1996. Slaying the Dragon: Segal, Spaeth and the Function of Law in Supreme Court Decision Making. *American Journal of Political Science.* 40: 1004–1017.

Brown, Rebecca L. 1993. Tradition and Insight. *Yale Law Journal.* 103: 177–222.

Brownstein, Alan. 2009. The Reasons Why Originalism Provides a Weak Foundation for Interpreting Constitutional Provisions Relating to Religion. *Cardozo Law Review de novo.* 44: 196–217.

Calabresi, Steven G. 2008. Text vs. Precedent in Constitutional Law. *Harvard Journal of Law & Public Policy.* 31: 947–960.

———. 2007. A Critical Introduction to the Originalism Debate. In *Originalism: A Quarter Century of Debate,* Steven G. Calabresi ed. Washington, DC: Regnery Publishing.

———. 2005. The Originalist and Normative Case against Judicial Activism: A Reply to Professor Randy Barnett. *Michigan Law Review.* 103: 1081–1098.

Calabresi, Steven G., and Livia Fine. 2009. Two Cheers for Professor Balkin's Originalism. *Northwestern Law Review.* 103: 663–702.

Calabresi, Steven G., and Gary Lawson. 2007. The Unitary Executive, Jurisdiction Stripping, and the Hamdan Opinions: A Textualist Response to Justice Scalia. *Columbia Law Review.* 107: 1002–1048.

Calabresi, Steven G., and Saikrishna B. Prakash. 1994. The President's Power to Execute the Laws. *Yale Law Journal.* 104: 541–666.

Canja, Jeffrey H. 2000. *Alden v. Maine* and State Sovereign Immunity: Original Intent or an Intent "Congenial to the Court's Desires"? *Cleveland State Law Review.* 48: 503–544. Carr, Edward Hallett. 1961. *What Is History?* New York: Random House.

Chemerinsky, Erwin. 2000. The Jurisprudence of Justice Scalia: A Critical Appraisal. *University of Hawaii Law Review.* 22: 385–402.

———. 1987. A Paradox without a Principle: A Comment on the Burger Court's Jurisprudence in Separation of Powers Cases. *Southern California Law Review.* 60: 1083–1114.

Chenoweth, Mark. 2009. Using its Sixth Sense: The Roberts Court Revamps the Rights of the Accused. *Cato Supreme Court Review.* 2009: 223–269.

Chernow, Ron. 2010 (June 26). The Feuding Fathers. *Wall Street Journal* W1.

Claeys, Eric R. 2004. Progressive Political Theory and Separation of Powers on the Burger and Rehnquist Courts. *Constitutional Commentary.* 21: 405–444.

Clinton, Robert N. 1987. Original Understanding, Legal Realism, and the Interpretation of "This Constitution." *Iowa Law Review.* 72: 1177–1280.

Colby, Thomas B., and Peter J. Smith. 2009. Living Originalism. *Duke Law Journal.* 59: 239–308.

Collier, Christopher. 1988. The Historians versus the Lawyers: James Madison, James Hutson and the Doctrine of Original Intent. *The Pennsylvania Magazine of History and Biography.* 112: 137–144.

Cooper, Charles J. 1994. Harry Jaffa's Bad Originalism. *Public Interest Law Review.* 1994: 189–215.

Corley, Pamela C., Robert M. Howard, and David C. Nixon. 2005. The Supreme Court and Opinion Content: The Use of the Federalist Papers. *Political Research Quarterly*. 58: 329–340.

Cornell, Saul. 2009. Heller, New Originalism, and Law Office History: "Meet the New Boss, Same as the Old Boss." *UCLA Law Review*. 56: 1095–1126.

Cosgrove, Charles H. 1998. The Declaration of Independence in Constitutional Interpretation: A Selective History and Analysis. *University of Richmond Law Review*. 32: 107–164.

Crane, Elaine. 1964. Publius in the Provinces: Where Was *The Federalist* Reprinted Outside New York City. *William & Mary Quarterly*. 21: 589–592.

Cross, Frank B. 2008. Chief Justice Roberts and Precedent: A Preliminary Study. *North Carolina Law Review*. 86: 1251–1278.

———. 1997. Political Science and the New Legal Realism: A Case of Unfortunate Interdisciplinary Ignorance. *Northwestern University Law Review*. 92: 251–326.

Cross, Frank B., James F. Spriggs II, Timothy R. Johnson, and Paul J. Wahlbeck. 2010. Citations in the U.S. Supreme Court: An Empirical Study of Their Use and Significance. *Illinois Law Review*. 2010: 489–575.

Cunningham, Sean B. 1997. Is Originalism "Political"? *Texas Review of Law & Politics*. 1: 149–189.

Czarkezki, Jason J., William K. Ford, and Lori A. Ringhand. 2007. An Empirical Analysis of the Confirmation Hearings of the Justices of the Rehnquist Natural Court. *Constitutional Commentary*. 24: 127–198.

Daly, John L. 1954. *The Use of History in the Decisions of the Supreme Court: 1900–1930*. Washington, DC: Catholic University of America Press.

Dam, Kenneth W. 1981. The Legal Tender Cases. *The Supreme Court Review*. 1981: 367–412.

Davies, Thomas Y. 2002. The Fictional Character of Law-and-Order Originalism: A Case Study of the Distortions and Evasions of Framing-Era Arrest Doctrine in *Atwater v. Lago Vista*. *Wake Forest Law Review*. 37: 239–438.

Detweiler, Philip F. 1962. The Changing Reputation of the Declaration of Independence: The First Fifty Years. *William & Mary Quarterly*. 19: 557–573.

Derfner, Armand. 2005. Why Do We Let Judges Say Anything about History when We Know They'll Get It Wrong. *Public Historian*. 27: 9–18.

Dewey, Donald O. 1971. James Madison Helps Clio Interpret the Constitution. *American Journal of Legal History*. 15: 38–55.

Durschlag, Melvyn R. 2005. The Supreme Court and the Federalist Papers. *William & Mary Bill of Rights Journal*. 14: 243–350.

Duxbury, Neil. 1995. *Patterns of American Jurisprudence*. New York: Oxford University Press.

Dworkin, Ronald. 1981. The Forum of Principle. *New York University Law Review*. 56: 469–519.

Eastman, John C. 2006. Politics and the Court: Did the Supreme Court Really Move Left Because of Embarrassment over *Bush v. Gore? Georgetown Law Journal.* 94: 1475–1492.

———. 1999. Taking Justice Thomas Seriously. *Green Bag.* 2: 425–433.

Edelman, Paul H., David E. Klein, and Stefanie A. Lindquist. 2008. Measuring Deviations from Expected Voting Patterns on Collegial Courts. *Journal of Empirical Legal Studies.* 5: 819–852.

Eisgruber, Christopher L. 2007. *The Next Justice: Repairing the Supreme Court Appointments Process.* Princeton, NJ: Princeton University Press.

———. 2001. *Constitutional Self-Government.* Cambridge, MA: Harvard University Press.

Epstein, Lee, and Jack Knight. 1998. *The Choices Justices Make.* Washington, DC: Congressional Quarterly Press.

Epstein, Lee, and Joseph F. Kobylka. 1992. *The Supreme Court and Legal Change: Abortion and the Death Penalty.* Chapel Hill: University of North Carolina Press.

Epstein, Lee, Jeffrey A. Segal, Harold J. Spaeth, and Thomas G. Walker. 2003. *The Supreme Court Compendium,* 3rd ed. Washington, DC: Congressional Quarterly Press.

Fallon, Richard H. Jr. 2008. Constitutional Precedent Viewed through the Lens of Hartian Positivist Jurisprudence. *North Carolina Law Review.* 86: 1107–1164.

———. 2001. *Implementing the Constitution.* Cambridge, MA: Harvard University Press.

———. 1997. Foreword: Implementing the Constitution. *Harvard Law Review.* 111: 54–152.

———. 1996. The Political Function of Originalist Ambiguity. *Harvard Journal of Law and Public Policy.* 19: 487–494.

Farber, Daniel A. 2000. Disarmed by Time: The Second Amendment and the Failure of Originalism. *Chicago-Kent Law Review.* 76: 167–194.

———. 1989. The Originalism Debate: A Guide for the Perplexed. *Ohio State Law Journal.* 49: 1085–1106.

Farber, Daniel A., and Suzanna Sherry. 2010. Building a Better Judiciary. In *The Psychology of Judicial Decisionmaking,* David Klein and Gregory Mitchell, eds. New York: Oxford University Press.

———. 2002. *Desperately Seeking Certainty: The Misguided Quest for Constitutional Foundations.* Chicago: University of Chicago Press.

Farrand, M. 1986. *Records of the Federal Convention of 1787.* _(Originally published in 1911.)

Fasolt, Constantin 2004. *The Limits of History.* Chicago: University of Chicago Press.

Festa, Matthew J. 2008. Applying a Usable Past: The Use of History in Law. *Seton Hall Law Review.* 38: 479–554.

———. 2007. Dueling Federalists: Supreme Court Decisions with Multiple Opinions Citing *The Federalist*, 1986–2007. *Seattle University Law Review*. 31: 75–106.

Finnis, John. 1994. "Shameless Acts" in Colorado: Abuse of Scholarship in Constitutional Cases. *Academic Questions*. 7: 10–41.

Fischman, Joshua B., and David S. Law. 2009. What Is Judicial Ideology, and How Should We Measure It? *Washington University Journal of Law & Policy*. 29: 133–214.

Flaherty, Martin S. 1995. History "Lite" in Modern American Constitutionalism. *Columbia Law Review*. 95: 523–590.

Frank, Jerome. 1930. *Law and the Modern Mind*. New York: Brentanos.

Friedman, Barry. 2009a. Reconstructing Reconstruction: Some Problems for Originalists (and Everyone Else Too). *University of Pennsylvania Journal of Constitutional Law*. 11: 1201–1238.

Friedman, Barry. 2009. *The Will of the People*. New York: Farrar, Strauss and Giroux.

Friedman, Barry, and Scott B. Smith. 1998. The Sedimentary Constitution. *University of Pennsylvania Law Review*. 147: 1–90.

Friedman, Lawrence M. 1998. Law Reviews and Legal Scholarship: Some Comments. *Denver Law Review*. 75: 661–668.

Gerber, Scott. 1995. *To Secure These Rights: The Declaration of Independence and Constitutional Interpretation*. New York: New York University Press.

Ghoshray, Saby. 2006. To Understand Foreign Court Citation: Dissecting Originalism, Dynamism, Romanticism, and Consequentialism. *Albany Law Review*. 69: 709–744.

Gibson, James L. 1978. Judges' Role Orientations, Attitudes, and Decisions: An Interactive Model. *American Political Science Review*. 72: 911–924.

Gillman, Howard. 1997. The Collapse of Constitutional Originalism and the Rise of the Notion of the "Living Constitution" in the Course of American State-Building. *Studies in American Political Development*. 11: 191–247.

Ginsburg, Douglas H. 2010. Originalism and Economic Analysis: Two Case Studies of Consistency and Coherence in Supreme Court Decision Making. *Harvard Journal of Law & Public Policy*. 33: 271–238.

Ginsburg, Ruth Bader. 2004. Looking beyond Our Borders: The Value of a Comparative Perspective in Constitutional Adjudication. *Yale Law & Policy Review*. 22: 329–337.

———. 2001. Foreward. *Supreme Court Decisions and Women's Rights: Milestones in Equality*, Clare Cushman, ed. Washington, DC: Congressional Quarterly Press.

Goldford, Dennis J. 2005. *The American Constitution and the Debate over Originalism*. New York: Cambridge University Press.

Graber, Mark A. 2003. Clarence Thomas and the Perils of Amateur History. In *Rehnquist Justice: Understanding the Court Dynamic*, Earl M. Maltz, ed. Lawrence: University Press of Kansas.

Greenberg, Mark, and Harry Litman. 1998. The Meaning of Original Meaning. *Georgetown Law Journal*. 86: 569–620.

Greene, Jamal. 2009a. Heller High Water? The Future of Originalism. *Harvard Law & Policy Review*. 3: 325–346.

Greene, Jamal. 2009b. On the Origins of Originalism. *Texas Law Review*. 88: 1–90.

———. 2009c. Selling Originalism. *Georgetown Law Journal*. 97: 657–719.

Greenhouse, Linda. 2008. Three Defining Opinions. *New York Times*, July 13.

Griffin, Stephen M. 2008. Rebooting Originalism. *University of Illinois Law Review*. 2008: 1185–1222.

Guthrie, Chris, Jeffrey J. Rachlinski, and Andrew J. Wistrich. 2007. Blinking on the Bench: How Judges Decide Cases. *Cornell Law Review*. 93: 1–44.

Hall, Matthew E. K. 2010. Bringing Down Brown: Super Precedents, Myths of Rediscovery, and the Retroactive Canonization of *Brown v. Board of Education*. *Journal of Law & Policy*. 18: 655–700.

Hamburger, Philip A. 1989. The Constitution's Accommodation of Social Change. *Michigan Law Review*. 88: 239–327.

Hansford, Thomas G., and James F. Spriggs II. 2006. *The Politics of Precedent on the U.S. Supreme Court*. Princeton, NJ: Princeton University Press.

Harvey, Anna, and Michael J. Woodruff. 2009. Confirmation Bias in the United States Supreme Court Judicial Database. *Paper presented at the annual meeting of the Midwest Political Science Association 67th Annual National Conference*.

Himmelfarb, Dan. 1990. The Constitutional Relevance of the Second Sentence of the Declaration of Independence. *Yale Law Journal*. 100: 169–188.

Holzer, Henry Mark. 2007. *The Supreme Court Opinions of Clarence Thomas, 1991–2006: A Conservative's Perspective*. Jefferson, NC: McFarland & Company.

Howard, Robert M., and Jeffrey A. Segal. 2002. An Original Look at Originalism. *Law & Society Review*. 36: 113–137.

Howe, Mark DeWolfe. 1965. *The Garden and the Wilderness: Religion and Government in American Constitutional History*. Chicago: University of Chicago Press.

Hume, Robert J. 2006. The Use of Rhetorical Sources by the U.S. Supreme Court. *Law & Society Review*. 40: 817–843.

Hurewitz, Daniel. 2004. Foundation for Change: *Lawrence v. Texas* and the Impact of the Historian's Brief. *Health and Human Rights*. 7: 205–216.

Hutson, James H. 1986. The Creation of the Constitution: The Integrity of the Documentary Record. *Texas Law Review*. 65: 1–40.

Irwin, John F., and Daniel L. Real. 2010. Unconscious Influences on Judicial Decision-Making: The Illusion of Objectivity. *McGeorge Law Review*. 42: 1–11.

Jaffa, Harry V. 1994. *Original Intent and the Framers of the Constitution*. Washington, DC: Regnery Gateway.

Jain, Sahiendra Pratap, and Durairaj Maheswaran. 2000. Motivated Reasoning: A Depth-of- Processing Perspective. *Journal of Consumer Research*. 26: 358–371.

Jenkins, Keith. 1991. *Re-Thinking History*. New York: Routledge.

Kahan, Dan M., Donald Braman, Paul Slovic, John Gastil, and Geoff Cohen. 2009. Cultural Cognition of the Risks and Benefits of Nanotechnology. *Nature Nanotechnology* 4: 87–90.

Kahan, Dan M., David A. Hoffman, and Donald Braman. 2009. Whose Eyes Are You Going to Believe? *Scott v. Harris* and the Perils of Cognitive Illiberalism. *Harvard Law Review*. 122: 837–906.

Kahan, Dan M., David A. Hoffman, Donald Braman, Danieli Evans, and Jeffrey J. Rachlinski. 2011. "They Saw a Protest": Cognitive Illiberalism and the Speech–Conduct Distinction. *Cultural Cognition Project Working Paper*. No. 63.

Kalman, Laura. 1998. *The Strange Career of Legal Liberalism*. New Haven, CT: Yale University Press.

Karlan, Pamela S. 2009. What Can Brown Do for You? Neutral Principles and the Struggle over the Equal Prot5ection Clause. *Duke Law Journal*. 58: 1049–1068.

Kay, Richard S. 2009. Original Intention and Public Meaning in Constitutional Interpretation. *Northwestern Law Review*. 103: 703–726.

———. 1988. Adherence to the Original Intentions in Constitutional Adjudications: Three Objections and Responses. *Northwestern University Law Review*. 82: 226–292.

Kelly, Alfred H. 1965. Clio and the Court: An Illicit Love Affair. *The Supreme Court Review*. 1965: 119–158.

Keown, John. 2006. Back to the Future of Abortion Law: *Roe*'s Rejection of American History and Tradition. *Issues in Law and Medicine*. 22: 3–38.

Kerr, Orin S. 2010. Applying the Fourth Amendment to the Internet: A General Approach. *Stanford Law Review*. 62: 1005–1050.

Kesavan, Vasan, and Michael Stokes Paulsen. 2003. The Interpretive Force of the Constitution's Secret Drafting History. *Georgetown Law Journal*. 91: 1113–1214.

Kissam, Philip C. 2006. Constitutional Theory and Ideological Factors: Three Nineteenth-Century Justices. *Kansas Law Review*. 54: 751–802.

Klarman, Michael J. 1995. Brown, Originalism, and Constitutional Theory: A Response to Professor McConnell. *Virginia Law Review*. 81: 1881–1936.

Kleinhaus, Emil A. 2000. History as Precedent: The Post-Originalist Problem in Constitutional Law. *Yale Law Journal*. 110: 121–161.

Knight, Jack, and Lee Epstein. 1996. The Norm of *Stare Decisis*. *American Journal of Political Science*. 40: 1018–1035.

Kozinski, Alex, and Harry Susan. 1997. Original Mean(der)ings. *Stanford Law Review*. 49: 1583–1605.

Kritzer, Herbert M., and Mark J. Richards. 2005. The Influence of Law in the Supreme Court's Search-and-Seizure Jurisprudence. *American Political Research*. 33: 33–55.

Kunda, Ziva. 1990. The Case for Motivated Reasoning. *Psychological Bulletin*. 108: 480–498.

Lain, Corinna Barrett. 2009. The Unexceptionalism of "Evolving Standards." *UCLA Law Review*. 57: 365–419.

Lash, Kurt T. 2004. The Lost Original Meaning of the Ninth Amendment. *Texas Law Review*. 83: 331–430.

Law, David. 2005. Generic Constitutional Law. *Minnesota Law Review*. 89: 652–742.

Law, Sylvia A. 1990. Conversations between Historians and the Constitution. *Public Historian*. 12: 11–17.

Lawson, Gary. 2002. Delegation and Original Meaning. *Virginia Law Review*. 88: 327–404.

Lawson, Gary, and Guy Seidman. 2006. Originalism as a Legal Enterprise. *Constitutional Commentary*. 23: 47–80.

———. 2002. The First "Establishment" Clause: Article VII and the Post-Constitutional Confederation. *Notre Dame Law Review*. 78: 83–100.

Lax, Jeffrey R., and Charles Cameron. 2007. Bargaining and Opinion Assignment on the U.S. Supreme Court. *Journal of Law Economics & Organization*. 23: 276–302.

Leuchtenberg, William E. 1992. The Historian and the Public Realm. *American Historical Review*. 97: 1–18.

Levin, Daniel. 2004. Federalists in the Attic: Original Intent, the Heritage Movement, and Democratic Theory. *Law & Social Inquiry*. 29: 105–126.

Levy, Leonard Williams. 2000. *Original Intent and the Framers' Constitution*. Chicago: Ivan R. Dee.

Lim, Youngsik. 2000. An Empirical Analysis of Supreme Court Justices' Decision Making. *Journal of Legal Studies*. 29: 721–752.

Lindquist, Stefanie A., and Frank B. Cross. 2009. *Measuring Judicial Activism*. New York: Oxford University Press.

Lindquist, Stefanie A., and David E. Klein. 2006. The Influence of Jurisprudential Considerations on Supreme Court Decisionmaking: A Study of Conflict Cases. *Law & Society Review*. 40: 135–162.

Liptak, Adam. 2010. Justices Debate Video Game Ban. *New York Times*, November 2.

Lofgren, 1988. The Original Understanding of Original Intent? *Constitutional Commentary*. 5: 77–114.

Lund, Nelson. 2009. The Second Amendment, Heller, and Originalist Jurisprudence. *UCLA Law Review*. 56: 1343–1376.

Lupu, Ira C. 1998. Time, the Supreme Court, and *The Federalist*. *George Washington Law Review*. 66: 1324–1336.

Lynch, Joseph M. 2000. The Federalists and *The Federalist*: A Forgotten History. *Seton Hall Law Review*. 31: 18–29.

Macey, Jonathan R. 1995. Originalism As an "ISM." *Harvard Journal of Law and Public Policy*. 19: 301–309.

Maggs, Gregory E. 2009a. A Concise Guide to the Federalist Papers as a Source of the Original Meaning of the U.S. Constitution. *Boston University Law Review*. 87: 801–848.

———. 2009b. A Concise Guide to the Records of the State Ratifying Conventions as a Source of the Original Meaning of the U.S. Constitution. *Illinois Law Review*. 103: 457–496.

Maier, Pauline. 2010. *Ratification: The People Debate the Constitution, 1787–1788*. New York: Simon & Schuster.

Maltz, Earl. 1994. *Rethinking Constitutional Law: Originalism, Interventionism, and the Politics of Judicial Review*. Lawrence: University Press of Kansas.

———. 1987. Foreward: The Appeal of Originalism. *Utah Law Review* 1987: 773–807.

Maltzman, Forrest, James F. Spriggs II, and Paul Wahlbeck. 2000. *Crafting Law on the Supreme Court*. Cambridge, UK: Cambridge University Press.

Manning, John F. 1998. Textualism and the Role of the Federalist in Constitutional Adjudication. *George Washington Law Review*. 66: 1337–1365.

Mason, Alpheus T. 1952. The Federalist—A Split Personality. *American Historical Review*. 57: 625–643.

McConnell, Michael W. 1998. Textualism and the Dead Hand of the Past. *George Washington Law Review*. 66: 1127–1142.

———. 1995. Originalism and the Desegregation Decisions. *Virginia Law Review*. 81: 947–1140.

———. 1992. The Fourteenth Amendment: A Second American Revolution or the Logical Culmination of the Tradition? *Loyola Los Angeles Law Review*. 25: 1159–1176.

McDonald, Robert M. S. 1999. Thomas Jefferson's Changing Reputation as Author of the Declaration of Independence: The First Fifty Years. *Journal of the Early Republic*. 19: 169–195.

McGinnis, John O., and Michael Rappoport. 2009. Reconciling Originalism and Precedent. *Northwestern Law Review*. 103: 803–856.

———. 2007. Original Interpretive Principles as the Core of Originalism. *Constitutional Commentary*. 24: 371–382.

McGowan, David. 2001. Ethos in Law and History: Alexander Hamilton, *The Federalist*, and the Supreme Court. *Minnesota Law Review*. 85: 755–898.

Meese, Edwin III. 1985. Address before the D.C. Chapter of the Federalist Society Lawyers Division. In *Originalism: A Quarter Century of Debate*, Steven G. Calabresi, ed. Washington DC: Regnery Publishing.

Melton, Buckner F. Jr. 1998. Clio at the Bar: A Guide to Historical Method for Legists and Jurists. *Minnesota Law Review.* 83: 377–472.

Merrill, Thomas. 2008. The Conservative Case for Precedent. *Harvard Journal of Law & Public Policy.* 31: 977–982.

Meyler, Bernadette. 2006. Towards a Common Law Originalism. *Stanford Law Review.* 59: 551–600.

Miller, Charles A. 1969. *The Supreme Court and the Uses of History.* Cambridge, MA: Harvard University Press.

Mohr, James C. 1990. Historically Based Briefs: Observations of a Participant in the *Webster* Process. *Public Historian.* 12: 19–26.

Monaghan, Henry P. 2004. Doing Originalism. *Columbia Law Review.* 104: 32–38.

———. 1988. *Stare Decisis* and Constitutional Adjudication. *Columbia Law Review.* 88: 723–773.

———. 1981. Our Perfect Constitution. *New York University Law Review.* 56: 353–396.

Munzer, Stephen R., and James W. Nickel. 1977. Does the Constitution Mean What It Always Meant? *Columbia Law Review.* 77: 1029–1062.

Murphy, Paul L. 1963. Time to Reclaim: The Current Challenge of American Constitutional History. *American Historical Review.* 69: 64–79.

Nagel, Stuart S. 1961. Political Party Affiliation and Judges' Decisions. *American Political Science Review.* 55: 843–850.

Nelson, Caleb. 2003. Originalism and Interpretive Conventions. *University of Chicago Law Review.* 70: 519–598.

Neuman, Gerald L. 2006. International Law as a Resource in Constitutional Interpretation. *Harvard Journal of Law & Public Policy.* 30: 177–190.

Nichol, Gene. 1999. Justice Scalia and the *Printz* Case: The Trials of an Occasional Originalist. *University of Colorado Law Review.* 70: 953–974.

Nickerson, Raymond S. 1998. Confirmation Bias: A Ubiquitous Phenomenon in Many Guises. *Review of General Psychology.* 1: 175–220.

Novick, Peter. 1988. *That Noble Dream.* Cambridge, UK: Cambridge University Press.

O'Neill, James. 1949. *Religion and Education under the Constitution.* New York: Harper and Brothers.

O'Neill, Jonathan. 2005. *Originalism in American Law and Politics: A Constitutional History.* Baltimore: The Johns Hopkins University Press.

Onuf, Peter S. 1989. Reflections on the Founding: Constitutional Historiography in Bicentennial Perspective. *The William and Mary Quarterly.* 46: 341–375.

Paulsen, Michael Stokes. 2008. A Government of Adequate Powers. *Harvard Journal of Law and Public Policy.* 31: 991–1004.

———. 2005. The Intrinsically Corrupting Influence of Precedent. *Constitutional Commentary.* 22: 289–298.

Perry, Michael J. 1991. The Legitimacy of Particular Conceptions of Constitutional Interpretation. *Virginia Law Review*. 77: 669–720.

Phelps, Glenn A., and John B. Gates. 1991. The Myth of Jurisprudence: Interpretive Theory in the Constitutional Opinions of Justices Rehnquist and Brennan. *Santa Clara Law Review*. 31: 567–596.

Phillips, Michael J. 2001. *The Lochner Court: Myth and Reality*. Westport, CT: Praeger Publishers.

Pierson, Charles W. 1924. The Federalist in the Supreme Court. *Yale Law Journal*. 33: 728–735.

Pinello, Daniel R. 1999. Linking Party to Judicial Ideology in American Courts: A Meta-Analysis. *Justice System Journal*. 20: 219–254.

Posner, Richard A. 2008. *How Judges Think*. Cambridge MA: Harvard University Press.

———. 2001. *Frontiers of Legal Theory*. Cambridge, MA: Harvard University Press.

———. 2000. Past-Dependency, Pragmatism, and Critique of History in Adjudication and Legal Scholarship. *University of Chicago Law Review*, 67: 573–606.

———. 1990. *The Problems of Jurisprudence*. Cambridge, MA: Harvard University Press.

Post, Robert, and Reva Siegel. 2006. Originalism as a Political Practice: The Right's Living Constitution. *Fordham Law Review*. 75: 545–574.

Powell, H. Jefferson. 1985. The Original Understanding of Original Intent. *Harvard Law Review*. 98: 885–948.

Prakash, Saikrishna B. 1998. Unoriginalism's Law without Meaning. *Constitutional Commentary*. 15: 529–546.

Primus, Richard. 2010. The Functions of Ethical Originalism. *Texas Law Review*. 88: 79–88.

Rakove, Jack. 2003. Confessions of an Ambivalent Originalist. *New York University Law Review*. 78: 1346–1356.

———. 1997. Fidelity through History (or To It). *Fordham Law Review*. 65: 1587–1610.

———. 1996. *Original Meanings: Politics and Ideas in the Making of the Constitution*. New York: Alfred A. Knopf.

———. 1990. *Interpreting the Constitution: The Debate over Original Intent*. Boston: Northeastern University Press.

———. 1987. Comment: Original Intent and the Constitution. *Maryland Law Review*. 47: 226–233.

Rehnquist, William H. 1992. Remarks on the Process of Judging. *Washington & Lee Law Review*. 49: 263–270.

———. 1976. The Notion of a Living Constitution. *Texas Law Review*. 54: 693–706.

Reid, John Phillip. 1993. Reweaving the Seamless Web: Interdisciplinary Perspectives on the Law. *Loyola of Los Angeles Law Review.* 27: 193–224.

Rice, Charles E. 1964. *The Supreme Court and Public Prayer: The Need for Restraint.* New York: Fordham University Press.

Richards, Mark J., and Herbert M. Kritzer. 2002. Jurisprudential Regimes in Supreme Court Decision Making. *American Political Science Review.* 96: 305–320.

Richards, Neil M. 1997. Clio and the Court: A Reassessment of the Supreme Court's Uses of History. *Journal of Law and Politics.* 13: 809–892.

Robertson, David. 1998. *Judicial Discretion in the House of Lords.* New York: Oxford University Press.

Rose, Gavin M., Jess Reagan, and Dino L. Pollock. 2010. Honoring the Legacies of Justice William J. Brennan, Jr., and Justice Thurgood Marshall. *Indiana Law Review.* 43: 441–466.

Rosenthal, Lawrence. 2011. Originalism in Practice. Chapman University School of Law Legal Studies Research Paper No. 11-01.

Rossiter, Clinton. 1964. *Alexander Hamilton and the Constitution.* New York: Harcourt, Brace & World.

Rubin, Phillip A. 2010. War of the Words: How Courts Can Use Dictionaries Consistent with Textualist Principles. *Duke Law Journal.* 167–206.

Ruger, Theodore W., Pauline T. Kim, Andrew D. Martin, and Kevin M. Quinn. 2004. The Supreme Court Forecasting Project: Legal and Political Science Approaches to Predicting Supreme Court Decisionmaking. *Columbia Law Review.* 104: 1150–1210.

Ryan, James E. 2006. Does It Take a Theory? Originalism, Active Liberty, and Minimalism. *Stanford Law Review.* 58: 1623–1660.

Samanaha, Adam. 2008. Originalism's Expiration Date. *Cardozo Law Review.* 30: 1295–1368.

Scalia, Antonin. 2007. Foreword. In *Originalism: A Quarter Century of Debate,* Steven G. Calabresi, ed. Washington, DC: Regnery Publishing.

———. 1997. *A Matter of Interpretation.* Princeton, NJ: Princeton University Press.

———. 1989. Originalism: The Lesser Evil. *University of Cincinnati Law Review.* 57: 849–866.

Schlesinger, Arthur M. 2007. Folly's Antidote. *New York Times,* January 1.

Schultz, David A., and Christopher E. Smith. 1996. *The Jurisprudential Vision of Justice Antonin Scalia.* Lanham, MD: Rowman & Littlefield.

Schulz-Hardt, Stefan, Felix C. Brodbeck, Andreas Mojzisch, Rudolf Kerschreiter, and Dieter Frey. 2006. Group Decision Making in Hidden Profile Situations: Dissent as a Facilitator for Decision Quality. *Journal of Personality and Social Psychology.* 91: 1080–1093.

Schwartz, Bernard. 1993. *Main Currents in American Legal Thought.* Durham, NC: Carolina Academic Press.

Segal, Jeffrey A., and Harold J. Spaeth. 2002. *The Supreme Court and the Attitudinal Model Revisited*. New York: Cambridge University Press.

————. 1993. *The Supreme Court and the Attitudinal Model*. New York: Cambridge University Press.

Sinaceur, Marwan, Melissa C. Thomas-Hunt, Margaret A. Neale, Olivia A.O'Neill, and Christophe Haag. 2010. Accuracy and Perceived Expert Status in Group Decisions: When Minority Members Make Majority Members More Accurate Privately. *Personality and Social Psychology Bulletin*. 36: 423–437.

Shaman, Jeffrey M. 2010. The End of Originalism. *San Diego Law Review*. 47: 83–108.

Shapiro, Carolyn. 2010. The Context of Ideology: Law, Politics, and Empirical Legal Scholarship. *Missouri Law Review*. 75: 79–142.

Sherry, Suzanna. 1995. The Indeterminacy of Historical Evidence. *Harvard Journal of Law & Public Policy*. 19: 437–442.

Slobogin, Christopher. 2009. Justice Ginsburg's Gradualism in Criminal Procedure. *Ohio State Law Journal*. 70: 867–888.

Smith, Christopher E. 1997. Clarence Thomas: A Distinctive Justice. *Seton Hall Law Review*. 28: 1–28.

Smith, Peter J. 2006. The Marshall Court and the Originalist's Dilemma. *Minnesota Law Review*. 90: 612–677.

————. 2004. Sources of Federalism: An Empirical Analysis of the Court's Quest for Original Meaning. *UCLA Law Review*. 52: 217–288.

Smith, Steven D. 1989. Law without Mind. *Michigan Law Review*. 88: 104–119.

Smith, Tara. 2009. Originalism's Misplaced Fidelity: "Original" Meaning Is Not Objective. *Constitutional Commentary*. 26: 1–58.

Solum, Lawrence B. 2009. *District of Columbia v. Heller* and Originalism. *Northwestern University Law Review*. 103: 923–982.

————. 2008. Semantic Originalism. *Illinois Public Law and Legal Theory Research Papers Series No. 07-24*.

Somin, Ilya. 2006. "Active Liberty" and Judicial Power: What Should Courts Do to Promote Democracy? *Northwestern University Law Review*. 100: 1827–1906.

Songer, Donald R., and Stefanie A. Lindquist. 1996. Not the Whole Story: The Impact of Justices' Values on Supreme Court Decision Making. *American Journal of Political Science*. 40: 1049–1063.

Sonpal, Rickie. 2003. Old Dictionaries and New Textualists. *Fordham Law Review*. 71: 2177–2226.

Spaeth, Harold J., and Jeffrey A. Segal. 1999. *Majority Rule or Minority Will: Adherence to Precedent on the U.S. Supreme Court*. New York: Cambridge University Press.

Spitzer, Robert J. 2008. *Saving the Constitution from Lawyers*. New York: Cambridge University Press.

Story, Joseph. 1833. *Commentaries on the Constitution of the United States.* Boston: Hilliard, Gray and Company.

Strang, Lee J. 2009. Originalism and the "Challenge of Change": Abduced-Principle Originalism and Other Mechanisms by Which Originalism Sufficiently Accommodates Changed Social Conditions. *Hastings Law Journal*, 60: 927–996.

———. 2006a. Originalism, the Declaration of Independence, and the Constitution: A Unique Role in Constitutional Interpretation? *Penn State Law Review.* 111: 413–480.

———. 2006b. An Originalist Theory of Precedent: Originalism, Nonoriginalist Precedent, and the Common Good. *New Mexico Law Review.* 36: 419–486.

Strauss, David A. 2009. The Death of Judicial Conservatism. *Duke Journal of Constitutional Law & Public Policy.* 4: 1–16.

———. 2008. Why Conservatives Shouldn't Be Originalists. *Harvard Journal of Law and Public Policy,* 31: 969–976.

———. 2007. Panel on Originalism and Precedent. In *Originalism: A Quarter Century of Debate*, Steven G. Calabresi, ed. Washington, DC: Regnery Publishing.

Sullivan, Kathleen M. 1992. Foreword: The Justices of Rules and Standards. *Harvard Law Review.* 106: 22–123.

Sunstein, Cass R. 2008. Second Amendment Minimalism: Heller as Griswold. *Harvard Law Review.* 122: 246–275.

———. 2005. *Radicals in Robes: Why Extreme Right-Wing Courts Are Wrong for America.* Cambridge, MA: Basic Books

Sutton, Jeffrey S. 2009. Role of History in Judging Disputes about the Meaning of the Constitution. *Texas Tech Law Review.* 41: 1173–1192.

Tamanaha, Brian. 2010. *Beyond the Formalist–Realist Divide.* Princeton, NJ: Princeton University Press.

Telman, D. A. Jeremy. 2009. Medellin and Originalism. *Maryland Law Review.* 68: 377–429.

tenBroek, Jacobus. 1938. Use by the United States Supreme Court of Extrinsic Aids in Constitutional Construction: Debates and Proceedings of the Constitutional and Ratifying Conventions. *California Law Review.* 26: 437–454.

Tetlock, P. E. 1985. Accountability: A Social Check on the Fundamental Attribution Error. *Social Psychology Quarterly.* 48: 227–236.

Thomas, Clarence. 1996. Judging. *Kansas Law Review.* 45: 1–8.

Tillman, Seth Barrett. 2003. The *Federalist Papers* as Reliable Historical Source Material for Constitutional Interpretation. *West Virginia Law Review.* 105: 601–620.

Treanor, William Michael. 1995. The Original Understanding of the Takings Clause and the Political Process. *Columbia Law Review.* 95: 782–887.

Volokh, Alexander. 2008. Choosing Interpretive Methods: A Positive Theory of Judges and Everyone Else. *New York University Law Review*. 83: 769–846.

Wahlbeck, Paul J. 1997. The Life of the Law: Judicial Politics and Legal Change. *Journal of Politics*. 59: 778–846.

Wahlbeck, Paul J., James F. Spriggs II, and Forrest Maltzman. 1998. Marshalling the Court: Bargaining and Accommodation on the United States Supreme Court. *American Journal of Political Science*. 42: 294–315,

Wells, Howell. 2009. Scalia's Time Machine Fails: Jurist Forced to Call Constitution "Living Document." *The Record*, April 2. Retrieved on June 16, 2012, from http://hlrecord.org/?p=11388.

White, G. Edward. 1988. *The Marshall Court and Cultural Change, 1815–1835*. New York: Cambridge University Press.

Whittington, Keith E. 2004. The New Originalism. *Georgetown Journal of Law and Public Policy*. 2: 599–614.

———. 1999. *Constitutional Interpretation: Textual Meaning, Original Intent and Judicial Review*. Lawrence: University Press of Kansas.

Wiecek, William N. 1988. Clio as Hostage: The United States Supreme Court and the Uses of History. *California Western Law Review*. 24: 227–272.

Wilkinson, J. Harvie. 2009. Of Guns, Abortions, and the Unraveling Rule of Law. *Virginia Law Review*. 95: 253–324.

Wills, Garry. 1984. *Cincinnatus: George Washington and the Enlightenment*. New York: Doubleday.

Wilson, James G. 1985. The Most Sacred Text: The Supreme Court's Use of *The Federalist Papers*. *Brigham Young University Law Review*. 1985: 65–136.

Wofford, John G. 1963–1964. The Blinding Light: The Uses of History in Constitutional Interpretation. *University of Chicago Law Review* 502: 31.

Wolfe, Christopher. 1996. *How to Read the Constitution: Originalism, Constitutional Interpretation, and Judicial Power*. Lanham, MD: Rowman and Littlefield.

Wray, Christopher. 2005. Originalism and Criminal Law and Procedure. *Chapman Law Review*. 11: 277–306.

Wright, R. George. 2008. Originalism and the Problem of Fundamental Fairness. *Marquette Law Review*. 91: 687–722.

Yoo, John C. 1999. Globalism and the Constitution: Treaties, Non-Self-Execution, and the Original Understanding. *Columbia Law Review*. 99: 1955–2094.

Index

abortion, 20, 39, 115, 160
abstraction of general principles, 37–41,
  53, 62, 70, 71–72, 117, 190; original
  principles-based originalism, 37–38,
  85, 87, 132; role in adaptation to
  changed circumstances, 34–35, 37,
  84–85
Ackerman, Bruce, 128
Adams, John, 3, 18
Adams, John Quincy, 69
admiralty jurisdiction, 87
adversary process, 166
affirmative action, 130
Alden v. Maine, 99–100
Aleinikoff, T. Alexander, 66
Alito, Samuel, 105, 133; on originalism,
  23–24, 103
Amar, Akhil Reed, 30, 48, 56
Amar, Vikram David, 103
amendments, 3, 8, 10, 24, 75; First
  Amendment, 25, 34, 68, 101, 128–29,
  158; Second Amendment, 14–15, 33,
  47, 104, 106; Fourth Amendment,
  35, 36, 95; Fifth Amendment, 46–47,
  134; Sixth Amendment, 181, 182, 186;
  Ninth Amendment, 61, 71, 95, 130;
  Eleventh Amendment, 99, 100, 112;
  Fourteenth Amendment, 38, 46–47,
  92, 93, 126. *See also* Bill of Rights
Anderson, Robert, IV, 117
Anti-Federalists, 50, 53–55, 69, 100, 180,
  182
appointments clause, 97
Aprill, Ellen P., 56
Arkes, Hadley, 61

Articles: Article II, 102; vs. Bill of rights,
  10, 12, 54–55, 71
Articles of Confederation, 61
Atascadero State Hospital v. Scanlon, 100
attitudinal model of judicial decisionmaking, 156–59, 161, 162, 163, 165,
  182
Austen-Smith, David, 54

Baade, Hans, 4
Baird, Vanessa A., 135
Balkin, Jack M., 5, 95; on abstract prin-
  ciples, 40; on due process, 47; on liber-
  alism, 16, 177; on originalism, 2, 6,
  16, 32, 38, 82, 85, 177; on reproductive
  rights, 70; on Second Amendment, 47
Ball, Howard, 128
Barber, Sotirios A., 68
Barkow, Rachel E., 176
Barnett, Randy E.: on judicial activism,
  11–12; on originalism, 2, 7, 11–12, 27,
  29, 41–42, 71, 192–93; on Scalia, 130,
  182; on unwritten principles, 40–41
Bartels, Brandon L., 160
Bassham, Gregory, 9, 13, 21, 26, 40, 89,
  108
Baum, Lawrence, 167, 168, 170
Beatty, David M., 18
Becker, Carl L., 109
Benesh, Sara C., 179–80
Benton v. Maryland, 95
Berger, Raoul, 11, 30, 58, 60, 69, 71, 94
Berman, Mitchell N.: on originalism, 2,
  5, 28, 29, 36, 38, 42, 43
Bernstein, Richard, 110, 112